GREENBERG'S GUIDE TO
MARBLES

DENNIS WEBB

GREENBERG BOOKS
A Division of Kalmbach Publishing Co.

Second Edition
Copyright © 1994 by Dennis Webb

Cover design by Sabine Beaupré
Cover photograph by Al Fiterman

Published by Greenberg Books
Division of Kalmbach Publishing Co.
21027 Crossroads Circle, Waukesha, WI 53187

Library of Congress Cataloging-in-Publication Data

Webb, Dennis.
 Greenberg's guide to marbles / by Dennis Webb—2nd ed.
    p.   cm.
 Rev. ed. of: Greenberg's guide to marbles / by Mark E. Randall and Dennis Webb, c1988.
 Includes bibliographical references and index.
 ISBN 0-89778-330-1
  1. Marbles (Game)—Collectors and collecting. I. Randall, Mark E. Greenberg's guide to marbles. II. Title. III. Title: Guide to marbles.
NK6215.W43 1994   93-16120
796.2—dc20   CIP

GREENBERG'S GUIDE TO
MARBLES

CONTENTS

	Preface and Acknowledgements	5
	Introduction	7
I	A History of Marbles	9
II	Stone Marbles	13
III	Ceramic Marbles	19
IV	Handmade Glass Marbles	27
V	Machine-Made Glass Marbles	38
VI	Marbles of Other Materials	54
VII	Game Boards and Miscellaneous Items	57
VIII	Marbles in Catalogs	63
IX	Containers and Packages	67
X	Glass Machine-Made Marble Production	72
XI	Glass Marble Formulas and Recipes	81
XII	Patents Related to the Marble-Making Industry	86
XIII	Patent Suits in the Marble Industry	93
XIV	United States Marble Companies	95
	Akro Agate Company	95
	Alley Agate Company/Lawrence Glass Novelty	
	Company/Alley Glass Manufacturing Company	100
	Alox Manufacturing Company	101
	C. E. Bogard & Sons Agate Company/Bogard Company	102
	Boston and Sandwich Glass Company	103
	Cairo Novelty Company	103
	Champion Agate Company	104
	Christensen Agate Company	105
	M. F. Christensen and Son Glass Company	106
	Davis Marble Works	107
	Heaton Agate Company	108
	Iowa City Flint Glass Manufacturing Company	109
	JABO, Incorporated	109

Jackson Marble Company 109
Kokomo Opalescent Glass Company 110
Marble King/Berry Pink Industries 110
Master Glass Company 114
Master Marble Company 114
Mid-Atlantic Glass Corporation/Mid-Atlantic of West Virginia 116
Navarre Glass Marble and Specialty Company 117
Nivison-Weiskopf Company 117
Peltier Glass Company 118
Playrite Marble and Novelty Company 121
Ravenswood Novelty Works 121
Vitro Agate Company/Gladding-Vitro Agate
    Company/Vitro Agate Corporation 122
XV   Foreign Marble Companies and Glass Houses 128
XVI   Price Guide 134
Dictionary of Marble Terms 146
Bibliography and Selected Literature 152
Appendix: U.S. Producers of Toy Marbles 157
Index 158

Preface and Acknowledgments

This book was inspired by my desire to document a significant part of Americana—marbles. My aim was to record the art of making marbles, from its earliest history to contemporary times. I also wanted to acknowledge those dedicated craftsmen, past and present, who made it all possible.

Greenberg's Guide to Marbles, second edition, was developed primarily from correspondence and interviews with people who are interested in marbles and in the history of the marble industry in the United States. Available published sources were consulted, but there are few publications devoted strictly to marbles or marble playing that cover more than a narrow part of the subject. The size and the broad focus of this book reflect the degree of cooperation I received from a large number of people, and thus my list of thank-yous is longer than most. Primary sources were given preference over other sources to the extent possible.

The hospitality and assistance of the people active in marble-making companies today have kept me aware that marbles in the United States are not just a part of history, but are still a part of our recreation and industries. The pioneers of the marble industry are gone now, but the people who make marbles today know the traditions and history of their craft, and have a great appreciation for the people and events that came before them. I cannot overemphasize the value of their contributions to this book. They donated countless hours in personal interviews and factory tours, and they also loaned or donated recent and older materials for photographic and other purposes.

The personal marble collections that were available to me furnished a superb cross section of marbles from the early decades of the twentieth century. I gratefully acknowledge the collectors who have made their marbles and stories part of this book: Gino Biffany, an authority on Peltier Glass Company marbles, who also reviewed an early draft of this manuscript; Jack Bogard, general manager of JABO, Inc., who shared the early history of his company; Jack Frier of Alox Manufacturing Company, who also gave me details on the early history of his company; J. Fred Early, son of the late John F. Early, gave me substantial information about his father's role in the Akro Agate and Master Marble companies; he also helped with sections on glass technology, gave me firsthand accounts of how various marble machines work, and provided helpful editorial comments and photographs; the late Roger W. Howdyshell, president of Marble King, who shared information about his company, including his scrapbook of newspaper clippings about the flamboyant Berry Pink, the first "Marble King"; Wallace S. Huffman, an authority on the Kokomo Opalescent Glass Company; Buck Lamp, of JABO, Inc.; Lewis L. Moore, former plant manager for Vitro Agate Corporation and consultant to Mid-Atlantic of West Virginia; and Naomi Alley Sellers, who provided information about her father, Lawrence O. Alley.

I would also like to thank Stanley Block of the Marble Collector's Society of America, for information regarding all aspects of the history of marbles; Robert A. Brown, marble maker, for information about contemporary ceramic marbles and for samples of his craftsmanship; and Beverly Brulé, collector, for editorial comments and photographs.

I am also grateful to Jeff Carskadden, collector and authority on ceramic marbles, for editorial comments and photographs, and for critiquing an early draft of this book; Lawrence M. Chapman, for information and for donating marbles to be photographed; Bertram Cohen, collector, for sharing his extensive collection of marble memorabilia; Michael J. Cohill, for information about the M. F. Christensen and Son Glass Company and other glass factories in the Akron area; Jim Davis, collector, for critiquing an early draft of this manuscript; and Claudia M. Del Toro, export manager, Vacor de Mexico, for her invaluable assistance.

I am also indebted to Rae Ecklund for critiquing the manuscript; Richard Gartley for information on ceramic marbles; Charles D. Gibson, of Gibson Glass, for details on making contemporary Swirl and Sulphide marbles; Joseph L. Jankowski, president of Peltier Glass Company, for information and documentation concerning Peltier's famous Picture Marbles; and Dave McCullough, of JABO, Inc.

I also gratefully acknowledge Mark Matthews, marble maker, for assistance; Donald Michels, of Champion Agate Corporation, for the early history of his company; Beverly Pearson for translations and transcription of personal interviews; Margaret K. Phillips, Vacor U.S.A national sales manager, for assistance; the United States Patent and Trademark Office, for assistance during intensive research on the first and second editions of this book and for the use of many illustrations; Dennis E. Webb, the author's son, for help with photography; and George Williams, of the Glass Swan, for details on making contemporary Swirl and Sulphide marbles.

I wish to thank the staff at Greenberg Books and Kalmbach Publishing Co., especially Bruce and Linda Greenberg; Allan Miller, for his support and encouragement; my editors, Marsha A. Davis, Martha Eliassen Bristow, and Mary Algozin; Al Fiterman, for his talented photography; Norm Myers, Maureen Crum, and Donna Price for their technical expertise; art director Lisa Bergman; and designer Gary Kachar.

Every effort has been made to correctly attribute all material in this book. If any errors have unwittingly occurred, I will be happy to correct them in future editions. Due to the passage of time, some names appearing in these acknowledgments represent individuals who, regrettably, are now deceased.

All marbles and related material in photographs are from the collection of Dennis Webb unless otherwise indicated in the caption.

—*Dennis Webb*

References

Several publications that may be of interest to other researchers and collectors are listed in the bibliography.

Marble Societies

Blue Ridge Marble Club
3410 Plymouth Place
Lynchburg, VA 24503

Buckeye Marble Collectors Club
473 Meadowbrook Drive
Newark, OH 43055

Canadian Marble Collectors Association
c/o Craig Gamache
10B Murdock Street
Georgetown, Ontario
Canada L7G 3L6

Cape Fear Marble Club
1212-A Columbus Circle
Wilmington, NC 28403

Hoosier Marble Club
7316 Halsted Dr.
Indianapolis, IN 46214

Kansas City Area Marble Club
P.O. Box 520111
Independence, MO 64052

Marble Collector's Society of America
P.O. Box 222
Trumbull, CT 06611

Marble Collectors Unlimited
P.O. Box 206
Northboro, MA 01532

The Marble Connection
P.O. Box 132
Norton, MA 02776

Midwest Marble Club
P.O. Box 161
216 Summit Ave.
Center City, MN 55012

National Marble Club of America
440 Eaton Road
Drexel Hill, PA 19026

Ozark Mountain Marble Club
P.O. Box 8668
Prairie Village, KS 66208

Southern California Marble Collectors Society
P.O. Box 6913
San Pedro, CA 90732-6913

Suncoast Marble Collectors Society
P.O. Box 60213
St. Petersburg, FL 22784-0213

Texas Marble Collectors
417 Marsh Oval
New Braunfels, TX 78130

West Virginia Marble Shooters Association
Route 3, Box 121-D
Bridgeport, WV 26330

Introduction

Words and terms used in playing the game of marbles have been the subject of several published studies. This picturesque slang includes many dozens of terms used nowhere else in any language. Phrases such as *fen sidings, dubs* and *tribs, cunny thumb,* and *marrididdles* were known and used by American children during the late nineteenth and early twentieth centuries, but have since largely faded from use.

Included in this interesting and extensive vocabulary are nicknames for marbles that are derived from the use of a particular type of marble rather than its physical appearance. For instance, a *taw* was a marble used as a shooter. Normally, taws were larger than the target marbles (ducks), but otherwise, taws shared no common design characteristics. Terms such as taw are of interest to folklorists and students of language, but are of little use in describing marbles used over a long period of time. The same nickname may have been applied to very different marbles by different generations of children.

Mel Morrison and Carl Terrison are the first known authors of an identification and price guide for marbles that named and described some major marble types and designs. Clare Ingram followed in 1972 with her booklet, *The Collector's Encyclopedia of Antique Marbles.* Both publications are scarce and are worthy additions to the library of any marble collector.

The Great American Marble Book, written by Fred Ferretti in 1973, dealt with marble games and included many of the terms concerned with playing the various games, and some names for types of marbles.

In writing this book, identifying marble types for collectors posed a challenge. In my attempt to describe all the marbles ever made or used in the United States, it was necessary to use a simple system. However, the system had to be one that still accurately described all the varieties of marbles present.

(Carpet bowls or lawn bowls are not addressed in this or the previous edition since many serious marble collectors do not consider them toy game marbles, primarily due to their size and method of play. Some early marble collectors did add them as a novelty to their collections due to their color and design. However, my major concentration is toy game marbles.)

The most basic characteristic by which to classify marbles is the material of which they are made: glass, stone, ceramics, metal, etc. All materials except glass are relatively simple; since there are not so many different varieties of marbles in the non-glass categories, an elaborate descriptive system is not necessary. The glass types, however, are much more complex. Both handmade glass and machine-made glass types occur in hundreds of varieties.

In describing machine-made glass marbles, several different naming systems exist. These include the brand names given by the companies that produced the marbles; for instance, Marble King's Rainbows and Vitro Agate's Aqua Jewels. There are also the names bestowed on particular marble designs by the users—the kids who played with them. These nicknames include Bumble Bee, Cub Scout, and Black Widow.

Sometimes these two names are the same; either the company adopted the names the kids gave their marbles, or the kids used the name put on the bag by the maker.

Developing individual names for the hundreds of different machine-made marbles made by all companies is beyond the scope of this particular project, and to do so would only tend to confuse collectors.

This book uses a more generic typology. The terms are applicable to machine-made glass marbles made by any company at any time, based strictly on description. The names themselves imply nothing about which company made the marble, or when. Such information is covered in the sections on individual marble types and in the chapter on marble companies.

In this system, the classification levels within glass machine-made marbles are according to whether the marble is a single color or multicolored, what design elements are present, and how opaque is the body glass. The opacity classification usually becomes part of the type name; in the vast majority of marbles the appropriate class is obvious.

Opaque allows no light to pass through the body of the marble. In other words, you cannot see through it. An example is a Chinese Checkers marble.

Translucent allows some light to pass through, but not clearly. A hazy glow of light can be distinguished through the marble. Examples include milk glass, custard glass, and Vaseline glass.

Transparent allows light to pass through clearly, if only around the design elements. For instance, in a Cat Eye, even though parts of the interior cannot be seen through, the marble's body glass (the non-design part) is still transparent.

Besides design patterns, certain other factors having to do with size or surface features—such as creases, roll marks, or rough "orange-skin" texture—tell more about the marble and help distinguish it from other types.

The identification chart in the machine-made glass marble chapter defines most categories of glass machine-made marbles. Also listed are marble manufacturers who are known to have produced that type of marble.

The measurements of the marbles described in this book are as stated by the manufacturers. Thus, marbles are described in both inches and millimeters.

Chapter I

• • •

A History of Marbles

Past and present—this is a group of special marbles representing a variety of materials, techniques, and eras. Clockwise, from left: Contemporary (1987) 2-inch handmade glass Swirl of gold glass with mica and yellow and orange spiral threads by Terry Crider; contemporary (1990) 2-inch ceramic Whirligig by Robert A. Brown; *antique 2⅛-inch handmade Latticino Spiral with four levels of multicolored threads; antique 1⅞-inch hand-decorated glazed Ceramic marble—the cobaltlike color of the body and figures are similar to ceramics from Holland. This marble is rare in size, color, and design.*

Kneeling in the dirt and knuckling down for a game of marbles —this is a childhood memory shared by many generations of Americans. Before television, long before Nintendo, marbles were everywhere. In school yards, on playgrounds, even on city sidewalks, playing marbles was a great American pastime.

But marble games are older than America, older than the discovery of the New World, older than the rise of civilization in Europe. No one knows exactly where or when the first games using marbles or objects like marbles were played. Historical evidence suggests that such pastimes were independently invented in several locations around the world at different times. In European history, marble games were known to the Greeks and Romans several centuries before Christ's birth.[1] The collection of the Metropolitan Museum of Art in New York contains

A selection of unusual marbles not often seen in collections. Top row: Czechoslovakian fortune-telling marble with thirty-two facets. Second row: Wirepull, German machine-made marble, maker unknown; Tomato by Vitro Agate, 1¼ inches, circa 1983; purple Goldstone, probably made in Italy; early machine-made marble regionally known as Watermelon, maker unknown; Burgundy by Vitro Agate, circa 1985; contemporary Tennessee flint marble by Carole A. Bowen; hollow Steelie, with X mark highlighted by chalk. Third row: Modern machine-made glass Tiger Eye by Master Marble, circa 1930s, rare and valuable; frosted transparent marble with faint mold mark around circumference, excavated from colonial site in Maryland; Codd bottle stopper marble; transparent molded marble; Custard Glass marble, colored with uranium oxide, circa 1930s, maker unknown; Vaseline glass marble, maker unknown; Confetti by Vitro Agate, experimental runs only, never mass-produced. Front row: Brown Bennington with screen marks from kiln; Backlash, with inner design of metal, by Champion Agate, scarce; black ballot box marble, also found in white, black used for a "no" vote and white used for "yes" vote; Maryland 350th Anniversary Celebration Commemorative marble showing state colors by Marble King; U.S.A. Bicentennial edition Slag by Champion Agate, circa 1976; Flame, by Champion Agate, made for a game to symbolize automobile flameout; early cage-type Cat Eye by Vitro Agate, circa 1950, transparent ruby body glass with opaque white striping.

fine examples of glass marbles from the Roman Empire, fourth century A.D., ranging in size from ½ inch to 2 inches. The legendary Berry Pink, an owner and founder of Marble King, had spheres of jade, emerald, silver and gold in his thirty-eight-hundred-marble collection. One of Pink's marbles was from King Tut's tomb, another was from an Aztec palace, and one from England was more than one thousand years old.[2]

Seven white marbles, apparently used by some of our Paleolithic ancestors, were found in the Drachenhohle Cave near Mixnitz in Styria, Austria. Thirty pebbles of a similar nature and date were found in the Wildenmannlisloch Cave, fifty-three hundred feet up in the Churfirsten Mountains of Switzerland. These marbles were not of local stone but had been brought a considerable distance.[3]

Excavation of Stone Age tombs in eastern Ireland yielded grave goods such as marbles or balls averaging one to two centimeters in diameter. Although the marbles were usually made of chalk, natural pebbles were also used, as were other materials such as baked clay, bone, and stone such as limestone, basalt, ironstone, serpentine, quartzite, and marble. Approximately forty marbles or balls were excavated from this five-thousand-year-old archaeological site.[4]

In western European history, marbles were noted as early as the fourteenth century and are mentioned in a French manuscript of that period. An English game, Fox and Geese, from circa 1450, required eighteen marbles and a playing board.[5] Boys are depicted playing marbles in a 1560 painting by Flemish artist Pieter Breughel the Elder. Marbles are mentioned in European literature fairly regularly thereafter.[6]

Whether European marbles first came to America with the English, French, Dutch, or others is not known. They were present at colonial Williamsburg, Virginia,[7] and at Fort Albany, Canada (1675–1720).[8] Stone marbles were found at the Fort Rivier Tremblente archeological site in

Manitoba, Canada; this site dates to a very narrow time period of 1793–1798. During the American Revolution, soldiers employed by the British brought marbles from their homeland to the American continent.

Even though new inhabitants brought their marbles with them, marbles were here before they arrived. American Indians already possessed marbles, or at least small stone or clay balls just like European marbles of the same period. These small balls have been found in prehistoric ruins in the Southeast, in the Southwest, and on the East Coast, predating the arrival of the first Europeans by several centuries.

From the early period of New World settlement until almost the last decade of the nineteenth century, American marbles were either homemade or imported from Europe. Soon afterward, however, the United States began to produce its own marbles commercially. By 1920, foreign imports had all but vanished due to competition from domestic products.

During the late 1920s and early 1930s, business was booming—the game of marbles was a fact of American life. Foreign competition was long gone and did not trouble the United States marble makers again for a number of years. Competition on the home front was fierce enough; after a series of court battles over patent infringements, the field was thrown wide open to newcomers by the ruling that certain crucial patents were invalid and that technology once monopolized was now available to everyone. The number of marble companies increased rapidly during the early 1930s and into the early 1940s.

Marbles were so prevalent, they even played a role in political demonstrations and protests. Shortly after World War I, the veterans of that war took to the streets of Washington, D.C., demanding immediate payment of a promised bonus. The situation became rather hectic when the mounted police were called in and bonus marchers threw marbles under the horses' feet, causing the animals to slip and fall. Horses and riders were injured. This sordid episode, called "The Battle of Anacostia Flats," prompted humorist Will Rogers to compliment the veterans by commenting that "they hold the record for being the best behaved of any 15,000 hungry men ever assembled anywhere in the world."[9] The bonus was not paid.

In the summer of 1932, the "doughboys" again pleaded for payment of the bonus that was promised in 1924 to be paid in 1945; the veterans needed that bonus to survive the Great Depression's worst year. But their pleas for relief fell on deaf ears. Facing mounted, armed troops, these destitute veterans again used the most inexpensive and plentiful weapons at their disposal—marbles. There were more than one hundred casualties in this "battle." They included two babies suffocated by the troops' tear gas attack.

To President Hoover, Congress, lawmen, and the newspapers, the demonstrators were not veterans but "red agitators." However, Hoover's own Veterans Administration surveyed the Bonus Army and found that 95 percent of them were indeed veterans.[10]

Through several wars, playing marbles was apparently a favored pastime among lonely American soldiers far from home. The author's collection of marble memorabilia includes photographs of members of the U.S. Army Fifth Infantry Division playing marbles while stationed in Iceland before World War II. More recently, the November 9, 1992, issue of *Time* magazine featured photographs of items brought by visitors to the Vietnam War Memorial; one item was a bag of marbles left as a tribute to a serviceman whose name appears on the wall.

The primary market for marbles was, of course, American children, and the domestic marble industry did its best to meet the demand. In the 1930s, however, the specter of foreign competition returned briefly. Japan purchased glass cullet from West Virginia glass factories to manufacture its own marbles and pressware. The cullet was transported by rail to the East Coast and then by ship through the Panama Canal. The cullet, which takes less energy to process than raw materials, was a cheap source of high-quality glass for Japanese manufacturers.[11]

By the late 1930s, demand was beginning to lag, largely due to the changing tastes in children's toys. As early as 1936 a magazine article[12] declared that things were not as rosy as they once were for the marble industry. By the post-World War II period, marbles were rarely seen in major mail-order catalogs.

World War II itself did not markedly affect the marble business as it did many industries. If anything, the industry benefited by the substitution of glass ball-bearings for steel bearings in some applications.[13] Glass is harder than steel, and if the glass bearings are cooled and tempered properly, they are quite durable.

Foreign imports again appeared in the early 1950s in the form of the Japanese Cat Eye marble. The enormous popularity of this design almost put the surviving American companies out of business. Some, however, were able to produce their own Cat Eye varieties and rebounded somewhat.

Since that period there has continued to be stiff pressure from Asian imports and, more recently, from Mexican imports. As the *Parkersburg (West Virginia) News* noted, "An economic dilemma arose due to the fact that the Japanese shipped marbles into the U.S. at prices that are below the cost of raw materials in the American marble industry. U.S. foreign tariff policy has seen U.S. small business sacrificed to Japanese interests, particularly the marble industry."[14]

After the Americans introduced their own Cat Eye designs in the mid-1950s, there were few truly new designs, with the exception of a few special-order promotional marbles, until the early 1980s. In 1983 and 1984, Vacor de Mexico introduced several radically new designs into the American market, as did the American companies Vitro Agate, Marble King, and Champion Agate. These designs reflected the use of marbles in new board games rather than a resurgence of interest in traditional marble-shooting games.

Some American marble makers who had been in the glassmaking business (their products including marbles) long before the Japanese "invasion" have discontinued production of toy marbles, and now make marbles for industrial uses only. (The colorful history of American marble makers is recounted in Chapter XIV.)

[1]Kelsie B. Harder, "The Vocabulary of Marble Playing," *Publication of the American Dialectic Society* (No. 23, Center for Applied Linguistics, Arlington, Va., 1955), p. 4.

[2]Personal conversation with Roger W. Howdyshell; and John Proctor, "Marble King," *The Family Circle*, Vol. 14, No. 25 (June 23, 1939).

[3]Ivar Lissner, *Man, God and Magic.* Translated from the German by J. Maxwell Brourejohn, M.A., (New York: C. P. Putnam and Sons; and London: Jonathan Cape, 1961), pp. 183, 188–189 and Figure 55.

[4]George Eogan, *Knowth* (London: Thames and Hudson, 1986), pp. 140, 144, 210.

[5]*Marble-Mania*, newsletter of the Marble Collectors Society of America, Trumbull, Ct., published periodically since 1976, Vol. 25 (January 1982), p. 1.

[6]Michael Olmert, "Points of Origin," *Smithsonian*, Vol. 14, No. 9 (December 1983), p. 40 (mention of marbles in early European literature).

[7]Mark E. Randall, "Marbles as Historical Artifacts" (Trumbull, Ct.: Marble Collectors Society of America, 1979), p. 12.

[8]Randall, op. cit.: 10

[9]Richard Ketchum, *Will Rogers—The Man and His Times* (American Heritage Publishing Company, 1973).

[10]Kenneth C. Davis, *Don't Know Much About History* (New York: Crown Publishers, 1990), pp. 274–275.

[11]Howdyshell, personal conversation.

[12]"Immies," *Fortune*, Vol. 13 (June 1936), p. 36.

[13]"The Marble Business Rolls Ahead," *Coronet*, Vol. 26 (September 1949), p. 120.

[14]*Parkersburg* (W. Va.) *News*, Jan. 9, 1955.

Chapter II

• • •

Stone Marbles

The earliest round game piece that could be considered a marble was probably made of stone. Man's knowledge and use of stone predated by millions of years his mastery of clay, the other naturally occurring material eventually used for marbles. The date of the first true marble is unknown, of course, but several writers have documented marbles from early Egypt, Rome, and Greece. On the North American continent, examples of round stone (and clay) marbles have been recovered from sites of prehistoric Indian occupation.

Non-flint, stone balls were obtained during general excavation of one burial mound in Indian Knoll, Kentucky, a large village site in the Green River Valley. The site is dated to the Woodland Period, Adena-Hopewell Culture (circa 1000 A.D.)[1] Small (1.8 millimeters) engraved stone marbles from the Hopewell Culture have been excavated from the Seip Mound,

Hopewell Group, in Ohio. These marbles are in the cabinets of the Ohio Historical Center in Columbus.[2] An unusual marble is nature's "cannonball," also known as a Moqui (mo-key), which is found in Utah in ironstone concretions at the base of the Navajo Sandstone Formation. These small balls are used for marblelike games by the Navajo.[3]

Marbles are documented in European literature by the fourteenth century A.D.;[4] and while the document that mentions them does not specify what they were made of, it is safe to assume that marbles of that period were made of both stone and clay. European civilization by that time had centuries of familiarity with the working properties of building stones such as granite, marble, and limestone. Because of its homogeneous internal structure and lack of fractures, limestone easily lends itself to small items such as marbles. Likewise, the mineral marble, which is metamorphic limestone, would have been easily workable into small spheres, and hence, so legend says, came the name of the objects themselves, "marbles."

Sometime during the following two centuries, marble workers expanded their inventory of base materials and began working in other, more exotic minerals, such as agate.

The popularity of stone marbles continued from these early times until the mid-nineteenth century, when glass was widely used for marbles. From that time on, agates, previously the most sought-after material for marbles, had to compete with this novelty, as did all other stone marbles as well. The price of the handmade glass marbles became considerably cheaper than agate marbles, since less labor was required to produce them, and by the last quarter of the nineteenth century glass marbles were widespread. Clay marbles were still the most common since they were the least expensive. Limestone marbles were also

Clockwise, from left: Red quartzite of unusual roundness from a Native American archaeological site in Maryland; handground stone sphere used in male puberty rites among indigenous people of New Guinea; white quartz stone from a Native American archaeological site in Alabama; nature's cannonball, also known as a Moqui, is found in southern Utah. These small, naturally formed balls were used by Native Americans for games similar to marbles.

A varied selection of early and contemporary stone marbles. In the back row, from left: Contemporary flint shooter, made of stone from Flint Ridge, Ohio, by Carole A. Bowen; contemporary sardonyx marble, also by Bowen; early agate marble with prized "bull's-eye"— some of these marbles exhibit more than one eye or ring around the prominent center ring; contemporary Oregon beach agate marble by J. W. Love; early, rare black agate marble with two white eyes (although only one eye is visible in this shot). In the middle row: Unpolished yellow quartz marble from the Mall in Washington, D.C., ground on-site by the late Robert "Bud" Garrett of Celina, Tennessee, at the Twentieth Annual Festival of American Folklife in 1986; contemporary machine-made marble of Virginia unakite by Carole A. Bowen; natural black agate shooter; handground natural green agate; carnelian sphere that was the head of a hat pin or bauble until an enterprising mibster cut off the pin, which is visible in the middle of the marble. In the front row: Early, common chalcedony marble, handground with prominent facets—players preferred the colorful bull's-eye over this transparent gray color; quartz sandstone with reddish veins of induced iron oxide, often called a Stonie in the Chicago area, and prized as a shooter because its rough surface provided a firmer grip than agate, often overlooked by collectors; rare shooter made of marble—note the reddish blush of iron oxide; natural tiger's-eye marble handmade in Germany—the golden reflection is caused by fine threads of asbestos; white opaque agate, probably from India and handground on one of the crude machines in use there.

common and inexpensive but not as easy to get as clays since, as far as can be determined, the limestone marbles were never made in the United States but were always imported from Germany.

Limestone marbles varied in size from about 5/16 inch up to about 1¼ inches, and with dyes that penetrated the surface, they could be changed from their natural shades of brown and gray or white to red, blue, purple, or green. These marbles were not turned by hand, as were agates, but were ground between a revolving water-driven beechwood platform and grindstones. Consequently, there are no grinding facets on limestone marbles. Occasionally, however, a flat area appears on these marbles. This is the remnant of a face or facet of the preform before it was ground to a spherical shape. The Untersberg (Germany) marble grinding mill, founded in 1683, produced thousands of limestone marbles each year until the last shipment in 1921. This part of Bavaria featured some 130 mills, driven by water power and operated by poor mountain farmers to supplement their income. Mass production of clay and glass marbles drove the stone marble mills out of business.[5]

Stone marbles, from the cheaper limestones to the more expensive agates, remained a major part of any child's marble collection up until World War I, which interrupted imports from Germany. The conflict severely damaged Germany's industrial capacity for production of both stone and glass marbles.

Shortly before World War I, machines were developed that expedited production of glass marbles. The effects of the war and these new machines were the beginning of the end for stone marbles of all types. The popularity of glass marbles persisted, and as prices became significantly lower in the second decade of the twentieth century, clay and stone marbles became less desirable items. Agates, which retained their pre-twentieth century mystique and attraction, remained the exception. But by that time, for the price of a single agate, a child could have a handful of the new glass marbles. So while he might keep a single prized agate shooter (preferably one with a bull's eye and colored red, symbolizing a direct hit and kill of the opponent's target marble), the remaining dozens or hundreds of his marbles would be clays, some limestones, and, by the 1920s and 1930s, almost exclusively machine-made glass marbles.

There were still a few limestone marble mills active in Germany in 1927, but these were in rapid decline. The company of Otto and Dieter Jerusalem of Idar-Oberstein, Germany, currently produces marbles of semiprecious stone from all over the world, but these do not include common limestone. The company's products include marbles of Wyoming jade, Brazilian and Moroccan agate, South African jasper, and Australian opal.

Besides agate, which is a variety of chalcedony, limestone, and the mineral marble, traditional stone marbles included those of flint, jade, alabaster, turquoise, amethyst, quartz, opal, calcite, and other chalcedonies, including carnelian (red was a highly preferred color), tiger's-eye, and onyx, which is banded agate. Tiger's-eye is caused by fibrous inclusion of asbestos. When cut properly and oriented, these will produce the famous "tiger's eye" effect.

Agate is first mentioned in literature by Theosphrastus (circa 372 B.C.), and he attributes its name to the river Achate in Sicily, where the stones are said to have been found for the first time.[6] This etymology is repeated by Pliny, who discusses agate to some extent and continues to say that it has been found in many other Mediterranean areas.[7] Agate nodules were considered the product of divine creation.

Gem cutting in two towns in southwestern Germany on the Idar and Nahe rivers, Idar and Oberstein (later combined to become Idar-Oberstein), began more than two thousand years ago. The area was a natural location for this activity because it had deposits of lithic material, as well as sandstone for grinding stones and swift streams for turning millstones. Despite the exhaustion of stone material, this area is still the gem-cutting center of the world.

The earliest record of agate being cut and polished is from 1497 in Idar and Oberstein. Agate from this region ranges from gray-blue to flesh-red in color and is similar to that found in southern Brazil. The agate deposits in the Permian Oberrotliegen geological formation were actively mined for at least five hundred years, and production ceased only when richer deposits were found in southern Brazil and Uruguay in the first half of the nineteenth century.[8] Huge imports of agate revived a declining industry.

This beautiful stone is prized as a marble for a variety of characteristics. Agate is composed of silicon dioxide (SiO_2) and registers at seven on the Mohs' hardness scale. Its hardness and toughness lend to a high polish, and its translucency and porosity allow artificial coloring. Its semi-transparent banded structure exhibits fluorescence, which varies with bands. In essence,

agate is the favorite material for a stone marble and continues to this day to be the choice for a shooter. No two agate marbles are alike.

Making an agate marble on the early water-powered mills was hard work. Rough agates were shaped by hammer and chisel into a preform corresponding to the diameter of marble desired; they were then ground on great sandstone wheels, often five feet in diameter. The sides of the wheels contained grooves of different shapes to fit the various forms of agates. Many grindstones were wide enough that two workmen could use one wheel, one workman on a side. Grinding was done by workmen who lay prone on a sort of a hollow bench and braced their feet against cleats nailed to the floor. With the pressure of their bodies, they forced the preform against the revolving grindstone. The agate emitted a bright light during grinding and was kept wet with a stream of water.[9] A large oil painting by Max Rupp depicting this operation hangs in the Museum Idar-Oberstein.

In earlier years, finer grades of agate were used to make jewelry; inferior grades were made into marbles. This accounts for the appearance of internal fractures and surface defects in apparently mint handground agate marbles. Collectors of agate marbles and marble shooters do not consider these flaws to be serious defects.

The effect of hand-turning on stone marbles may be seen by holding the marble so that a light reflects off of the surface. As the marble is turned gradually, the light jumps from facet to facet. These facets result from holding the marble against the grinding wheel and rotating it back and forth to obtain the round shape.

Modernization of the mills was inevitable, and electricity replaced water power. Now discs impregnated with emery or diamond dust make a preform before it is ground on a modern sphere machine. Sphere-ground

A marble mill (Kugelmühle) at Untersberg, Germany, established in 1683. Untersberg is a small village in the southeastern corner of Bavaria, near the German-Austrian border. An exhibit of marbles made at the mill is displayed at a nearby resort hotel. The marbles appear to be made of local fossilized rock as well as limestone. Photo by Jason Glick.

A marble mill in the Idar-Oberstein area of Germany, showing gemstone cutters at work. They lie prone in front of sandstone cutting wheels that weigh about three tons each. The wheels are used to cut agate and other gemstones. Courtesy and permission by Deutsches Edelsteinmuseum Idar-Oberstein. Copyright Gerhard Hosser, Idar-Oberstein 1990.

agates are smooth and round, easily distinguished from the earlier hand-ground agates with facets. One does not need a "paper trail" to tell the antique from the modern agates made on a sphere machine. The facets are visible to the naked eye; one should look closely or in some instances use a low-power magnifying glass.

The majority of agates are colorless in nature, but some natural colors do occur. Red and brown are the most common due to the presence of iron oxide or iron hydroxide. Black is a natural color but scarce, making a handground black agate marble rather rare. Green also occurs in the form of moss agate, attributed to manganese oxide, and a natural blue is obtained from Africa.[10]

Agates may be colored naturally, or artificially using heat and chemicals. The art of dyeing has been practiced in Idar-Oberstein since the 1820s and has been perfected over the decades. Details of the coloring process are a commercial secret. The desired color is determined by the properties of the chemical. In contrast, carnelian is exposed to the rays of the sun to darken the color. Coloring by this method is still practiced in India, but coloring by exposure to direct flame is much quicker.

Nowadays, most agate is colored. An early principal listing shows colors and the coloring agent. In addition to the chemical, heat is employed as a catalyst.

Color	Coloring Agent
Red	Iron oxide
Blue	Turnbull's blue
Apple-green	Nickel oxide
Black	Carbon
Bluish-green	Chromic oxide
Blue	Berlin blue
Brown	Caramel

The brown (caramel) coloring is obtained from sugar by heating. Black is obtained by use of a concentrated sugar solution, following heat treatment with sulfuric acid. The sugar provides the carbon and sulfuric acid provides the catalyst. Generally, this dangerous process requires two to three weeks.[11] The absorption of the coloring agent varies with the porosity of the individual layers of the agate. White layers, consisting of dense quartz aggregates, absorb little or no color.

Contemporary handground stone marbles. Clockwise from top: Natural fine-grained quartzite; limestone; black flint; and fine-grained quartzite, dyed yellow.

The coloring of agates was discovered by accident in 1819; the first color was black. Nowadays, it is difficult to tell the difference between natural black agates and those that have been dyed. However, the dyed agate will show black specks like black pepper when examined under a microscope.[12] Other colors may be obtained by modification of the above methods. A large wholesaler of agate material advertises "White agate also dyed as red, yellow, green and coral green," so the possibilities of coloring are probably endless.

The main sources of agate today are South America and India. The Oregon coast, around Newport and Agate beaches, is noted for its exotic stone material. This is one of the finest agate hunting areas in the world and the leading cutting center for these gems in North America.

Clay and glass marbles have been used to promote candy and the famous popcorn confection, Cracker Jack. The Bloomer Candy Company of Zanesville, Ohio, once put agate marbles inside its chocolates. In the 1930s, when the company moved to a new plant on the other side of Zanesville, several large casks of agate marbles were hauled away by one of the workers and were used to pave his driveway. The driveway has since been covered with concrete, but the marbles are still believed to be there.[13]

A stone marble seldom seen in major marble collections is the Stonie, given its name by Chicago area marble players in the 1920s. Close examination of this white opaque stone marble reveals a coarse surface without facets; a "ding" made by an opponent's shooter results in a snowball-like surface fracture. Several geologists state that it is made of quartz sandstone—densely cemented quartz crystals—and that the natural reddish color and veins are probably an induced iron oxide. The stone is not a beautiful marble and was not a popular shooter, but serious shooters considered it an advantage over an opponent using an Aggie or a glass marble since its rough surface provided a firmer finger grip. Some authors call this type of stone marble an Alabaster.

MODERN STONE MARBLES

As a result of the interest in marble collecting in the last few years and as a spin-off of mineral collecting, there has been a great increase in the availability of newly made, semiprecious stone marbles. United States production of these marbles is on sphere machines or modified bead-making machines, which produce perfectly round examples, except where a mineral is a conglomerate of different materials, some of which have sections that are harder than others. The hard sections grind down more slowly, sometimes producing odd shapes. There are also a large number of stone marbles being imported from India. These are usually gray agate; apparently at some phase of their production they are turned by hand and then finished off by polishing. The hand-turning produces a less than perfectly round overall shape, but the final polishing removes the individual grinding facets seen on older hand-turned agates.

Robert "Bud" Garrett of Celina, Tennessee, was the earliest known maker of flint sphere-made marbles in the United States. His handmade specimens vary in size but are priced about the same regardless of size, since a similar amount of effort goes into making small ones and large ones.

Garrett made flint marbles for over sixty years for local marble shooters and was featured on NBC News on August 7, 1983, when the "Tennessee Shootout" was televised. Garrett also appeared in June 1986 at the 20th Annual Festival of American Folklife in Washington, D.C., which was sponsored by the Smithsonian Institution.

Garrett used only local native flint material, first chipping a rough cobblestone into as near a sphere as possible. Then it was ground down on a rough grinding wheel to remove the edges. Finally, it was placed in a concave preform die made of silicon carbide and held against a hard rubber wheel, which turned the rough sphere. The turning wheel caused it to rotate and grind itself into a smoother sphere against the silicon carbide die. The final phase of production was to place the sphere in a polishing drum.

There are several craftsmen of handmade marbles in the Tennessee-Kentucky border area, near Celina, Tennessee, who use local flint for their shooters. Dalford Farmer, a well-known marble maker, was featured in *The Tennessee Magazine*, September 1992.[14]

Ohio is known for a fancy variety of flint; Ohio flint is hard and fine-grained, but its outstanding characteristic is that it occurs in bright colors and complicated patterns. The general area around Flint Ridge State Park is famous for this flint, which is a choice material for tools and weapons of Native Americans. Recently, Ohio flint has become a favorite stone for modern flint sphere-made marbles. Carole A. Bowen of Portland, Oregon, makes spheres from this colorful stone and from Tennessee black flint. Ed Kepley of Independence, Missouri, advertises himself as a marble maker specializing in spheres of agate, fiber-optic glass, and tiger's-eye materials.

[1]William S. Webb, *Indian Knoll* (Knoxville, Tenn.: University of Tennessee Press, 1974), p. 231.

[2]Jeff Carskadden, personal correspondence, July 12, 1992.

[3]Trainoff, R & A Enterprises. Personal correspondence.

[4]Michael Olmert, "Points of Origin," *Smithsonian*, Vol. 14, No. 9 (December 1983), p. 42 (mention of marbles in early European literature).

[5]Stefan Pfnur, Gasthaus und Pension Zur Kugelmühle a.d. Almbacklamm, personal correspondence.

[6]Theosphrastus (372–287 B.C.), a treatise *On Stones*.

[7]Pliny the Elder (Gaius Plinius Secundus A.D. 23–79), *Natural History* (A.D. 77).

[8]Si and Ann Frazier, "Quartz Building Blocks," *Lapidary Journal*, February 1990, p. 91.

[9]*Leaflet 8* (Chicago: Field Museum of Natural History, Department of Geology, 1927), p. 125.

[10]*Leaflet 8*, ibid.,125.

[11]June Culp Zeitner, special editor, *Lapidary Journal*, personal correspondence.

[12]Ibid.

[13]Betty Bernard, "Chocolate Covered Marbles," *Buckeye Marble Collectors Club Newsletter*, June 1991, p. 2.

[14]Cathleen Cope, "The Rolley Holers," *The Tennessee Magazine*, September 1992, pp. 7–10.

Chapter III

• • •

Ceramic Marbles

Ceramic marbles—known to marble players and collectors as Clays, Chinas, and Benningtons, among many other names—are made of the second-oldest material used for marbles. Only stone marbles could possibly be older, but the question is not pertinent to the history of marbles in the New World. Both stone and clay marbles were well developed before European immigration to the Western Hemisphere. It is a safe assumption that both arrived with the earliest settlers.

Documented examples of early ceramic marbles include excavations at Fort Albany in James Bay, Canada, which was occupied between 1675 and 1720; pre-1776 Williamsburg, Virginia; and Fort La Cloche in Ontario, Canada, 1850–1870.[1] The majority of marbles found on many colonial sites are of plain gray or brown clay, although a few limestone and flint marbles have been found on seventeenth and eighteenth century colonial sites.[2] Some "agates" made from the mixing of two clays of different colors, generally gray and a reddish-brown, are also found on these sites.[3] Ceramic marbles, particularly non-glazed clays, are the most common type of marble found in excavations of sites inhabited during the last quarter of the nineteenth century.

The earliest information concerning porcelain marbles goes back to the last third of the eighteenth century in an area south of Thuringia, Germany, which had several porcelain factories. One of the factories began to specialize in porcelain marbles. The manufacturing method was as follows: The malleable porcelain mass was passed through pipes, then cut into appropriate pieces, pressed into plaster molds with lengthwise grooves, and with swift turning motions made into spheres. The marbles were then dried, painted in colors, and fired. The majority of the marbles had a banded design.[4]

Many of the ceramic marbles found in the United States and Canada were imported from Germany, although other European countries had ceramic marble industries. There were probably dozens of attempts at local production in the United States, but only a few are documented. The earliest of which there is a good record was Frazey Pottery in Zanesville, Ohio, in 1818.[5] The extent to which these marbles were distributed outside the Ohio region is not known.

China marbles were made by the Indiana Pottery Company in Troy, Ohio, as early as 1844. This is the earliest documentation for production of this type of marble in the United States. A fine account of this factory and the marbles made there is contained in the classic book by Jeff Carskadden and Richard Gartley, *Chinas—Hand-Painted Marbles of the Late 19th Century.*[6]

By 1884 Samuel C. Dyke was making clay marbles in Akron, Ohio,[7] and another factory was opened in 1889 by A. L. Dyke. The two factories had consolidated by 1891 and operated as the American Marble & Toy Manufacturing Company until about 1900.[8] About the same time as the Dykes' consolidation, another Ohio resident, Matthew Lang, applied for a patent for a machine to produce clay marbles. Other American ceramic marble makers of the period included J. F. Brown, in Akron; in 1895, Brown's factory produced one hundred thousand clay marbles per day.[9]

Little research has been done in other areas of the United States, but judging from the reported number of companies from Ohio, it is probable that the number of ceramic marbles produced in the United States beginning in the early nineteenth century was not as insignificant as previously believed.

Most surviving packages of ceramic marbles are clearly marked as German imports. The German marbles were packaged in cardboard cartons and boxes, intended for retail display, from which single marbles could be sold. The McKinley Tariff Act required labeling country of origin after 1891; all cartons and packages of imported marbles produced after that date would be so labeled. American-made marbles did not have to be labeled, so the origins of all unmarked packages are unknown. Some could very well be American-made.

Jeff Carskadden and Richard Gartley[10] provide the following overview of ceramic marbles:

1. Earthenware—fired at a low temperature
   a. Common Clays (including homemades)
   b. Pipe Clays or Plasters (white kaolin marbles, usually with concentric parallel lines)
   c. Yellowware (unglazed or clear lead glaze)
   d. Whiteware (white, out-of-round, porous, partially glazed, often decorated with a few concentric lines or spirals)
2. Stoneware or Crockery—medium firing
   a. Benningtons (brown manganese glaze or blue cobalt glaze)
   b. Agateware or Lined Crockery (several colors of clay mixed together)
   c. Salt-glazed (orange peel-like surface, sometimes decorated with blue)

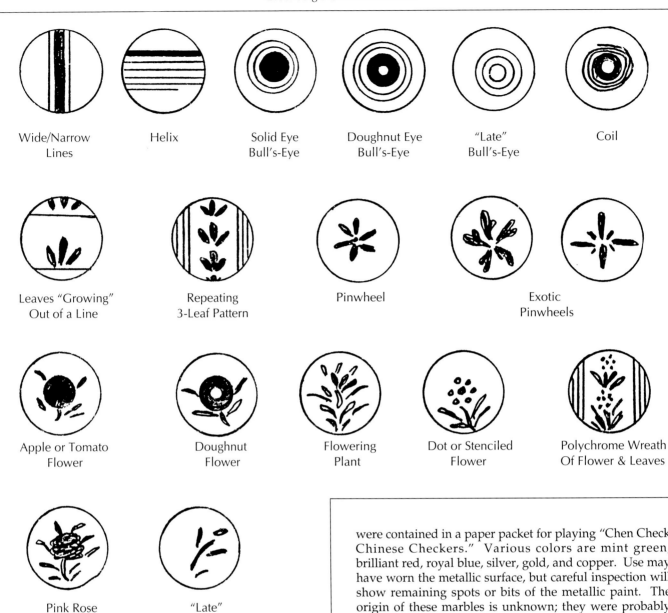

Wide/Narrow Lines · Helix · Solid Eye Bull's-Eye · Doughnut Eye Bull's-Eye · "Late" Bull's-Eye · Coil

Leaves "Growing" Out of a Line · Repeating 3-Leaf Pattern · Pinwheel · Exotic Pinwheels

Apple or Tomato Flower · Doughnut Flower · Flowering Plant · Dot or Stenciled Flower · Polychrome Wreath Of Flower & Leaves

Pink Rose Or "Pinkie" · "Late" Flower

Chinas can be decorated with a great variety of designs.

3. Porcelain—fired at high temperature; fine kaolin clay; includes Chinas (white-glazed or unglazed, with or without designs)

Common among the earthenware ceramic marbles is the clay homemade marble. Although the Clays or Commoneys were cheap, many boys preferred molding the marbles themselves to buying them. A detailed method for making clay marbles is contained in *Youth's Companion*, February 15, 1912. The article contains step-by-step procedures for making a mold, for making a device to gauge the amount of clay necessary, and for drying and baking the marble.[11] Commercially made clay marbles were usually well-rounded and often painted.

"Metallic Clay" marbles recently came to the attention of James "Jim" H. Davis, a noted collector. The marbles were contained in a paper packet for playing "Chen Check Chinese Checkers." Various colors are mint green, brilliant red, royal blue, silver, gold, and copper. Use may have worn the metallic surface, but careful inspection will show remaining spots or bits of the metallic paint. The origin of these marbles is unknown; they were probably made during the heyday of Chinese Checkers, 1930–1940.

At the end of the nineteenth century there were many English manufacturers producing ceramic marbles,[12] and while it is quite possible that some of these marbles may have been imported to the United States, English imports have not been documented.

Imports of German ceramic marbles were cut off during World War I (1914–1918) and may not have been resumed afterwards, due to the damage to that industry. Based on marble selections offered in catalogs of the period, the glazed Ceramics (Chinas and Benningtons) disappeared several years before World War I. In the Sears Roebuck and *Our Traveler* catalogs of 1903, there are several glazed ceramic types offered, but none after that year. So, by the beginning of the war, clays were the only ceramic marbles still offered. If the war hurt Germany's marble business, it did not entirely end sales of clay marbles in the United States. The Sears catalogs offered plain or painted clay marbles every year from 1916 through 1928; these may have been produced in the United States.

Clays were quite inexpensive. The November 1918

Yellowware marbles from Zanesville, Ohio area, circa 1870. Elizabeth Reeb and Jeff Carskadden Collections.

edition of *Little Folks*, of Salem, Massachusetts, advertised "American Painted Marbles" at forty cents a bag, each bag containing one thousand.

In general, Ceramics suffered the same fate as the other marbles that had been popular for the last half of the nineteenth century. With the development and improvement of machine-assisted glass production by M. F. Christensen, Horace Hill, John F. Early, and others, beginning in 1902 and continuing through the 1930s, the whole nature of the marble industry changed. It is surprising that clay marbles survived as long as they did, but their long-lived popularity was probably due to their low cost.

There are reports of clays still being sold in stores by the mid-1930s,[13] and the Christensen Agate Company had a large stock of clays on hand when it closed in 1933. In the early 1970s, reproductions of antique clays appeared in antique stores and flea markets, and in the early 1980s, at least one German firm, H. E. Hopf, offered clays as part of its regular line of marbles. (See Chapter XV on foreign marble companies.)

Earthenware marbles (clay or yellowware) are the simplest type, being composed of baked clay. As described above, clays were often homemade, in which case they were the natural color of the clay, usually tan, reddish, or brown. Commercial varieties were either plain or painted. When painted, the marble had either a single color or a speckled covering of color. The bright painted or dyed colors date from the 1890s and were made in Akron, Ohio.[14] Gartley and Carskadden date the pipe clay to the late nineteenth century.

In the colored earthenware marbles, the color was poorly baked on; in examples found today the color is usually worn off. In some cases, however, the coloring was mixed with the clay before baking and survived in better condition. Even in the latter case, the colors were earth tones, and it is difficult to determine whether they were dyed or are the natural color of the clay.

Most earthenware clays mature at about 2,000 degrees Fahrenheit and will deform if fired higher; stoneware and porcelain bodies mature between 2,250 and 2,400 degrees Fahrenheit.[15]

Whiteware marbles, which Gartley and Carskadden named and described for the first time, have been dated from excavations in the New Orleans area to the early or mid-1880s through about 1900–1910. They believe that this type is either an American or more probably an English imitation of the German porcelain type.

Brown stoneware marbles are often called Benningtons by collectors. For some time it was thought that they might have been made by potteries in Bennington, Vermont, where a similar brown glaze was applied to other wares. However, there are many examples of the brown and blue marbles from Germany, in original cartons, and there is no direct evidence that any were made in the Bennington area. Bennington marbles are also found in a variety of sizes, colors, and designs.

Benningtons are characterized by a number of "burn spots" or "black eyes" in the glaze, which are the result of the marbles being stacked together in a mass in the furnace during the firing phase.[16] The still-liquid glaze on the marbles' surface would run a bit before solidifying. After baking, the marbles were broken apart, leaving small scars or black eyes on the surface. Finer, individually made examples will have only a single mark, where the marble rested on the bottom of the furnace. Some of the blues and browns have window-screen marks on a flattened side, which indicates that these marbles were on the bottom of the pile and were squashed into the screen on the furnace floor by the weight of other marbles. Frequently, there is a surface roughness due to adherent grains of sand, suggesting the rather careless manner in which these marbles were made. These characteristics are helpful in distinguishing an early clay-ceramic marble from a contemporary one. The most common colors of Benningtons are brown and blue. A combination of these colors is called "fancy," and in some cases green is also present, resulting in a rather rare type. Some white Benningtons do exist.

Agateware color combinations include glazed and unglazed white with randomly swirling fine blue and green lines of color, and both blue and brown on white in a splotchy pattern. The catalogs of the 1880s, 1890s, and the 1903 editions mentioned above offer "Chinas" or "glazed" pottery marbles. These porcelain or stoneware marbles were fired at higher temperatures than the clays and consequently were harder and more expensive.

In Gartley and Carskadden's significant analysis of excavated materials from New Orleans, they cite the "earliest archaeological examples of imported German hand-painted porcelain . . . marbles" from a circa 1850–1860 cistern and mention pre-circa 1850 examples of agateware marbles from other sites. They also say that indications from excavations are "that most of the earlier decorated porcelain marbles were unglazed."

The relatively large number of decorated porcelain marbles from the New Orleans excavations enabled Gartley and Carskadden to propose dates for several of the known decorative schemes:

1. Intersecting sets of parallel lines/checkered pattern: date throughout the circa 1850–World War I period.

2. Single set of parallel lines around circumference, often with other decorative features on the "poles" such as leaves, flowers, or daisy wheels: fairly early in the period,

with dated examples from circa 1850–1860 and circa 1855–1865 sites.

3. Bull's-eyes: throughout the circa 1850–World War I period in general, but with "a" (below) generally earlier, "c" generally later, and "b" lasting throughout.

　　a. Large dot in center of eye surrounded by one or two narrow rings.
　　b. Wide central ring surrounded by one or two narrower rings.
　　c. All narrow concentric rings and always glazed.

4. Spirals: throughout the circa 1850–World War I period.

5. Leaves: popular throughout the circa 1850–World War I period.

6. Pinwheels (four to thirteen leaves or flower petals radiating from a central dot): early in the period, one dated example from circa 1850–1860.

7. Flowers and berries: uncertain dating, but indications are that the designs become more complex toward the end of the decorated ceramic period.

Early decorated and undecorated, glazed and unglazed ceramic and clay marbles, and crockery marbles commonly called Chinas. Grouped by type. Top row: Four colored clay marbles; single china marble with pinwheel and repeating three-leaf pattern; five glazed china marbles with multiline patterns of various colors. Middle row:

Three ceramic marbles, white unglazed and highly glazed color; five glazed Benningtons; one large unglazed and two small glazed marbles exhibiting the helix pattern. Bottom row: One unglazed, single Bull's-Eye marble and one glazed, three-color Bull's-Eye; single lined crockery marble.

It is possible that other countries in Europe were in the porcelain marble business before the Germans. By at least the 1860s and 1870s, porcelain marbles were being imported to England from the low countries (Netherlands, Belgium, and Luxembourg).[17]

In the white porcelain examples, the painted designs were common; but as the designs appear to have been applied after the initial firing of the marble itself, they do not survive well. In many cases, the white Chinas were not glazed and do not appear to have had a design applied at all. Some Porcelains featured decorated cherubs that were applied by decal. These were thought to be made by companies that made porcelain cane heads or parasol handles with cherubs. The Jeff Carskadden Collection and background data concerning the cherubs are outstanding.

The 1895 Montgomery Ward catalog lists "American Majolica Marbles," implying that they were produced in the United States, and calls them a new item. The term majolica is used to indicate brightly colored ceramics of some type, but the exact type of marble offered in the catalog is unknown.

Carskadden, Gartley, and Reeb[18] list two companies that made porcelain marbles in Ohio; one in Akron, which

A selection of modern, handmade ceramic marbles by Robert A. Brown of Ironton, Ohio, who is known worldwide for his craft. Brown recognizes the need to distinguish contemporary marbles from earlier ones, so most of his marbles are dated, signed, or initialed—an effort appreciated by antique dealers and serious marble collectors. Museum-quality ceramic marbles by this master craftsman are a refreshing addition to the line of marbles now collected.
Top row: handpainted 1992 Christmas marble featuring poinsettia on one side, holly on the other; Sugar Daddy with applied flower decals and glaze; Spongeware; first dated marble featuring hallmark "R. B. 86; orange Bennington; four-color Bennington featuring an eerie "mask" with yellow eyes, black irises, and a yellow nose is a colorful, *collectible aberration, not signed or dated. Second row: Chambered Nautilus, which looks like a ceramic marble but is actually a glass marble with special modifications by Brown; Polka Dot; Polka Dot (note dot on dot); handpainted clipper ship in three colors; Big Blue, which symbolizes the view of earth from outer space. Third row: Handpainted osprey with fish in beak; Funny Faces, six versions handpainted with six firings; three-colored feathered geometric; handpainted grapevine labeled "Concord R. B. 87," one of several fruit designs. Fourth row: Rosalita, entirely handpainted; two highly glazed multicolored geometrics. Bottom row: Corkscrew; handpainted strawberries with hallmark "Robert A. Brown 1987." Courtesy of Robert A. Brown.*

made marbles for a few years after 1894, and another porcelain company, which was established in 1916 and was producing Porcelains in 1923. This is quite a late date for this type, and it is surprising that there was enough demand for this "old" type to sustain production. The exact colors and designs produced by these two companies are not known.

For at least the last forty years, a stonelike marble has been produced for industrial uses, and it is often confused with (and sometimes misrepresented as) an antique stone or ceramic marble. These industrials are aluminum oxide compounds, white when new, extremely hard, and up to 3 inches in diameter. By the time these ceramic marbles have been worn down to about ¾ inch in diameter, they are discarded from certain uses such as ore-grinding, and are stained with rust colors. When worn down, they exhibit a seam around the middle that is slightly larger in diameter than the marble. These marbles are smooth and "heavy."

MODERN CERAMIC MARBLES

No one knows for certain when ceramic marbles began making a comeback. Most probably, the trend began several years ago when marble collecting revived and there was a demand for this type of marble. A list of makers known at this time includes Robert A. Brown, Ironton, Ohio; Michael Maday, Napa, California; and Marlow Peterson, Dayton, Utah. There are more contemporary craftspeople making glass marbles than ceramic marbles.

Overall, Robert Brown may be considered the top craftsman in the contemporary clay marbles field because of his numerous, imaginative designs. His colorful marbles are at present collectible and of museum quality. He has been singled out as a dedicated master craftsman whose designs range from the traditional, antique types to more modern motifs. The first of Brown's handmade marbles offered to the public bore a handpainted rose with green leaves, and Brown's hallmark, "R B 86." Following are descriptions of some of his marbles and methods.

Bennington-style (large size, up to three inches): The recipe for commercial clay marbles includes raw sugar, which imparts "toughness" or strength. Adding the sugar results in a marble that, if dropped on a concrete floor, will bounce without breaking. Brown rolls a dab of recipe clay in a circular motion by hand and sets it aside to dry. After drying, the marble is fired at 2,055 degrees Fahrenheit (Cone .02. A cone is a visible device to measure temperature.) Kiln ventilation is not necessary for the first firing. After cooling, the marble is ground to roundness on a belt-driven, water-cooled, fine-grade grinding wheel. The edge of the wheel is concave, and Brown turns the marble constantly with his fingers to make it round. This type of marble is not ground to perfection, as are geometrics, which must be truly round spheres to acquire uniform striping on a lathe. A colored glass glaze is applied after air-drying, and the marble is returned to the kiln for a second firing at 1,860 degrees Fahrenheit (Cone .06). After cooling, a decal may or may not be applied. If a decal is applied, the marble is then fired at 1,550 degrees Fahrenheit (Cone .015) with an automatic cone setting of approximately four hours and with exhaust ventilation for the first three hours. For colored and decal types, this ventilation is necessary because accumulated gases may damage the marbles. Various colors are used, which distinguishes these modern marbles from antique Benningtons.

Bennington-style (smaller size): The same procedures are followed as in making the larger sizes, but the marbles are not sized on a grinding wheel. Contemporary Benningtons are made in white, blue, brown, green, mottled, and fancy colors.

Big Blue: Big Blue is a porcelain marble with an off-white body color and numerous variegated bluish lines swirling throughout the body and design surface. The surface is truly representative of what earth looks like from outer space. This limited edition classic collectible is fired at a rather hot temperature of 2055 degrees Fahrenheit (Cone .02) and bears a signature reading "Robert A. Brown" and "1992." Big Blue III, a marble of nearly 3 inches in diameter, is serially numbered and will be limited to one hundred. This beautiful marble may be seen displayed on a stand of matching colors.

Corkscrew: This marble is a recent design and another first. Clay preparation is very critical. White commercial clay is kneaded into a stick several inches in length and about 1 inch square and set aside. Four lengths of two different colored clays are rolled out about ¼ inch or less in diameter, and then placed on the flat surfaces of the square piece of white clay. (Colored clay is made by adding dry powdered color glaze to white clay. A variety of color designs are possible through use of different clay colors.) The entire mass is then rolled and twisted into a 1-inch stick. The rolling and twisting must remove any entrapped air because the rapid expansion of an air bubble literally causes the sphere to explode, damaging the kiln liner and possibly injuring the marble maker as well.

Dexterity and finesse in the rolling and twisting gives the clay mass a screwlike appearance. Blank marbles are cut off with a specially designed knife that pushes the colors toward the center of the stick. Each segment is hand-rolled into a rough sphere and air-dried. The sphere is fired at 2,055 degrees Fahrenheit (Cone .02); after cooling, it is ground into a round sphere by hand on a water-cooled grinding wheel, like the large Bennington. After drying, a clear glaze is applied and the marble is fired at 1,860 degrees Fahrenheit (Cone .06). After cooling, Brown adds his signature and the date. The marble is then given its final firing at 1,330 degrees Fahrenheit (Cone .018). Only a flat underglaze, which requires finishing with a coat of clear-transparent glaze, works well in this design. There is no difficulty in recognizing this contemporary clay design since no similar antique ceramic design exists. This should become a very popular collectible. Its display or exhibition along with various Akro Agate Corkscrews would be outstanding.

Decal: This type encompasses a wide range of design possibilities. The marble is made like the Bennington. A decal is applied on top of a white gloss glaze and then fired.

Gem China: These marbles are quite similar to the antique Chinas, and are made like the Benningtons. About 90 percent of them are finished unglazed. Stripes or bands of various colors are added on a lathe before the final firing. Colored body clay may also be used.

Geometrics: These marbles are prepared essentially like the Benningtons, and the design possibilities are endless. Rings are added with a fine hair brush while the marble is turning on a lathe. Various colors are used; however, a separate firing is required for each color. Antique and marble collectors can distinguish between the antique and contemporary types since the contemporary ones have straight, even lines due to the use of the lathe, whereas the antique ones have wavy lines since they were applied by hand.

Brown made a glazed, feathered prototype in 1992 with three circling colors of green, blue, and black. This single marble was signed and dated with day, month, and year. But Brown did not repeat this design because of the time and effort involved in making it.

Handpainted China: The same procedures for making the Benningtons are used to make marbles bearing the Pennsylvania Dutch hex sign motifs or variations, except that after the marbles are sized and dried, they are then painted with an underglaze and permitted to air-dry. A clear glaze is then applied, dried, and fired at 1,860 degrees Fahrenheit (Cone .06). Marbles featuring paintings of various types of fruit, particularly a cluster of Concord grapes, are quite beautiful.

Hand-decorated: Again, these are made like the Benningtons. After they are fired and rounded, the marbles are painted with an underglaze and fired, then dipped in a clear glaze, permitted to air-dry, and fired at 1,860 degrees Fahrenheit (Cone .06). Hand-decorated marbles may also be underglazed. An outstanding example of a hand-decorated marble is the first annual Christmas marble, which depicts the green leaves and red berries of the American holly. It also bears Brown's trademark "RB 86." This is another first; subsequent marbles have a full signature applied by decal or hand and the year. For this type of marble, Brown also uses Pennsylvania Dutch hex signs, which give him an endless variety of patterns.

Leopard Skin: The Leopard Skin is a spin-off of the Polka Dot (below), having a black glaze with orange dots. All are signed and dated. Few of these colorful marbles are made, and they are highly collectible.

Polka Dot: This is a glazed ceramic marble first made in 1991 with a yellow glaze and a multitude of orange, red, green, black, purple, and blue dots on the entire surface. One design type is unique in that it contains a dot on a dot. Considerable time and effort are expended in making this signed and dated marble, as well as the above-mentioned Leopard Skin. The size ranges from 7/8 inch to 1¾ inches.

Pontil: This design does not have a pontil mark per se as found on early handmade glass marbles. However, the name does describe the design very well. The Pontil marble is shaped and fired following similar methods as for Benningtons. It is made from a rounded ball of clay fired at 2,055 degrees Fahrenheit (Cone .02) and then ground for roundness. Next, the marble is dipped in glaze. Various color combinations are possible. All colors used are gloss glaze, such as white and possibly two other colors such as brown and green. For this combination, a white gloss glaze is placed in a small, open shallow container; brown gloss glaze is then poured on one side and green on the other side of the white. Using a two-tined fork, the marble is dipped into the container, which results in three distinct stripes dripping from the top of the marble to the bottom. The excess glaze at the bottom gathers in a "teat," giving the marble a pontil look. The marble is air-dried on three small stilts embedded in a platform, then fired at about 1,330 degrees Fahrenheit (Cone .06) to 1,400 degrees Fahrenheit (Cone .06).

Spongeware: The Spongeware marble is made using the same procedures as in making the Bennington. A variety of colors unlike that found in the earlier Benningtons such as orange, green, red, and yellow are used. Random application of color, variety of colors, and absence of burn marks or black eyes are the signatures of this contemporary type.

Sugar Daddy: These beauties are made like the Bennington except that excess raw sugar is added to the clay, and fired with a clear glaze. The excess sugar bubbles to the surface, showing brown spots. A decal signature and date are added.

Whirligigs: These marbles have various color rings representing Joseph's coat of many colors. The rings are added while the marble is spinning on a lathe. Firing order is then followed like the Bennington. This is an attractive, colorful marble, particularly in large sizes up to 3 inches.

Brown fires all of his marbles on props made by inserting three short stainless steel pins into a flat ceramic base. This method negates the formation of a black ring (black eye) as found in earlier mass-produced ceramic marbles that touched each other and the sides of the kiln. This modern refinement means, however, that fewer marbles can be fired per batch. In the case of the Pontil marble, only four marbles may be fired at a given time; hence, these are in a higher price range than other designs.

Firing of a marble with a signature or hallmark may differ. The firing of a marble with a decal signature and date is from 1,480 degrees Fahrenheit (Cone. 015) to 1,330 degrees Fahrenheit (Cone .018); whereas a signature and date applied by hand is fired at 1,860 degrees Fahrenheit (Cone .06).

Most if not all of Brown's handmade marbles have either a hand-applied hallmark (initial and year) or a full signature and year applied by decal or hand. Marble collectors and antique dealers should have no difficulty in distinguishing his contemporary ceramic marbles from the antique ones. The differences are obvious, considering the size of types such as the large Bennington and Whirligig, the bold and vivid colors, the new designs such as the Whirligig, Sugar Daddy, Pontil, and Corkscrew, and the addition of a hallmark or signature and date.

Brown is discontinuing many of his earlier designs, giving preference to a new design type consisting of hand-painted scenes such as Clipper Ship, Funny Faces, Osprey, and Spirit of St. Louis. These marbles will be signed by hand and dated; in some cases they will be limited editions. Much artistic skill and effort are expended on these highly collectible marbles.

In the spring of 1990, Michael J. Maday entered the circle of makers of contemporary clay-porcelain marbles, having found that the antique ones were rather dull and plain. He follows techniques similar to those of other contemporary marble makers. A new type introduced is produced through Raku firing, which is a unique process originating in Japan. Raku is named for the sixteenth-century potters credited with developing the earthenware items used in the tea ceremony. The ware is glazed and placed in a red-hot kiln, quickly withdrawn when the glaze melts, and covered with straw. These marbles are characterized by smoke-filled cracks and metallic lusters.

The pit-fired marbles are unglazed and usually black. Most of Maday's marbles are stoneware. Various types of firings include bisque, pit raku, and salt-firings.[19]

Porcelain marbles made by Marlow Peterson are normally in the standard size of about ¾ inch. His line includes a variety of colorful glazes of the Bennington type, sand of different colors rolled into the marble, beautiful flowers or other decals fired permanently into the glaze, and "Limited Edition Marbles" made for some of the marble shows, which have gold writing fired into the marble. Some are even numbered and dated. A three-page article in the June 1991 issue of *Rock & Gem* magazine highlights the various types of marbles made by Peterson.

[1]Mark E. Randall, *Marbles as Historical Artifacts* (Trumbull, Ct.: Marble Collectors Society of America, 1979), p. 10.

[2]Jeff Carskadden, personal correspondence, July 12, 1992.

[3]Ivory Noel Hume, *A Guide to Artifacts of Colonial America*, (Alfred A. Knopf, 1969), p. 320.

[4]Deutsches Spielzeugmuseum, Thuringia, Germany.

[5]Jeff Carskadden, Richard Gartley, and Elizabeth Reeb, "Marble Making and Marble Playing in Eastern Ohio," paper presented at the Third Annual Symposium on Ohio Valley Urban and Historic Archaeology, March 23, 1985.

[6]Jeff Carskadden and Richard Gartley, *Chinas—Hand-Painted Marbles of the Late 19th Century* (Zanesville, Ohio: The Muskingum Valley Archaeological Survey), pp. 10-12.

[7]Stout, cited in Carskadden, Carskadden, Gartley, and Reeb.

[8]Carskadden, Gartley, and Reeb, ibid.

[9]Carskadden, Gartley, and Reeb, ibid.

[10]Jeff Carskadden and Richard Gartley, personal comments.

[11]"Making Marbles," *Youth's Companion*, February 15, 1912, p. 9.

[12]*Marble-Mania*, newsletter of the Marble Collectors Society of America, Trumbull, Ct., Vol. 21 (January 1981), p. 4.

[13]Randall, ibid.

[14]Carskadden, personal correspondence, July 12, 1992.

[15]Glenn C. Nelson, *Ceramics, A Potter's Handbook* (New York: Holt, Rinehart and Winston, 1971).

[16]Robert A. Brown, personal conversation.

[17]Leslie Daiken, *Children's Toys Throughout the Ages* (New York: Frederick A. Praeger, 1953), p. 34.

[18]Carskadden, Gartley, and Reeb, ibid.

[19]Michael J. Maday, personal correspondence

Chapter IV

● ● ●

Handmade Glass Marbles

Various types of early handmade glass Swirls, including rare cut cane marbles. Many have dings and fractures attesting to their antiquity. Four marbles in the foreground are of special interest.

From left: a beautiful and rare cranberry Lutz marble; a white opaque marble with two red swirls, quite rare; a canary Ribbon Swirl; and a lemon Lutz. Robert Payton and Dennis Webb Collections.

The first handmade glass marbles were attributed to the Venetians.[1] Although Venetian glassmakers were certainly capable of such production, it was the Germans who gave the glass marble industry its international reputation. The earliest record of handmade glass marbles coincides with the invention of marble scissors at a glasshouse in southern Thuringia, Germany, around 1846. This original tool made marble production faster but still required great skill and dexterity, particularly to make Sulphides. The preferred material for marbles was many-colored, threaded glass rods.[2] The history of the Greiner family glasshouse of Lauscha at Sonneberg shows that the marble scissors invented by Johann Christoph Simon Karl Greiner made it possible to produce multicolored glass spheres. A similar tool had already been used to create animal's eyes and "glass blobs over the lamp."[3] It is not known exactly when German marbles began appearing as a major import to the United States.

Other European countries were producing marbles, including handmade glass marbles, in the same period. A method for manufacturing "marble glass" was patented on April 25, 1892, by C. F. E. Grosse (country of patent unknown). The glassman took molten glass and worked it

Closeup of Lutz marbles. In The Collector's Encyclopedia of Antique Marbles, Clara Ingram refers to these lovely marbles as Goldstone Spirals.

off the glass. After the marble cooled somewhat, it was placed in a wooden drum. The marble maker rotated the drum with a foot extension (pedal) until the marble was completely cooled and rounded.[6] Generally, the marble bore a single rough cutoff mark, which is the signature of this type of handmade glass marble.

Mel Morrison and Carl Terrison describe a slightly different process: the glass rods were banded together and heated just to melting, and then the glassworker twisted the rod, forming the marble. The new marble was still attached to the original rod by a thin glass thread that was cut off, leaving the cutoff scar.

There were sporadic attempts at clay and glass marble production in the United States, and while some may have been locally successful, there was no serious competition against the tide of the German marbles until shortly after the turn of the twentieth century. One American company that made handmade glass marbles (Swirls and possibly Sulphides) was the Iowa City Flint Glass Manufacturing Company, which produced glassware from early 1881 until early 1882.[7] Another possible American maker was the Sandwich Glass Company, but information regarding its marble-making activities is sketchy and conflicting. Since American and German marbles were produced by the same methods, they are indistinguishable.

For the last quarter of the nineteenth century, semiprecious stone (mainly agates) marbles from Germany and handmade glass marbles from Germany or the United States were the most sought-after marbles. A combination of events changed this and ended the German dominance of the marble market: the beginning of World War I, which halted German imports and destroyed the German glass industry, and the development in the United States of semi-automatic marble-making machines. By the mid-1920s handmade glass marbles were not nearly as popular as they had been, having been replaced by the new machine-made glass marbles, which were made only in the United States.

As the saying goes, there is no explaining taste. The German and American handmade glass marbles were undoubtedly the most beautiful marbles ever produced, but they passed from the scene after almost a half-century of preeminence. Their beauty has only recently been reproduced by American glass craftsmen who have revived this art.

The August 1993 issue of *Early American Life* magazine depicts $50,000 worth of rare handmade antique marbles from the collection of Bertram M. Cohen.[8]

on the end of a punty. The punty, sometimes called a pontil, was an iron rod $\frac{3}{8}$ inch in diameter and about 30 inches long, with a rivet-like head about $\frac{5}{8}$ inch in diameter; it was the primary tool for handling molten glass. The punty was sometimes fitted with a leather sleeve to prevent slipping. The gob of molten glass on the tip was called a "gather." When the glass was in a suitable working mass—not too stiff and not too runny—the glassman sprinkled it with a fine colored powder called flux. He then reheated the mass, which was still on the end of the punty, in a furnace to fuse the flux.[4]

The Bristol Glass Works in England manufactured glass marbles in the mid-nineteenth century,[5] but it is not known which, if any, countries besides Germany exported their products to the United States. By the 1880s, however, the German marble industry, which produced not only glass marbles, but those made of clay, stone, and porcelain as well, was virtually the only outside supplier of marbles to the United States.

Production methods for handmade glass marbles changed little over the decades. In most cases, the glassworker began with a hot mass of glass about 6 inches long on the end of a blowpipe. The glassworker rolled the glass across a grooved iron sheet on which other small rods of colored glass had been laid. This colorful rod was then covered with clear glass. This process could be repeated a number of times, forming several layers of variously colored rods of glass. When the final design was achieved, the glassworker pulled and twisted the rod out to a smaller diameter and a length of about 6 feet. These rods could later be pulled to the desired diameter of the marbles to be produced. The actual marbles were cut off the end of the rod with marble scissors.

The marble scissors resembled tongs with a thimblelike cup on one side and a knife blade on the other. The end of the hot glass rod was forced into the cup and twisted. The round bottom of the cup formed one rounded portion of the new marble, and the twisting motion helped form the complete sphere. The tong handles were then squeezed shut, bringing the blade across the mouth of the cup to cut

MAJOR HANDMADE GLASS MARBLE TYPES

Swirl: handmade glass type. The most common type of handmade glass marble, encompassing many sub-types:
Banded: Occurs in Transparent or Opaque. The swirling

glass design is composed of two to eight intermittent bands or ribbons of color on the surface of the marble. If it is a Transparent marble, there is no inner design present.

Clambroth: Historically, this type is named after the color of the body glass, an off-white color, or the color of clambroth.[9] The Clambroth is considered similar to Candle Swirls but with no inner core; it has only the outer swirls—usually four or five.[10] This type with a black body glass has been called Clambroth Swirl.[11] Other marbles have also been called Opaque Glass Spirals[12] and Clambroths, which contain any color as long as they are opaque and covered with thin lines of colored glass evenly spaced in a swirl from top to bottom.[13] The swirls may be thick (wide), medium, or thin, running from one pontil to the other pontil; they stop a distance from each pontil point. Multiple stripes of several colors on white opaque (Clambroth color) command a higher price. Currently, collectors accept the following color combinations: opaque white body glass with lines of blue, red, green, and yellow; red and blue; blue and brown; and black body glass with white lines.

Divided, Split, or Open Core: Occurs in transparent bodies only; the design is composed of a central core of differently colored glass threads in a gently twisting pattern from one end of the marble to the opposite end. The twisting group of threads is open in the middle, allowing the center of the marble to be seen. The marble is also called Latticino or Net Core. It may or may not have additional threads closer to the outside of the marble.

Indian or Joseph: The marble was so named because of a belief that this type was produced in India, but there is no hard evidence to support this theory; another explanation for the name is that the bright colors are reminiscent of colorful American Indian blankets. It may also be called Joseph in view of its coat of many colors. The Indian Swirl occurs in Opaques and in dark Transparents they can be distinguished by holding them up to a strong light. What appears to be a black Opaque may actually be a purple or blue Transparent. A fine example with transparent green was shown at the Blue Ridge Marble Club meet in 1991. The entire outer surface of the marble is covered in a thin mixture of colored lines of glass that move from one pole of the marble to the other in unison. Some of the bands of color may fade in and out, as they are thinly applied to the very surface of the marble.

Lutz: The Lutz name designates the presence of "goldstone," which is found in the Banded type (both Opaque and Transparent). Credit for originating this technique is given to Nicolas Lutz, who worked at the Boston and Sandwich Glass Company in Massachusetts from 1869 to the closing of the factory in 1888. Clara Ingram in an early book gave this marble the rather descriptive name of Goldstone Spiral.[14]

Some sources question whether Lutz marbles were made there. Dr. Henry D. Watson, an authority on antique glass, says that "the Boston and Sandwich Glass Company did make marbles, for in excavations at the site a considerable number of them were found, but mostly imperfect or broken. It is intimated that these marbles may have been imported. Yet, this is thought to be unlikely; it seems more probable that such marbles were actually made at Sandwich. It is presumed, however, that the colored canes from which these swirled marbles were molded [sic] were importations, for a large number of them have been found in excavations at Sandwich."[15] It is also not certain whether the Lutz was made as a novelty by the glassmen or whether it was a production item like their paperweights and other famous glass. Germany and other European countries did make the Lutz and were fully aware of the methodology.

Peppermint: This design is composed of definite ribbons of color that do not fade in and out; the entire surface is completely covered with red, white, and blue bands. The body is clear, but this can only be seen at the cutoff points where the spiraling bands come together.

Ribbon or Lobed Core: As above, occurs only in Transparent. The central core is similar to that of the Divided Core type, in that the center of the design is open, but in this case the design elements are much thicker than the threads of the Latticino type. They are either the wider "ribbon," which may be composed of two or more colors,

A group of early handmade glass marbles. Top row: Divided Core Swirl; Onionskin. Center: End of Day. Bottom: Latticino Core; Onionskin. The Onionskins are opaque marbles with a transparent body and two pontil marks. One may see through the marbles at the marks. The highly collectible End of Day is similar to the Onionskin but has only one pontil mark. Swirls have two. Divided Core Swirls are not common, particularly if the body glass is other than transparent white; Latticino Swirls are more common.

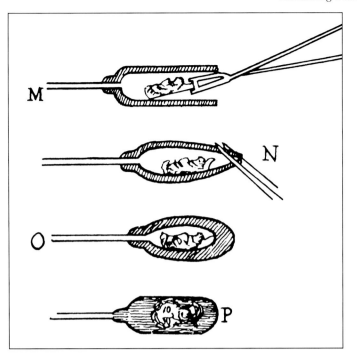

Generally, handmade marble production was concentrated in Lauscha, Germany, around the time Johann Greiner invented the so-called "marble scissors," circa 1850. It was in that era that the first Sulphides were made. This diagram from Curiosities of Glass Making, written by Englishman Apsley Pellatt in 1849, shows a gypsum figure being inserted into glass.

or they may be the still wider and much thicker "lobe."

Solid Core: Also occurs only in Transparent. The core in this case is composed of a single element: a gently twisting central core of several different colors of glass.

Micaceous (Micas or Glimmers): The presence of many small flecks of ground mica distinguishes this type. Patent No. 201,100 (application filed October 3, 1883; renewed April 23, 1884) Specification forming part of Letters Patent No. 201,100, dated July 1, 1884, to John Charles De Voy of Sandwich, Massachusetts, describes the use of mica in glassware.

Particles of mica were immersed in a bath of silver nitrate for about forty-eight hours, after which they were removed and dried. A preheated punty with a gather of molten glass on the end was rolled into the particles of silver-coated mica and then submitted to intense heat in a glass furnace, which caused the glass to flow over the mica and firmly adhere to it. Due to the mechanics of the handmaking process, a swirling effect can be seen in the glass, but it is not very strong due to the sparseness of the inner design elements. Micas are always transparent, and the only design variations are in the color of the body glass and the amount of mica in the marble. Sometimes a fine thread of differently colored glass occurs in the center of a Mica, and its origin is unknown. The body glass colors of Micas include clear, turquoise, light to dark blues and greens, gold, purple, and red.

David Gruening, an internationally known glass artist from West Barnet, Vermont, made a Mica in clear crystal for his annual limited edition marble in 1987. One is signed, numbered, and dated "DG 33 87." Charles D.

Gibson, of Milton, West Virginia, a maker of modern Swirl marbles, uses iron pyrite flakes instead of mica.

Opaque: The handmade glass Opaque is not a common type. The much more colorful types were more popular with children. The most common use of Opaque marbles, at least in black and white, was in voting ceremonies, where a black marble signified a "no" vote, and a white signified a "yes"; hence, these are called ballot box marbles. To "black ball" someone meant to vote against them by dropping the black marble in the ballot box. Cutoff marks are often quite pronounced. No effort was made to polish them down because they were not to be used for games, and it was not as important that these objects be perfectly round. Besides black and white, the opaque type occurs in green, blue, yellow, and red. Singer & Wheeler's 1894–95 catalog from Peoria, Illinois, advertised ballot marbles, No. 00, white or black, at 50 cents per one hundred.

Translucent: Also called Semi-Clearies, these marbles are simply a more translucent variety of the Opaque type; they also lack any decoration other than the single basic body glass color and occur in the same colors as the Opaques (except black).

Transparent: Also called Clearies, these are like the Opaque and Translucent types in that they lack any design aside from the single body color and they occur in the same colors (except black).

A common type of Transparent is the bottle marble. Developed in England in the early 1870s, it was used with a type of bottle called a Codd bottle, named after its developer. The marble was part of a closure device for carbonated beverages. It debuted in the United States shortly after it appeared in England. It was patented here in 1873.[16] This was a complex bottle to produce, however, and soon other methods of sealing liquids in bottles were developed.[17] When the bottles were empty, children often broke them and removed the marbles. These marbles are distinguished from other Transparents by the presence of a mold mark or line around their circumference. This indicates that the bottle marbles were made in spherical molds like bullets, rather than being twisted off as true marbles were. However, some do exist without these marks. They are clear, azure, opaque black, and translucent light green in color. The Codd bottle is described in Patent No. 138,230 granted April 29, 1873, to Hiram Codd of England. The patent uses the term "ball-stoppers" rather than marbles.

Although these bottles (and marbles) were supposedly used only for a few years, many of them have appeared on the domestic antique market in recent years. Quantities of marble-stoppered bottles with English brand names on them can be readily obtained. The excellent condition and relative abundance of these bottles seems to deny that they might be more than one hundred years old. There are also records of the use of this type of bottle in the Orient, in the post-World War II period, and in Cuba well into the twentieth century. A 1940 article[18] mentions marbles being used as stoppers in nonrefillable bottles. This particular use involved machine-made marbles. Master Glass and Champion Agate shipped many marbles to Havana, Cuba, for placement into "nonrefillable" bottles to prevent "the unscrupulous from refilling bottled-in-bond with Old Radiator."[19]

It is possible that the original English bottle and marble molds were sold to other companies and used much later than the 1870s. All in all, dating these types of bottles and marbles is very uncertain.

Glass ingots are often mistaken for old Transparent marbles. These are light green glass spheres about one inch in diameter, not perfectly round, and usually scarred and chipped, with an orange-peel surface. They have been manufactured for the production of fiberglass for many years.

Slag: The French chemist, J. A. Chaptal, working for the queen of Naples in the late eighteenth century, succeeded in making a new form of marble glass by mixing volcanic slag with the batch of ingredients. The resulting glass was velvety purple. Objects in lava glass were also made in Bohemia, and in the 1880s the fashion was taken up in England under the name of slag glass.[20] Another type of slag glass is produced by skimming silicate slag off of molten metal and mixing it with clear glass.[21]

The Slag is opaque only, with a single swirling design color added to the body color; the two colors are intermingled, but not enough to blend into each other. The design pattern is generally a spiral, but it is not definite enough to be a Banded Opaque Swirl. Dark colors are the most common, particularly dark brick red. Pontil marks identify handmade Slag marbles.

End of Day: According to legend, at the end of the work day, workers in marble factories would each make a single marble for their children. The End of Day title encompasses all of those unique marbles that were made not for sale but as gifts. They are usually large, in excess of one inch, and normally they are opaque with the colors only on the outermost layer. The design is usually a random collection of many colors in a gently spiraling pattern. The End of Day marbles have only one cutoff mark, since this type was individually pulled rather than being one of many cut from a single rod.

Onionskin: This marble is so named because the design layer is like the layer of an onion. Unlike the End of Day, the Onionskin has two pontil cutoff marks.

Sulphide: Related to the other types only in that they are made by hand, the Sulphides are large transparent marbles. They range from 1 inch to 3 inches in diameter. In their centers are silvery figurines of people, animals, and other items. Rarely is there more than a single figure in each marble. If a pontil cutoff mark is present, it will be well polished. In rare cases there are other design characteristics added, such as a ground surface for an animal to stand on. The body color is almost always clear, and only in rare examples is the body glass or enclosed figure colored. Sulphides were made individually, rather than being one of a series cut from a single rod, as were the majority of handmade glass marbles.

The early history of the Sulphide marble is sketchy in that any glass references address cameo encrustations or "crystallo ceramie" and not marbles per se. A Sulphide is a figure that may be inserted into a cameo, paperweight, or marble. In early days, the prime interest was in cameos, but in later years Sulphide figures played a major role in making paperweights. Making Sulphide marbles was secondary for many years. However, the methodology for making cameos and paperweights was easily applied to making a Sulphide marble. The first attempts in making crystallo ceramie originated in Bohemia and then traveled quickly to France.

Experiments in Sulphide marble making were many. Pierre Honoré Boudon de Saint-Amans secured the first recorded patent in France in 1818 for perfecting (not inventing) the Sulphide.[22] A description of this process follows: A copper mold is prepared, the size and depth depending upon the size and thickness of the cameo to be encrusted. The first workman pours in molten crystal from his dipper; a second levels the surface with his copper palette knife and inserts the cameo, face downwards; a third workman pours more molten crystal on the back of the cameo, which is thus between two layers of crystal; the second man with his palette knife gently presses the mass in the mold. An apprentice carries the hot mold in a pair of tongs to the oven. Two minutes of baking generally is sufficient to set the crystal, no matter how large the object.[23]

The most successful method is contained in a patent acquired one year later by Apsley Pellatt, No. 4424, December 18, 1819. "The figure intended for encrustation must be made of materials that will require a higher degree of heat for their fusion than the glass within which

Early handmade Sulphide marbles. The bodies are transparent glass and the figures are made of a clay-glass paste. Top row: Leaping frog and sheep. Bottom row: Horse. The original owner of the horse Sulphide said that it is more than one hundred years old. Robert H. Payton Collection.

it is to be encrusted; these are china clay and super-silicate of potash, ground and mixed in such proportions . . . should be slightly baked, and then suffered gradually to cool; or the cameos may be kept in readiness till required for encrustation, for which purpose they should be reheated to redness in a small Stourbridge clay muffle. A cylindrical flint glass pocket is then prepared, one end adhering to the hollow iron rod (see [p. 30] Step M) with an opening at the other extremity, into which the hot composition figure is introduced; the end (Step N) is then collapsed and welded together by pressure, at the red heat, so that the figure is in the center of the hollow glass pocket or muffle. The workman next applied his mouth at the end of the tube (Step O), while rewarming the glass at the other extremity; but instead of blowing, he exhausts the air, thus perfecting the collapse, by atmospheric pressure, and causing the glass and composition figure to be one homogeneous mass (Step P)."[24] A Sulphide figure is composed of china clay mixed with sand and a flux of potash—in other words, a clay-glass paste. (The Stourbridge clay muffle is a small oven used for heating or melting an object. It is named for a town in England.)

Jokelson[25] says that Sulphides were made in the United States and in Germany from about 1878 to 1926. He does not distinguish which country produced them until the later date, but he admits that good information on the manufacture of Sulphides is not available. The Iowa City Flint Glass Manufacturing Company reportedly produced Sulphides during the short time they were in business (1881–82) according to Righter.[26] The Sulphide industry in Germany may have been damaged in World War I, but it is not clear whether it was destroyed.

Overall, dates for Sulphide production vary widely from one source to another. A 1941 article[27] says that they were made "40–50 years ago"; in 1966[28] it was reported that they were made by hand in Germany from about 1840 to about 1926, and from then until about 1950 by machine. A 1972 *Antique Trader* article[29] does not give a beginning date but claims that production ceased in 1930.

The first appearance of Sulphides in American catalogs was in 1894 and 1895,[30] and they last appeared in 1914.[31] Catalog references sometimes called them "Figured Glass" marbles. They were always one of the most expensive types; in the 1894–1895 Montgomery Ward catalog, they were priced at three cents to fifteen cents each, depending on size. Clay marbles at the same time were about ten for one cent; Agates were eight cents to twenty cents each.

Sulphides exhibit one of three different surface finishes: completely smooth; with a single cutoff mark; or with a seam entirely encircling the marble, as if it were made with a mold.[32]

In the early 1970s, plastic reproductions were made. Some mint-condition glass specimens that appeared around that time may be reproductions, but their origin is unknown. The enclosures in the reproductions are less silvery than the genuine Sulphides. It is also reported that

The limited-edition Population Portrait by artist Mark Matthews of Archbold, Ohio. The series consists of six jars, each containing eighty-one handmade glass marbles. Matthews' marbles and jars are in the collections of several museums and have won numerous awards. Photo by Jerry Anthony.

in the mid-1960s glass Sulphides were being made in Murano, Italy, for a New York importer.

Animal figures enclosed in Sulphides include the following: ape, bear, beaver, boar, buffalo, camel, cat, chicken, cow, crane or stork, dog, donkey, duck, eagle, elephant, fish, flying horse, fox, frog, goat, hedgehog, hippopotamus, horse, lamb, leopard, lion, lizard, mink, monkey, mule, otter, owl, parrot, pig, pigeon, porcupine, quail, rabbit, raccoon, ram, rat, rooster, seal, sheep, squirrel, turtle, weasel, wolf, and wolverine. Since the figurines are often indistinct, some of the animals named above may be the same character, for instance, mink, otter, and weasel. Some marbles contain figures of people: ape man, baby, children (boys and girls), Christ on cross, clown, Little Red Riding Hood, man, President McKinley, W. C. Fields, Santa Claus, woman, and Queen Victoria. Other: angel, cannon, coin, crucifix, drum, flowers, letters, numerals (0–9 and Roman numerals), pocket watch, rocking horse, ship, teddy bear, and train. There also are combination figures: child and dog, dog and bird, girl with book and doll, cow and calf, and couple dancing.

According to the January 1991 issue of *Marble-Mania*, the rarest Sulphide marbles contain two figures, colored figures, double-sided figures, or three figures. The rarest subjects are inanimate objects such as trains, cannons, watches and so forth; next are religious symbols and people, including U.S. presidents. The rarest Sulphide of all is one with colored body glass, since Sulphides are usually made of clear glass.

An interesting use of Sulphide marbles appears in a National Historic Landmark on Martha's Vineyard, Massachusetts. The Flying Horses Carousel in Oak Bluffs, was built in 1876 and brought to the Vineyard from Coney Island in 1884. The horses' eyes are "clay figurines of animals like bears—and eagles—eyes so rare and valuable that one owner painted them black so no one would steal them." The color photo by Allison Shaw highlights the horse's shining eyes made of Sulphide marbles.[33]

MODERN HANDMADE GLASS MARBLES

In 1974 interest in handmade glass marbles was reborn in California. The basic technique was the same as in the nineteenth century, but few modern examples could be confused with the earlier handmade.

The revival was lead by Richard Marquis, and by the late 1970s Jody Fine and Steven Maslach were also prominent. The list of other makers active in the late 1970s through the early 1990s includes the following:

Robert Barrett	Steven Lundberg
William R. Bavin (London)	Steven Maslach
	Mark Matthews
Geoffrey Beatem	Michael Max
Barry Besett	Michelle and William
Harry Bessett	McKinney
Harry Boyer	Fulton Parker
Christopher Constantine	Ed and Amy
James Cooprider	Pennebaker
Terry Crider	Stefan Pfnuar
Robert Dane	(Germany)
James "Jim" Davis (Indiana)	Marquis and Ro Purser
	Joseph Rice

James C. "Jim" Davis (West Virginia)	Joe St. Clair
	Thomas St. Clair
Leonard Dinardo	David Salazar
Lynn Dee Dinning	Joshua Simon
Jody Fine	Josiah Simpson
Dudley Giberson	Russell C. Stankus
Charles D. Gibson	Douglas Sweet
David Gruenig	Genie Jorgenson Wald
James Holmes	Rolf Wald
Richard Iorio	George Williams
Robert Lichtman	Kathy Young
Brian Lonsway	Joseph Zimmerman[34]

The Zenith Glass Works is also reported to be producing modern handmade glass marbles. The new marbles are more perfectly round and well-polished than their nineteenth century counterparts; design techniques are more imaginative, from the variety of color combinations and arrangement of threads to totally new techniques such as the application of the *murrini* design by Dick Marquis and Ro Purser. Murrini are the cross sections of colored glass canes known to paperweight collectors as *millefiori*. Marquis and Purser's murrini include profiles of many different kinds of animals, all combined into a sphere.

Some contemporary collectors do not consider these modern examples true marbles. However, their similarities to the earlier handmade marbles in basic design and production methods make them part of the long heritage of glass marbles in the United States.

Mark Matthews of Matthews Art Glass is one of the leading glassmen and is nationally recognized for his limited edition jars. Since 1985 Matthews has been the resident glass artist at the Sauder Farm and Craft Village in Archbold, Ohio. His work has been in numerous shows and exhibitions and is held in private and public collections. Matthews takes a broad view of historical glass techniques in the concept and development of his marbles.

His limited-edition Population Portrait series is an example of his artistic vision. The jar itself is approximately $23\frac{1}{4}$ inches by $6\frac{3}{4}$ inches, with a 5-inch diameter and a $\frac{3}{8}$-inch wall. Approximately $\frac{1}{8}$ inch of the wall's thickness at the upper $\frac{3}{8}$ inch of the rim has been cut from the outside of the top to permit the dome lid to fit. The foot of the jar is acid etched, leaving an unetched ring on the bottom where the artist inscribes his signature and the title, date, logo, and edition number.

Each marble in the jar has a special mark to show that it belongs with that particular jar. Every jar contains eighty-one marbles. According to the artist, these marbles as "individuals sacrifice their autonomy for the power of the group and yet they retain their individual voices. This tension between the individual and the group mirrors a basic axiom of our human civilization." A listing of most of the designs contained in the series follows.

Beach Ball: This marble features six segments of opal colors; it looks like a beach ball. $1\frac{5}{8}$ inches.

Blue Jetson: This unusual marble is made of copper-blue glass with an hourglass-shaped bubble, with a ring bubble encircling the equator. $1\frac{7}{8}$ inches.

Clambroths: All of these have seventeen stripes. One has opal red stripes over an opal kelly green core. The other seven feature pastel opal backgrounds with highly

Contemporary handmade glass marbles. The large marbles at the rear were made by U.S. marble makers. Back row: A white and lavender Swirl by George Williams of the Glass Swan. Second row: A red, white, and blue Swirl by Jim Davis of Mid-Atlantic Corp.; a contemporary Sulphide with a squirrel figure by Gibson Glass. Third row: A rare rosé-cranberry glass marble with swirl design and iron pyrite flecks, by Gibson Glass; Sulphide marble containing a

"trapped air" figure "3" by Mark Matthews. This award-winning marble is signed and dated. Smaller types carry the "double m" logo of his glass house. Dennis Webb Collection. The smaller marbles in the foreground were handmade in Germany (formerly East Germany) by an unknown glasshouse. Their distinguishing features are opaque body glass, in some instances, and spirals that reverse direction at midpoint. Bertram M. Cohen Collection

chromatic transparent stripes of the same color as the core. Set of eight, 1¼ inches.

Clambroth Shooter: Twenty-one alternating red, green, and blue stripes cover a translucent white background. 1⁷⁄₁₆ inches.

Clear Cube: Trapped air forms a cube bubble in the center of this marble. There are also three open square bubbles oriented around the cube. 1¹⁵⁄₁₆ inches to 2¹⁄₁₆ inches.

Clown Murano Latticino: This marble boasts thirteen entirely different latticino canes on a translucent white background. It is a population portrait within itself. 2¼ inches to 2³⁄₈ inches.

Eccentrics: Five identical groups of three stripes are featured on an opal background. The experimental color format does not follow any particular color system. Set of six, 1½ inches.

Equilateral Triangle: This geometric design consists of a

system of small interlocking black and white equilateral triangles using a special technique that Matthews refers to as the graal technique. 2¼ inches to 2³⁄₈ inches.

4-Vane Ribbon: The 4-vane ribbon core consists of two vanes of enamel white and two vanes of a rich transparent color that represents one color of a six-color wheel. Four pastel stripes of pink, blue, green, and yellow accent the ribbons. Set of six, 1½ inches.

4-Vane Ribbon Shooter: These are the same as the 4-vane ribbons. The transparent core color vanes are a brilliant red. 2¼ inches.

Gumballs: Transparent color over a white core gives this marble its name. Each represents one color of a twelve-color wheel. Set of twelve, 1 inch.

Half Full/Half Empty: Radical modern. The design is slightly twisted; half is solid and half is clear. Cutting between the two halves are transparent white stripes.

There are two opal accent colors on each side. Set of three, 1½ inches.

Hugo Largo: This is a three-level design consisting of an opaque blue solid core with two different canary yellow accents at the four corners of the blue core. The next level is a seventeen-stripe cage of opal red. The third level is a group of black and white stripes bordered by one tight, heavier pair of black and white. 3½ inches to 3¾ inches.

Indian Corn: These colorful marbles are made of satin iridescent cobalt blue glass with rows of spots that resemble corn kernels. 1⅞ inches to 2 inches.

Latticinos: All have twelve latticino canes over opal backgrounds. Some are four identical groups of four. Some are four identical groups of three and some are six identical groups of two. Set of five, 1⅞ inches to 2¹⁄₁₆ inches.

Lobe Core: This attractive marble has seven lobes of chartreuse and pink transparent stripes on white. 1¹⁵⁄₁₆ inches to 2¹⁄₁₆ inches.

Pink Air Twist: Gold ruby glass is combined with four long parallel helical bubbles. 1¾ inches to 1⅞ inches.

Pink Iridescent Pearl: This marble of gold ruby glass has a predominantly green satin iridescent surface. 1¾ inches.

Rainbow: In this complex marble, a fifteen-stripe color rainbow surrounds an alternating black and white stripe latticino core. 1⁹⁄₁₆ inches.

Reverse Twist: A multicolored Onionskin format twisting in opposite directions from each pole forms a chevron at the equator. 1⅝ inches.

Ribbon Lutz: Transparent analogous colors cover translucent white. Thick goldstone stripes are bordered with enamel white. Set of six, 1⅛ inches.

30-Stripes: Thirty stripes of alternating analogous colors ripple on a black matrix. Set of twelve, 1½ inches.

Transparent Ribbons: This marble has an analogous core with two transparent and one opal color. Stripes are the opposite color of the core area and form four identical groups of four analogous stripes. Set of eight, 1⅜ inches.

Zig Zag: Matthews uses the graal technique to create a black and white, zig zag pattern. 1⅞ inches to 2 inches.

Matthews is equally recognized for single handmade marbles, some but not all of which are included in the portrait jar series. Some are sold in sets containing a variety of colors of the same design. At present Matthews offers a Ribbon Lutz set, Clambroth set, Ribbon set, 30-Striper set, 4-Vane Ribbon set, Clambroths, Ribbons, large Ribbons, Solid Core, three-sided Solid Core, 3-Vane Ribbon, 4-Vane Ribbon, Reverse Twists, Peppermints, Clouds, Clear Jetson, Clear Air Twist, Pink Air Twist, Clear Cube, experimental Air Patterns, olive green Latticino, early turquoise Latticino, yellow Latticino, plaid Latticino, Hugo Largo Red and Blue Core, black and white Zig Zags, and Latticino Cores.

A slide featuring Matthews' Ice Blue Air Trap Number Spheres was among one hundred slides selected for the *New Glass Review*, published by the Corning Museum of Glass in Corning, New York.[35] It is an honor to be recognized in this prestigious publication.

George Williams of the Glass Swan, Inc., in Jane Lew, West Virginia, started as a glassman in 1959 and has been a glassblower since 1961. Williams makes off-hand pieces such as apples, peaches, strawberries, pears, paperweights, and now marbles.

Williams has made contemporary Clambroths, the Lutz-type in silver and gold, and other fair representations of the earlier glass types. A real attraction at Williams' glasshouse is that visitors may make their own marbles under his supervision. The use of cobalt (Bristol) blue in body glass is outstanding. A strong light is necessary to penetrate this deep color. Williams' contemporary glass marbles reflect craftsmanship of the highest order.

A growing interest in handmade glass marbles brought about the recent revival of the Sulphide. Joe St. Clair was one of the earlier makers and employed Charles D. Gibson. Gibson later formed Gibson Glass in Milton, West Virginia. Through this connection he was able to purchase 95 percent of the St. Clair Sulphide figure molds. However, he prefers to purchase ready-made figures from a California firm rather than use the St. Clair molds.

Gibson described and demonstrated some of the artful manipulations required in making a contemporary Sulphide. The initial step in making a Sulphide marble is the heating from 1,000 to 1,900 degrees Fahrenheit of a previously heat-treated ceramic figure; it must be the same or greater temperature as the body glass. The preheating causes any gas within the ceramic to be expelled; otherwise the gas will appear between the ceramic and the body glass as silvery bubbles. A gather of molten transparent glass is withdrawn with a punty from a melting pot and sheared off into a preheated, hollow, hemispherical metal cup. A preheated Sulphide figure is then inserted downward into the gob. A second gob is placed on top off the first gob with a punty; the two gobs stick or weld together. At this point, the combined mass is then lifted up and out of the iron mold by the punty. It is then placed on the arms of a bench where the master glassman rolls the punty shaft forward and backward with one hand and shapes the gob with the other hand, using a cup. The crucial shaping is accomplished with a cherry wood cup with a hemispherical recess that is mounted on the end of a paddle. The cup is constantly dipped in water to prevent overheating and burning. Several sizes are on hand. Some craftsmen use a carbon cup (graphite) or metal shaping cup lubricated with beeswax. The punty with the nearly completed Sulphide is lifted from the bench, and another team member holds the Sulphide upright in a doughnut-shaped, asbestos-covered ring on a metal rod. The two then place it on a table, and another team member snaps the Sulphide off the punty. The Sulphide, which bears a scar or cutoff mark, is melted (fire-glazed) with a gas torch, resulting in a near-perfect sphere. The process is not yet complete, since the important step of annealing—or tempering—must occur. The newly formed Sulphide is carried in the asbestos ring to an annealing oven for this final step.

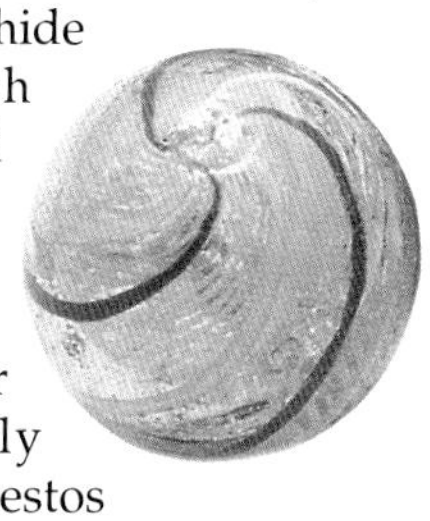

Some antique Sulphides show a ring around the circumference where the two gobs of glass were welded together, areas where the Sulphide was inserted into the body glass, or a shear-punty mark on one end. In contrast, the contemporary Sulphide marble contains a figure modern in design and color and does not contain the aforementioned identifying marks.

Gibson does not initial, sign, or date his Sulphide glass marbles. One rare example does contain a "G" on the bottom of the figure.

In addition to the Sulphide, Gibson also makes Swirls of extraordinary beauty. One prime example is his Snakeskin, and another is a sphere with light pink, transparent body glass containing a reflective substance. In this instance, the reflective material is not treated mica as in earlier days, but iron pyrite flakes.

The efforts of Gibson Glass do not end here. The line includes paperweights and other deco glass objects. Occasionally, Gibson is commissioned to make special glass objects. In 1990 ARMCO Steel Company commissioned Robert A. Brown from Ironton, Ohio, to make a promotional glass Sulphide marble for official company use only. It became a cooperative effort of Brown and Gibson and is the first dated Sulphide.[36]

Brown made the clay figure (slug) Sulphide, which was round and flat, bearing the ARMCO Steel Company logo on one side and the date "1990" on the other. The slug was passed to Gibson for completion of a 2⅛-inch to 2¼-inch clear crystal marble. The raw figure was heated to 2,100 degrees Fahrenheit to burn out any oxygen and thus prevent bubbles from forming around the figure. (In earlier days, bubbles formed because Sulphides were fired by coke or charcoal, which produced lower temperatures than modern methods and failed to expel all of the oxygen.) The number made is not known but is believed to be small. All Sulphides that were made went to ARMCO; however, ARMCO permitted Brown to make six serially numbered prototypes as collector's marbles. They are for sale by Brown; a certificate of authenticity indicating the serial number is issued to avoid duplication.

James C. "Jim" Davis of West Virginia, a glassman of several years, began making glass marbles recently. He has progressed considerably in his efforts, producing some unique designs worthy of inclusion in any marble collection. At present, Davis is producing marbles for display and sale at Mid-Atlantic of West Virginia, Inc., in Ellenboro, West Virginia.

An outstanding example of a contemporary handmade glass marble is the Caramel Slag, which is made by another Jim Davis of the marble world, in Redkey,

Indiana. The scrap glass for making this colorful marble was recovered from the dump site of the Indiana Tumbler and Goblet Company (1894–1903) in Greentown, Indiana, by Wallace S. Huffman of Kokomo, Indiana. These marbles are engraved "J. D. 1989."[37]

Another contemporary glass marble maker is David Gruening of Gruening Glassworks in West Barnet, Vermont. He has been a full-time glass professional since 1972, and his art is well known to collectors of handmade glass marbles. His formal credentials include a master's degree in chemistry from the University of Maryland. Gruening has complete control of the glass process, from building the furnaces and tools to manipulating glass formulas and melting methods, thus creating from sand, rare metals and fire a striking gem-like material than can be shaped into a myriad of exciting marble designs. His work reflects a combination of European and American techniques, along with his own new and innovative design methods. Each of his own handmade pieces is initialed or signed and dated to ensure appreciating value. An outstanding example of his expertise is the Sunset, made in 1989; this particular marble also is numbered, i.e. "37 DG 89." This beautiful handmade marble defies description.[38]

Jody "Captain Marble" Fine, owner of J. Fine Glass of Berkeley, California, produces handmade marbles in modern designs, as well as those that attempt to duplicate the earlier swirls. Jody is preparing a series of Sulphide marbles that will include figures of endangered species designed and hand-colored by renowned artist Ken Butterfield. The first few designs will include sea turtles and whales and should be available in early 1993. The new Sulphides should be high on the list of collectibles. They should also be welcomed by environmentalists.[39]

Josh Simpson, of Josh Simpson Contemporary Glass in Shelbourne Falls, Massachusetts, looks to the planet earth for his inspiration. He hides bits of earthly information in every piece and often puts as much information into a piece as he can, necessitating the use of a hand lens to see and appreciate the planet. Simpson believes his marbles will be around for hundreds of years for someone in another country to discover.[40]

A note of caution: Initials and dates engraved on contemporary handcrafted marbles made of scrap glass may be obliterated by flame treatment. The marbles may be sold or traded as "early machine-made" rather than "contemporary handmade."

[1]Mel Morrison and Carl Terrison, *Marbles—Identification and Price Guide* (private publication, Falmouth, Maine, 1968).

[2]Herbert Kuhnert, *Recordbook of the Thurning Glass Factory Stories* (Wiesbaden: Franz Steiner Verlag, 1973), p. 247.

[3]Kuhnert, ibid.

[4]Albert Christian Revi, *Nineteenth Century Glass* (1967), p. 242.

[5]*Marble-Mania*, newsletter of the Marble Collectors Society of America, Trumbull, Ct., Vol. 21 (January 1981), p. 4

[6]Deutsches Spielzeugmuseum, Zonneberg, Thuringia, Germany.

[7]Mariam Righter, *Iowa City Glass*; private publication, copyright by Dr. J. W. Carberry (1982), p. 32.

[8]Mini Handler, "Lutz, Clambroth and Onionskin," *Early American Life*, August 1993, pp. 10–11.

[9]James R. Ridpath, *National Marble Club of America Newsletter*, Vol. 4, No. 15 (September 30, 1989).

[10]Morrison and Terrison, ibid.

[11]Clara Ingram, *The Collector's Encyclopedia of Antique Marbles* (Paducah, Ky.: Collector Books, 1972).

[12]Paul Jockelson, *Sulphides: The Art of Cameo Incrustation* (New York: Thomas Nelson and Sons, 1968), p. 67.

[13]Everett Grist, *Antique Collectible Marbles* (Paducah, Ky.: Collector Books, 1984), p. 24.

[14]Ingram, ibid.

[15]Dr. Henry D. Watson, "Antique Marbles of Stone, Pottery and Glass," *American Collector* (July 1942), pp. 6-7 and 15.

[16]Dessamae Lorraine, "An Archaeologist's Guide to 19th Century American Glass," *Historical Archaeology*, Vol. 2, p. 42 (marble-stoppered bottles).

[17]Marian Klamkin, *The Collector's Book of Bottles* (New York: Dodd, Mead & Co., 1971) (marble-stoppered bottles).

[18]Enrique C. Canova, "West Virginia: Treasure Chest of Industry," *The National Geographic Magazine*, Vol. 78, No. 2 (August 1940).

[19]William C. Blizzard, "West Virginia's Marble King," *Charleston (W.Va.) Sunday Gazette Mail* (October 4, 1959), 4D; and Donald G. Michels, personal conversation.

[20]Keith Middlemas, *Antique Glass in Color* (Garden City, N.Y., 1971), p. 89.

[21]Derek David and Keith Middlemas, *Colored Glass* (1968), p. 118.

[22]Paul Hollister Jr., *The Encyclopedia of Glass Paperweights* (1969), p. 255.

[23]Mary Martin, "The Crystal Cameos of France," *House and Garden* (December 1926).

[24]Apsley Pellatt, *Curiosities of Glass Making* (London, 1849).

[25]Paul Jokelson, *Sulphides: The Art of Cameo Incrustation* (New York: Thomas Nelson and Sons, 1968), p. 67.

[26]Righter, ibid., p 3.

[27]*Hobbies* (November 1941), p. 56 (article on sulphides).

[28]Roger C. Miller, "Swirl and Sulphide Playing Marbles," *The Spinning Wheel* (November 1966), p. 20.

[29]"Interesting Antiques—Marbles," *The Antique Trader* (May 16, 1972), p. 43.

[30]City Products and Montgomery Ward catalogs.

[31]City Products.

[32]Joyce Stanton, *Marble-Mania*, Vol. 3 (July 1976), p. 4.

[33]Katherine Imbrie and Patricia Mandell, "You Can Go Around on Horseback," *Yankee* magazine, August 1993, p. 45.

[34]"Contemporary Handmade Marble Makers," *Marble-Mania*, Vol. 35 (July 1984), p. 2; and Plate 64 of MCSA Photographic Series.

[35]*The New Glass Review*, The Corning Museum of Glass, No. 13 (Corning, N.Y., 1992).

[36]Charles D. Gibson, Gibson Glass, and Robert A. Brown, personal conversation and correspondence.

[37]Wallace C. Huffman, personal conversation and correspondence.

[38]David Gruening, personal correspondence.

[39]*Marble Mate No. 1*, Japan Marbles Association (Tokyo, 1992), p. 6.

[40]Ibid.

Chapter V

• • •

Machine-Made Glass Marbles

The machine age revolutionized the American marble industry in two major stages. In the first stage, machines were used to form the marbles; however, men still manipulated the molten glass. These marbles are called "semi-machine made."

In the second stage of modernization, the craft became fully mechanized, largely due to the inventions of Horace Hill and John Early, two early innovators in the marble world. Their significant patents resulted in a higher-quality marble and raised production until the United States became the world's leading marble manufacturer

This chapter describes various types of both major classifications of machine-made glass marbles: semi-machine-made and fully machine-made. Actual descriptions of manufacturing methods are contained in Chapter X, and relevant patents are discussed in Chapter XII.

SINGLE-COLORED MARBLES

Solids and Opaques: Single color only, complete absence of any design elements except occasional minor swirling pattern in the glass due to incomplete mixing.

These are most commonly known as Chinese Checkers,

A boxed set of Akro Agate Chinese Checker marbles in opaque colors of blue, red, yellow, green, white, and black. The set is mint with dividers.

even though the type was present about a decade before the introduction of this particular game in the late 1930s. A 1938 magazine article calls the game "new."[1] Standard colors throughout the marble industry are green, yellow, black, blue, white, and red, made and packaged to match the six colored triangles on the board.

Solids have been a popular type for over a half-century, beginning in the early 1920s and continuing today, primarily due to the simple design. The lack of design elements other than a single color makes this type ideal for use in games, where the primary need is to distinguish one game token from another.

Similar reasons also apply to industrial uses where shape, size, and hardness are important, but design is not. Industrials are often colored, usually dark blue or black; this is primarily due to the fact that used glass, or cullet, can be used, and when mixing many colors of used glass together, the product is a dark color. When new, or recipe, glass is used for industrials, it usually lacks much coloring, and the resulting marble is a Transparent type.

Solids were made by all the major marble companies in the United States from early in the machine-made period. Since there is little variation from company to company or through the years, solids are almost impossible to assign to a particular company or period. A few generalities can be made: prior to the 1950s, perhaps before the 1940s, larger sizes of Solids were produced than in later times. The reason for this larger size is not known. The most common size made presently is ⁵⁄₈ inch or ¹¹⁄₁₆ inch; the earlier types included ¾ inch and slightly larger. It should be kept in mind that the smaller sizes were made during the earlier periods as well. It cannot simply be said that all the larger ones are older than all the smaller ones. It is interesting to note that really large sizes, larger than ⁷⁄₈ inch, are quite rare. This is probably due to the fact that the large sizes were almost exclusively shooters, and marble players wanted fancy shooters, not single colors.

Makers of Solids

Akro Agate	Heaton Agate
Alley	JABO
Alox	Kokomo Opalescent
Bogard	Marble King
Cairo	Master Marble
Champion Agate	Peltier
M. F. Christensen	Vacor de Mexico
Christensen Agate	Vitro Agate

Clears or Transparents: Single color only, complete absence of any design elements except occasional (unintentional) minor swirling pattern in the glass due to incomplete mixing.

The description is exactly like that of the Solids, except that in this case the coloring agent is faint enough so that the marble is transparent. It is only logical that the Clears and the Solids should share many of the same characteristics and history, since the only difference is the amount of coloring. The production methods are not different—the glass feed and shearing mechanisms used to produce the two types are the same. So if the technology was available to produce Solids, it could also produce Clears.

Commonly called Clearies or Puries, Clears are popular and have been for about the same period as the Solids, from at least the 1920s through the present. Like the Solids, the Clears had an ancestor in the fully handmade varieties, so some demand for a transparent marble existed long before the automation of the production process. A likely reason that Clears were not one of the first types produced by machine (that is, during the period from 1910 to the 1920s) is that the handmade Clears were not as popular as other handmade types. They were not beautiful, to say the least. Akro Agate did, however, produce large numbers of Clears in the mid-1920s for use in reflectors and road signs.

A common artifact usually mistaken for an early machine-made glass marble, or a handmade type, is a glass ingot intended for use in making fiberglass. These are clear glass spheres about 1 inch in diameter, usually light green, and the orange peel surface is often chipped due to rough handling at the glass factory.

Makers of Clears

Akro Agate	Marble King
Alley	Master Marble
Bogard	Mid-Atlantic of West Virginia
Cairo	Peltier
Champion Agate	Ravenswood
Heaton Agate	Vacor de Mexico
JABO	Vitro Agate

Translucents: This type is known by many names— Alabaster, Cloudy, Custard, Milk Glass, Semi-Clear, Semi-Clearie, and Vaseline. All of these terms describe this type of marble well. Visually, it is simply halfway between the Transparent/Clear and the Opaque/Solid types; it was not an easy type of glass to make. John F. Early and Henry T. Hellmers, the Akro Agate chemist, with the help of the Corning Glass Company, developed the alabaster glass process in the United States in 1928; it had been in use for some years before that in Europe.

The Translucent single-colored marble was a rather low-demand type—both in the handmade days and after the development of machine production—and consequently is rare today, except for the revival type below.

The histories of Solids, Clears, and Semi-Clears diverge somewhat after the introduction of machine production. Whereas the Solids and Clears came back into demand after a few years, the single-colored Semi-Clears never really did. They were produced by only a few companies and never in great quantity. Certain machine-made Semi-Clears will sell for $10 in the marble collectors' market today, but a Solid or Clear can be had for pennies. This demonstrates the scarcity of the translucent type.

Translucence itself was not unpopular; indeed, Semi-Clear marbles with designs were a mainstay of the heyday of the marble industry during the 1920s and 1930s. Translucents with patches of color are not rare at all and were produced by several companies, to be packaged and sold right along with other popular types. However, the non-design Semi-Clear did not fit into any category. It was not pretty enough for a marble player and not distinct enough to be used for board games, where Solids or Clears were preferred.

A recent revival of a type of Translucent appeared in 1985 in the form of Opalescent marbles. These are basically single-colored marbles with no interior or exterior design elements. However, ingredients are added to the basic glass recipe to produce a mother-of-pearl or opalescent appearance throughout the body and on the surface, thus yielding a multicolored marble. On July 8, 1857, Jules Joseph Henri Brianchon of Paris, France, registered a method for producing "the rich tint of shells, or the reflections of the prism" on glass and china.

In modern production, Vitro Agate used a "mother of pearl" chemical sold by Englehart Chemical Company. The machine operator sprayed the chemical onto the marbles in the annealing bucket or lehr, after they left the production line but before they cooled.[2]

Makers of Translucents

Akro Agate (early types)	Mid-Atlantic of West Virginia
Champion Agate (Opalescent)	Peltier (Opalescent)
Marble King (Opalescent)	Vacor de Mexico
Master Marble (early types)	Vitro Agate

Frosteds: Also called Camphor glass, Frosteds are single-colored and would be transparent except for surface alteration by a light acid bath that etches the glass, removing the polished surface and leaving a satiny finish, transforming the marble into a Translucent type.

A glass-frosting process is contained in Patent 9,453 from 1852. Marbles are frosted by dipping them in a hydrofluoric acid formula and then rinsing them in clear water. The frosting process is considered an operational and safety hazard due to the corrosive characteristics of hydrofluoric acid, which is used extensively in glass etching. Generally, because of safety concerns, marble factories contract with other glass factories to conduct frosting.

To produce the matte surface, a mixture of potassium fluoride and hydrofluoric acid may be used (one hundred parts water, ten parts of potassium fluoride, and one part hydrofluoric acid). The commercial name is Jack Frost and the methodology is "one dip and two rinses." In the last step of the process, the marbles are rolled or rubbed on clean fabric to dry them and remove any residue.[3]

This is a very recent type, seen occasionally in the late 1970s, but some examples may have been made by individuals for unknown reasons except to create something different. Frosteds were seen on the retail market first in 1983, sold by the House of Marbles in London and the Pioneer Balloon Company. Retailers sell marbles produced in Mexico, the United States, and probably the Orient (Japan, Korea, or China), so the Frosteds could be made by anyone. Vitro Agate made some Frosteds at one time experimentally but did not produce quantities for sale.

The marbles at left are frosted glass, and those at right are Carnival Glass. The Frosteds were made by the Vitro Agate Company and frosted (bathed in acid) by Fenton Art Glass. Samples courtesy of Lewis L. Moore, former plant manager. The Carnival Glass marbles were made by Champion Agate Company. To produce them, hot marbles of transparent or translucent glass are sprayed with a chemical that produces the metallic sheen. Samples courtesy of Dave McCullough, former plant manager for Champion Agate.

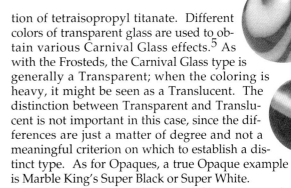

The frosted types sold by the House of Marbles are called Frosties and are offered in ½-inch size only, in blue, clear, green, and orange.

Makers of Frosteds

Champion Agate	Vacor de Mexico
Marble King	Vitro Agate

Carnival Glass: Also known as Lustered or Metallic Lustered, these marbles have a single color of body glass; surface alteration produces a metallic sheen that varies from blues and greens to golds and reds, depending upon the amount of this exterior coloration added. Carnival Glass marbles have the lustered exterior surface of Depression era Carnival Glass, but less of its orange color. The luster is not simply an outer layer of glass applied by the cold shear or veneering method, nor is it the result of a change in the basic recipe of the body glass, as is true in the case of the Opalescents.

During Roman days, glass was buried in damp earth for a long time to achieve an extremely attractive surface decay. Attempts have been made since then to duplicate the iridescent color. A patent for producing iridescent colors on glass was issued to Thomas Wilkes Webb of Stourbridge, England, on August 29, 1877. His process used a closed chamber wherein fumes from the evaporation of tin and other metallic salts played directly upon the surface of the glass enclosed in the chamber.

Carnival Glass as we know it today received its name from prizes given at games of chance at carnivals during the Great Depression. This highly decorative pressware was also sold in dime stores. It was manufactured by placing the oven-hot colored glass object over fumes of burning sulfur and then quickly returning it to the oven for further baking. In essence, the color is on the surface. It is unlikely that this method was used to color marbles; however, the possibility exists that it could be adopted for use.[4]

At present, Gibson Glass sprays hot marbles with a compressed air gun containing a commercial solution of tetraisopropyl titanate. Different colors of transparent glass are used to obtain various Carnival Glass effects.[5] As with the Frosteds, the Carnival Glass type is generally a Transparent; when the coloring is heavy, it might be seen as a Translucent. The distinction between Transparent and Translucent is not important in this case, since the differences are just a matter of degree and not a meaningful criterion on which to establish a distinct type. As for Opaques, a true Opaque example is Marble King's Super Black or Super White.

A new silver color of Carnival Glass appeared on the market in 1984, sold by several companies. Vacor de Mexico calls its variety Silver. The House of Marbles, retailing for an unnamed maker (probably Vacor de Mexico), sells the silver Carnival Glass also; it calls its product Lustered Rainbows and Lustered Clears. The House of Marbles offers a Lustered China as well, which is a Patched Opaque type with the same lustered finish (see Patched Opaque). United States makers entered this market in 1986, with two makers producing their own varieties (Champion Agate's Pearls, and Marble King's Supers—Super White, Super Black, Super Gray, etc.).

Makers of Carnival Glass

• The House of Marbles' catalog illustrations are as follows: Lustered Rainbow: 30 millimeters (1 inch); color illustration is light green, and the smaller Lustered Clear: 17 millimeters (¹¹⁄₁₆ inch); colors shown are clear, orange, blue, and light green.

• Vacor de Mexico's Silver comes in sizes from 9 millimeters to 30 millimeters and is offered in surface colors of gold, green, red, and blue. The body glass of the marble is usually light green.

• Marble King's Supers: black, white, or gray Opaque Opalescents, and Clear Transparents; ⁹⁄₁₆ inch.

• Champion Agate's Pearls: Opaque black; Translucent white; Transparent green, light blue, dark blue, clear, and red. Color names are Ebony, White Pearl, Evergreen, Sky Blue, Cobalt Blue, Clear, and Ruby; ⁹⁄₁₆ inches.

• Peltier Glass Company produces deco items (nuggets or flats) in the Opalescent finish, but no marbles.

MULTICOLORED MARBLES WITH EXTERIOR DESIGN ONLY

When examining Transparents or Translucents, it can be easily determined whether the design elements extend below the surface. With Opaques, however, it is sometimes more difficult, since the interior cannot be seen. In an effort to cut cost on production, a lower quality body glass is often encased in a thin layer of more expensive colored glass in a process called veneering. It is difficult to determine whether a marble is veneered by looking at the outside. One may only ascertain the body color by breaking the marble.

This description brings up something to keep in mind about the designs on a marble. On a marble that has surface design only, the design is applied to the molten body glass as it leaves the marble machine's orifice in a continuous molten stream. This stream is moving in a linear fashion—that is, in a straight line—before being sheared or cut

A group of promotional marbles popular among collectors. In the back row are a Marble Collectors Unlimited marble, a special edition Greenberg marble, and a Big Blue Marble. In the second row are two West Virginia promotional marbles and two Qualatex marbles.

The front row contains an Ing-Rich marble, a Comic Marble, and two Marble King logo marbles. From the collections of Beverly Brulé, Roger W. Howdyshell, Lawrence M. Chapman, and Qualatex Pioneer Balloon Company.

off into a gob. Anything added to it will exhibit straight lines indicating the direction in which the body glass was flowing. These perfectly straight lines, however, are then altered by the rounding of the body they are residing on. This is similar to square letters on a balloon; when the balloon is blown up (or rounded), the letters' edges become curved. The larger the design element, the more apparent this distortion. On a single patch, the edges are often quite curved, but when the design element is a small strip of color (ribbon), the curvature is less apparent.

The presence of exterior design only is a good time marker for archaeologists because it did not appear until the late 1920s, with the development of feeding and shearing mechanisms that made it possible to apply separate colors of glass (see Chapter X).

When the exterior design involves words and pictures, rather than just areas of color, it was applied with a decal. A decal was applied while the body glass was still hot, but the marble itself had already been formed.

Words, Boy's Face, Mountains: Called "Promotional Marbles," these are special order or promotional marbles. Each type is distinctly different, varying with the particular order.

Famous examples include the "Big Blue Marble," exhibiting those words and produced by Marble King around 1974 as part of International Telephone and Telegraph's promotion of the annual national marbles

tournament. The term is said to have originated with Michael Collins, an astronaut of the Apollo 11 flight, who said at a press conference that the earth looked like a big blue marble from outer space.[6] Aside from the inscription, this is a Patched Opaque (blue on white) marble, made only in 1-inch diameter; the imprint is sky blue in color. This marble is a recent but rare collectible.

Another example, "Almost Heaven, West Virginia" or "Almost Heaven" with a picture of mountains on the opposite side, is a Patched Opaque (yellow and red on white) marble, made to promote the state of West Virginia by Marble King in 1978. A Marble King Promotional made in 1978 had the words "Marble King" and a picture of a boy wearing a crown. The boy's head is a perfect circle, like a marble. This is also a Patched Opaque (blue on white).

A Promotional made for the Ingram-Richardson Manufacturing Company, Beaver Falls, Pennsylvania, has an imprinting in red of "*ING-RICH*BEAVER FALLS*PA." This type is not too well known and very collectible. A survey of the collection of Stanley Snider, a Georgia resident, shows that nineteen different colors were used, and that the marbles have a striking resemblance to marbles made by Akro Agate.[7] Recent finds include a Lemonade and Oxblood marble and a green and white Translucent marble, both made by Akro Agate, bearing the above imprint.

The Esso Oil Company used marbles made by Marble

King as a promotional product; the oil company placed small red-, white-, and blue-striped drums of ³⁄₈-inch Cat Eyes and Rainbows (not a special design) at its service stations as gifts to customers. With a fill-up a customer could take a handful.

Other examples include marbles given away with cereal, Coca-Cola, Cotes Bakery, Cracker Jack, Mr. Peanuts, Orange Crush, Popsicle, and R. C. Cola. On and off from the 1930s to the present, different types of marbles, from Patched Opaques in the 1930s to Cat Eyes in the mid-1950s, have been included in or hung on containers of all of the above products. Marble King has been a front-runner in the promotional arena, but others including Vitro Agate and Champion Agate have also been active.

Contemporary printed marbles are being made by Vacor de Mexico for distribution by Vacor USA. The company's line includes Garfield, Travelog, Looney Tunes, Cosmos, Bullwinkle, and Pink Panther, using 14mm and 25mm size marbles made by Vacor de Mexico. Contemporary imprints designed for private and commercial advertising usage and custom imprinted marble pouches to match the imprinted marbles are made by Vacor de Mexico. Vacor USA, a division of Vacor de Mexico, was incorporated to continue sales of Vacor de Mexico's products.

Comic Characters' Faces: These are the most famous and perhaps the most unusual collectibles of the middle machine-made marble period. Popularly called Comics or Comic Strips, these Patched Opaques sport the faces of one of twelve different characters from the comic strips (plus Tom Mix, the famous cowboy of the silent screen) on the opaque white, yellow, or blue body glass opposite a colored patch: Orphan Annie, Bimbo, Betty Boop, Emma, Andy Gump, Herbie, Kayo, Koko, Moon Mullins, Sandy, Skeezix, and Smitty.

Comics were produced beginning 1933 by the Peltier Glass Company, which produced all of the above-named characters; boxes containing sets of these marbles are labeled "PICTURE MARBLES," and Peltier's box of a dozen sold for 25 cents. (James H. Davis's profile of the Peltier Picture Marbles characters is contained in *Marble-Mania*, April 1991, Volume 62.)

Contemporary examples called Comic Strip Marbles by some collectors are made by Harold D. Bennett of Cambridge, Ohio. The figure is applied by decal and fired in a kiln. Bennett's type is 1 inch in size and has a distinctive marble design similar to Marble King's Rainbow; the figures are in a variety of single and multiple colors. A marble collector should be fully knowledgeable about the two major types since some contemporary ones are sold as earlier Peltier Picture Marbles. The contemporary type is a

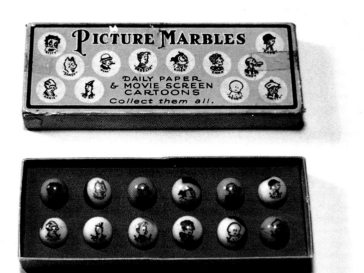

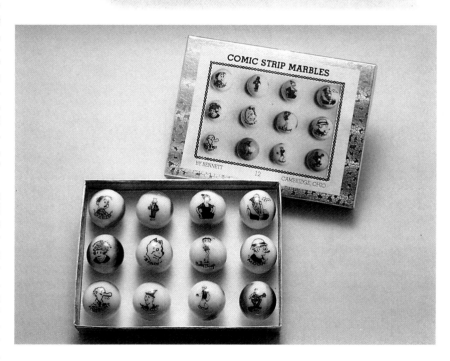

Above: The original Picture Marbles made by the Peltier Glass Company, courtesy of collector Beverly Brulé. Complete boxed sets are very scarce.
Below: Contemporary "Comic Strip Marbles" by Harold D. Bennett of Cambridge, Ohio. The marbles are 1-inch rainbows by Marble King, Inc. This type has been sold as "antique" or as the famous Peltier Comic Marbles. If one is in doubt about a prospective purchase, one should compare a known example with the unknown. The Bennett marbles are normally sold in a boxed set of twelve.

worthy addition to a collection, particularly if the marble collector has a complete set of the earlier Peltier marbles to display alongside them. Bennett also makes imprinted marbles of other figures and captions.

Confetti: This major new design was first made by Vacor de Mexico in the early 1980s. It is achieved by sprinkling small, confettilike pieces of colored glass on the still-plastic marble in the rollers. Lewis L. Moore of Vitro Agate suggested the name of Confetti for this new type.

Vacor de Mexico's Confetti is opaque with a black

MACHINE-MADE GLASS MARBLES IDENTIFICATION CHART

	Opacity	Type Names	Known Companies Production (Brand Names)
Single-colored marbles NO DESIGN ELEMENT PRESENT	Opaque	Opaques, Solids, Chinese Checkers	Akro Agate, Alley, Alox, Bogard, Cairo Novelty, Champion Agate, Heaton Agate (Marine Gems), Marble King, Master Marble, Mid-Atlantic, Peltier Glass, Vacor de Mexico (Opals), Vitro Agate (Aqua Jewels)
	Transparent	Transparents, Clears, Clearies	Akro Agate (Glassies), Alley, Bogard, Cairo Novelty, Champion Agate, Heaton Agate, Marble King, Master Marble, Mid-Atlantic, Ravenswood Novelty, Vacor de Mexico (Crystals), Vitro Agate
	Translucent	Translucent, Vaseline, Milk Glass, Custard	Akro Agate, Master Marble (Litho, Meteor, and Cloudy)
SURFACE ALTERATIONS (A) Frosted Surface	Translucent	Frosted	Champion Agate, Marble King, Mid-Atlantic, Vacor de Mexico, Vitro Agate
(B) Metallic or Lustered Sheen	Translucent	See "Multicolored Marbles, Exterior Design Only."	
Multicolored Marbles (A) Exterior Design Only			
(1) Words	Opaque	Promotionals	Marble King
(2) Comic Character Faces	Opaque	Comics, Comic Strips, Picture Marbles	Peltier Glass
(3) Dappled, Mottled Surface	Opaque	Dappled	Vacor de Mexico (Galactica), only maker
(4) Spotted, Dotted or Speckled Surface	Opaque/Transparent	Confetti Guinea	Vitro Agate (Confetti) Christensen Agate Co. (Guinea)
(5) Metallic or Lustered Sheen on Surface	Opaque	Carnival Glass, Lustered	Champion Agate (Pearls), Marble King, Vacor de Mexico (Meteor), Vitro Agate
	Transparent	Carnival Glass, Lustered	Champion Agate (Pearls), Marble King (Supers), Vacor de Mexico (Silver), Vitro Agate
	Translucent	Carnival Glass, Lustered	Champion Agate (Pearls)
(6) Single-Colored Patch (well-defined)	Opaque	Patched	Akro Agate, Alley, Heaton Agate, Marble King, Master Glass, Master Marble, Peltier Glass, Ravenswood, Vitro Agate
	Transparent	Patched	Marble King (Rainbows), Vitro Agate (Conquerors)
	Translucent	Patched	Akro Agate, Marble King (Rainbows), Vitro Agate (Conquerors)
(7) Single-Colored Patch (streaky, ragged edges)	Opaque	Brushed	Akro Agate, Master Glass
	Transparent	Brushed	Akro Agate, Master Glass, Master Marble (Comet), Vitro Agate (Conqueror)
	Translucent	Brushed	Akro Agate, Master Marble

	Opacity	Type Names	Known companies production (brand names)
(8) Single-Colored Patch (as above, with misty streaks on other part of surface)	Opaque Transparent Translucent	Patched & Brushed	Vitro Agate
(9) Four-Striped or Different Colors	Opaque	Striped Opaque	Vacor de Mexico (Pirate), only maker
(10) Ribbons, Rings, &/or Patches	Opaque	Patched & Ribboned, or Ribboned only (see also Patched Opaque)	Alley (Ribboned, Patched & Ribboned), Kokomo, Marble King, (Patched & Ribboned), Master Glass (Ribboned only), Peltier Glass (Ribboned only), Vacor de Mexico (Patched & Ribboned), Vitro Agate (Patched & Ribboned, All Reds)
(B) Interior Design Only			
(1) Vanes, Leaves, Blades or Petals	Transparent	Cat Eye	Bogard, Champion Agate, Heaton Agate, H. E. Hopf, Marble King, Master Glass, Peltier, Vacor de Mexico (Zebra), various Oriental companies, Vitro Agate
(2) Many Filaments of Different Colors	Transparent	Tiger Eye	Master Marble (Tiger Eye), only maker
(C) Both Interior & Exterior Design			
(1) Two Even Halves of Different Colors	Opaque	Half & Half	Kokomo, Vitro Agate
(2) Vanes, Leaves, Blades of Petals (thick, wide at surface)	Transparent	Picasso	Vacor de Mexico (Picasso), only maker
(3) Single-Colored Surface Patch (with misty streaks on interior)	Transparent Translucent	Patched & Brushed	Vitro Agate
(4) Randomly Swirling, Variegated Glass	Opaque	Swirl & Slag	Alox, Akro Agate, Alley, Champion Agate (Old Fashioned) Christensen Agate, Heaton Agate, Marble King, Ravenswood, Vitro Agate
	Transparent	Swirl	Alox, Akro Agate, Alley, Champion Agate (Whirlwind), Christensen Agate, Heaton Agate, Peltier, Ravenswood Novelty
	Translucent	Swirl	Alley, Heaton Agate
(5) Spiral, Coil, Corkscrew	Opaque Transparent Translucent	Swirl	Akro Agate, only maker Akro Agate, only maker Akro Agate, only maker
(6) Ribbons, Rings &/or Patches	Opaque Transparent Translucent	See "Exterior Design Only" Patched & Ribboned, or Ribboned Patched & Ribboned, or Ribboned	Peltier Glass (Opalescent, Rainbo) Marble King (Ribboned, Rainbow)

45

body. It is speckled with colors of yellow, blue and white, orange and blue, red, and green. When two colors are present on a single marble, it appears that one was applied, then the other, rather than a mixture of the two at once.

Vacor calls its marble Galaxy because, according to the company's catalog, "they have an infinite number of colored dots, simulating a galaxy." The House of Marbles sells this Vacor type under the name Spotted. Black is a natural color for this type's design, since most colors display well against it. This marble is available in ⁹⁄₁₆-inch and 1-inch sizes.

Unlike the Galaxy, the surface decoration on the Vitro Agate marble called Confetti consists of separately defined dots of color, rather than a dappled look. Several colors are mixed on each Confetti, but only occasionally do the dots overlap or touch each other, as on the Galaxy. They feature opaque black or transparent clear and green body glass. Dot colors include red, orange, white (opaque), yellow, dark and light blue, and green. Vitro Agate in Parkersburg made this design on an experimental basis only in 1984 in 1³⁄₁₆-inch and ¾-inch sizes.

Single Patch (well-defined edges): Patched marbles are seen in Opaque, Transparent, and Translucent. They have been a popular type for many years beginning by at least the early 1930s.

The Transparent variety may not have been made as early as the Opaque or Translucent varieties, but it was produced until the early 1960s, longer than the others. The Opaque and Translucents were made through the 1940s but essentially disappeared with the advent of the Cat Eye in the early to mid-1950s. Perhaps because of a vague similarity between the Transparent Patched and the (transparent) Cat Eye, the Transparent variety survived a little longer.

The patch of color is usually a "rounded square"—that is, it is approximately the same dimensions on all four sides, but the sides are not perfectly straight, having been rounded in the manufacturing process.

The House of Marbles (retailer only) offers a Lustered China in 17 millimeters (¹¹⁄₁₆ inch) that is a Patched Opaque with the metallic surface sheen; maker unknown.

Makers of Single Patch

Akro Agate	Marble King
Alley	Master Marble
Heaton Agate	Peltier
Kokomo Opalescent Glass	Vitro Agate

Single Patch (ragged edges): The Brushed Patch may only be a Patched as above, but with thinly-applied design color. This may be true of the Opaque and Translucent varieties in particular, but the Transparents seem to be quite distinct.

The Patched and Brushed Patch may also be just the same type, made by different makers who applied different amounts of design color to the marble. If this were policy rather than chance, the different makers would pro-

duce either Patched or Brushed Patch, but not both types.

Judging from the quantity of the Brushed Patch available, it was a popular type and probably made for the same period as discussed above (late 1920s or early 1930s through early to mid-1950s).

Makers: Probably made by several companies, but only verified as made by Akro and packaged as Hy-Grade, in a cloth mesh bag with a paper label.

Double Patch (well-defined edges): This is a variety of the Single Patch above, but seen only in Opaque. The two patches are of different colors, generally on a white opaque body.

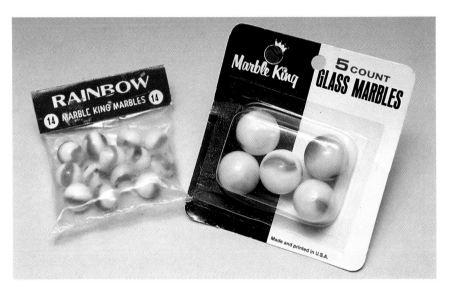

Early "14-count" packet of Rainbow marbles by Marble King. Note rare multicolored marbles. The legend on the reverse side of the bag says, "Each bag includes Shooter." This packet contains thirteen marbles and no shooter. Also, a five-count blister pack of Rainbow shooters. The back side of the package lists "Words that marble players use and what they mean," and "Tips to remember."

They are probably contemporary with the Single Patch, beginning late 1920s through mid-1950s.

Four well-defined stripes: Called Striped Opaque, the stripes are of different colors. Stripes are not rectangular near the ends like Ribbons but taper to a point. The stripes converge at the poles of the marble and come in stripe colors of red, yellow, green, and blue on white or black opaque body.

This is a new and quite distinct type introduced in 1983. Although it is a simple design and easy to produce, especially given the past sixty years of automated production technology, it has not been done until recently.

Striped Opaques are available in three sizes from 9 millimeters to 30 millimeters.

Maker: Vacor de Mexico: Pirate.

MULTICOLORED MARBLES WITH EXTERIOR DESIGN ONLY OR INTERIOR AND EXTERIOR DESIGN

Patched and Brushed: These marbles have a well-defined patch covering one-fourth to one-third of the surface area; the remainder of the body glass is covered or filled with

Old Japanese Cat Eyes with box.

thread-like strands of generally white or whitish color. Sometimes two patches are present on different sides of the marble.

Depending on the amount of striping added to the body glass, this type may be Transparent, Translucent, or almost Opaque with only small areas of body glass remaining clear.

Patched and Brushed marbles are common and probably are contemporaneous with other Patched and Ribboned or Brushed types from the late 1920s to about the early 1950s.

Rectangular Ribbons of Color: With or without a single patch (all well-defined), Ribboned or Patched and Ribboned versions occur in Opaque (exterior design only), Transparent, and Translucent (exterior only, or interior and exterior).

In the Opaque, the ribbons lie flat on the surface; they sometimes dip slightly beneath the surface and are seen to emerge a little farther on. Many combinations of wide and narrow ribbons and patches can be seen, including one narrow and two wide ribbons, three narrow, two narrow and one patch, etc. They all appear to be the same type, and variations probably are due to manufacturing procedures. Veneering was used on the Opaque type during some periods, but not all. The same manufacturers made the same designs by non-veneering, switched to the veneering method, and returned to non-veneering over a period of years.

In the Transparents and Translucents, the ribbons are sometimes flat on the surface, but in other examples they are perpendicular to the surface they intersect. There are usually two to four separate ribbons, and the body glass is sometimes quite "seedy" (i.e., it has many tiny bubbles suspended in it).

The width of the ribbons varies considerably from quite narrow to almost square. The ribbons are usually near the middle of the marble but are sometimes closer to the end, forming a ring-like pattern. There is almost always a dividing line in the ribbons, so that the longest continuous band of color is from one-third to two-thirds of the marble's circumference.

This was a long-lived type of marble. Some examples date back to the late 1920s. The Transparent and Translucent varieties may have been later arrivals than the Opaques, but the timing is uncertain. Ribboned marbles were last sold in the mid to late 1950s, while the Opaques are still widely sold today with little change in design over the past three decades.

Makers of Patched and Ribboned or Ribboned
•Alley (Opaque Ribboned, and Opaque Patched and Ribboned)
•Kokomo Opalescent Glass
•Marble King (Transparent Ribboned, Patched and Ribboned Opaque)
•Master Glass (Patched and Ribboned Opaque)
•Peltier
•Vacor de Mexico: Agate (Patched and Ribboned Opaque)
•Vitro Agate (Patched and Ribboned Opaque)

MULTICOLORED MARBLES WITH INTERIOR DESIGN ONLY

Cat Eyes: This type is determined by the presence of strands or ribbons of color that have been described as blades, vanes, leaves, or petals. From one to ten of these blades is seen, depending on the type. The body glass is transparent; some very early Japanese Cat Eyes (Type I) contain colored transparent body glass rather than clear. Blades may be all of one color in a single marble, or the blades may be of different colors. In some types, each blade is of more than one color (see U.S. Type II).

There was one attempt to produce what is called a Cat Eye in 1939 and 1940 by the Heaton Agate Company. The marble did not succeed as a popular design, however, and was discontinued.

The introduction into the United States of the Cat Eye as we know it today began about 1951 as a Japanese import. The domestic marble industry at the time had already been suffering from more than a decade of declining demand for its marbles, and the instant and enormous popularity of this foreign marble was the final blow for several companies. During the next couple of years there was a frantic scramble among American companies to duplicate the design as a matter of survival. By 1955 Marble King and Vitro Agate had succeeded in producing their own designs. In time other companies also produced Cat Eye designs.

The Cat Eye marble is not as popular today as in the past and is not considered collectible in any but the rarer varieties. However, the larger size of Cat Eye with a transparent colored body glass or with multiple colors is highly collectible. The smaller Cat Eye of the 1955 era design and color is no longer called a Cat Eye, at least not in Dallas, Texas, where these marbles are called "uglies."[8] One hesitates to speculate why this name was bestowed.

The Oriental manufacturers are still an important force in this market, with Cat Eyes being produced in Japan, Taiwan, Hong Kong, Mexico, Germany, China, and Korea.

Cat Eye Types: All Cat Eyes made by all companies over the past three decades can be divided into eight major types. Note that as in other descriptions of marble types, the colors listed do not necessarily constitute the total range of possibilities. A manufacturer's equipment may be limited to one size of marble, as it is not easily adjustable for size, but any marble-making machine can handle any color of glass. Colors produced by any one company are limited only by the desire of that company to produce a certain color, and whether it has the correct formula to do so.

1) Japanese Style: This is the earliest style, present in the United States from 1950 or 1951 and still sold today. The simplest of the Cat Eye designs, the single-colored Japanese style has four wide, well-defined blades that cross each other at a 90-degree angle. The blades form a cross-shaped pattern when the marble is viewed from the end. The four blades are always together at the center, from tip to tip. In general, the earlier examples are absolutely free of seedy glass, while later examples exhibit a few bubbles.

The multicolored Japanese style was developed later than the single-colored Japanese style. The different colors and slight changes in structure of the internal design may have been the result of competition from the American companies in the late 1950s or early 1960s.

The multicolored Japanese style has from three to seven blades that are less well-defined than the single-colored type. The blades meet at the tips, and usually at the center. Their angles of intersection are less regular than the single-colored. The blades are of a single color, with three colors per marble.

Color combinations include white, green, and purple; white, green, and red; white, yellow, and blue; yellow, green, and light blue; and yellow, green, and red.

The large sizes of multicolored Japanese-style Cat Eyes are very similar to Vacor de Mexico's Picasso type, but the Picasso has much thicker blades that are thick at the surface of the marble. Vacor also makes Cat Eyes but does not call the Picasso a Cat Eye.

2) Japanese "Cage" Style: This type has six or more narrow but well-defined blades rather than the standard four. The blades meet at the tip but bend away from the center, in an evenly spaced arrangement like the bars of a cage. Like the introduction of the Japanese multicolored type, this style may have been the result of American influence in the late 1950s or early 1960s and was evidently a short-lived type, as examples are fairly scarce.

There are single- and multicolored varieties, exhibiting colors of green, yellow, blue, red, and white. In the multicolored examples, there is one color per blade and three colors per marble. The blades of the same color are grouped next to each other, so that the pattern is three white blades, three green blades, and three red blades. Other combinations include white, blue, and yellow and red, white, and yellow.

3) U.S. Type I: This type originated in early 1955 and is still made today. Single- and multicolored types are presently made; the single-colored type was produced prior to the multicolored, but exactly how much earlier is not known.

The U.S. Type I has from three to six usually well-defined curving blades that meet at the tips and sometimes at their centers; odd numbers of blades are the result of production errors rather than design, since the design of the machines produces even numbers of blades. The curve is in a sideways manner in each blade. There is a mix of wide and narrow blades within each marble. The blades in Marble King's variety are more well defined than those of Master Glass; the latter are often thin enough to allow light to pass through. Some of Master Glass' examples are almost cagelike in that the blades bend away from the center.

Marble King's single-colored types include red, yellow, yellowish-orange, green, dark green, light blue, dark blue, bluish-white, and white. Their bi-colored type has colors of blue and yellow, two blades each, alternating in sequence—blue, yellow, blue, yellow—as the marble is turned. This particular type was made for only a very short period in 1958, prior to the fire that year that destroyed the St. Marys location. The Marble King four-color marble includes red, dark blue, dark green, and yellow; the six-color type colors include red, green, blue, yellow, and others.

Master Glass' single colors include red, yellow, green, blue, white, and purple.

4) U.S. Type II, or "Cage" Type: This type has four to eight wavy blades, usually well defined. The blades are narrower than the U.S. Type I or the Japanese types and tend to be about midway between the center of the marble and the outside. The blades in the Type II are like separate strands of color that just happen to run more or less from one point near the surface of the marble to another point on the opposite side, but they form much less an "X" or cross pattern than the other types do.

Type II is single- or multicolored and appeared at the same time as the U.S. Type I, late 1955 or early 1956. The multicolored variety of the Type II is harder to separate from the single-colored variety because color variations occur within a single blade, rather than each blade being a

separate and distinct color. For instance, the outer edges of a blade might be blue, but with yellow inner edges.

The multicolored examples exhibit only two colors per marble and are as described above; the two colors are on the same blade.

U.S. Type II was made by Vitro Agate, the developer of this style. There is a slight difference between the Cat Eye made at Vitro in Anacortes, Washington, and the original style made in Parkersburg, West Virginia. The difference may be seen by comparing the two styles.

5) U.S Type III: This type is identified by a single blade running from pole to pole. It was developed and made only by Peltier. Peltier knew of the Japanese type but chose not to make a Cat Eye marble like the four-bladed Japanese type. Instead, Peltier developed its own design of a marble that "looks like a cat's eye," a single blade similar to the pupil of a cat's eye. This style has recently been dubbed "banana," despite the use of various colors other than yellow for the blades.

6) Korean Type I: This type of Cat Eye is defined by three blades with three opaque white, yellow, and reddish-orange colors.

7) Korean Type II: Two types, each with six blades in the

A selection of Old Fashioneds, which are multicolor Opaque Slags, and Transparent Whirlwinds made by Champion Agate. With these marbles, Champion attempted to duplicate similar designs of the Ravenswood Novelty Works (see photo on page 123 to compare). Note: The black marble with silvery lines is called a Whirlwind even though the body glass is opaque.

color combinations of orange, yellow, and white; and orange, yellow, and blue. Sold by Imperial Toy Corporation, Los Angeles, California.

8) Mexican Type I: This type has four to six blades containing a single color or a combination of two colors. The design is quite similar to the U.S. Type I, but the blades are not as well defined. Vacor de Mexico makes this style of Cat Eye, which enjoys international recognition via distribution by the House of Marbles and Vacor USA.

TIGER EYE: Not to be confused with the mineral tiger's-eye, this is a glass machine-made type. Similar in description to the cage-type Cat Eye, it is nonetheless a distinct variety by type, maker, and time. It is considered rare and highly collectible.

It is distinguished from the Cat Eyes in that it is characterized by the presence of many very fine filaments of different colors running from a cutoff line on one side of the marble to the other side. The cutoff or gathering line in this case is a line where the strands all end, rather than the single point of the Cat Eye. The strands are of as many as five or six colors per marble in randomly arranged sequence around the marble. The strands are quite near the surface and also almost fill the transparent interior of this attractive marble.

Colors present in this type, in any combinations possible, include white, yellow, red, blue, green, and purple.

The Tiger Eye described above was produced by the Master Marble Company from 1930 to 1935. Vitro Agate also produced a design called a Tiger Eye in the 1950s, but examples are not available. It is not known if it resembled the Master Marble Tiger Eye or not.

MULTICOLORED MARBLES WITH INTERIOR AND EXTERIOR DESIGN

Half and Half: Two differently colored halves split an opaque body fairly evenly; there is some waviness where the colors meet, but not the spiraling pattern of the Opaque Spirals. Not veneered, the coloring extends into the interior. Half and Half is not a factory brand name.

This is a fairly scarce, distinct type, and the two colors are usually quite cleanly separated. Marbles of this type were made by Peltier Glass Company, and often called Peerless Comic Marble, as the base for the Peltier Picture Marbles. Also made by Vitro Agate in the 1940s and 1950s, the unusual ¾-inch size faded from popularity during the 1950s.

Picasso: So named by the only maker of this type, Vacor de Mexico, this is a Transparent with four blades or vanes like a Japanese-style Cat Eye, but the blades are much thicker and are fairly wide when they intersect the surface, which the Cat Eyes do not do.

Like the Cat Eye, the Picasso's blades run from point to opposite point and are joined at the center. The only distinctions of this type from the Japanese-style Cat Eye seems to be the thickness of the blades and the fact that they extend clear to the surface.

Colors are one to a blade and two to a marble in alternating sequence. Colors include red and white, blue and white, and yellow and white.

This is a recent style, present by 1983 and still produced in 1992.

Swirl-Slag: Transparent and Translucent varieties are also known as Akro Swirls by company officials, or Variegated Glass, and are characterized by randomly swirling striping in tinted body glass. The earliest reference to Slag marbles is by Mel Morrison and Carl Terrison; Clara Ingram comments about and shows a color photo of various Slag colors.

Slag or marble glass was made in purple and white, blue and white, green and white, canary yellow and white, and dark amber or brown and white.[9]

Transparent and Translucent: Only one or two colors of striping are present in each marble. The single-colored striping variety is one of the earliest of collectible semi-automatically machine-made marbles, and certainly the most common, but still a desirable specimen for any collection. These were the first machine-produced glass marbles to be made without any cutoff mark.

Known among collectors as an Akro Swirl, this type of marble was actually made by several companies besides Akro, both before and after Akro made the type. The early Swirls had striping that varied in size within each marble, and the marbles varied in size rather than being in consistent ¹/₁₆-inch increments. In the later types, probably produced after the late 1920s, the size of the marbles is much more uniform, being made, as they are now, in ¹/₁₆-inch increments. There is still variation in the size of the striping, but not as much as in the earlier type.

In Transparent and Translucent Swirls, the striping is white in either a tinted or clear body glass. The white striping inside the marble's tinted body glass picks up the color of the body glass, and appears to be a different color than white, but can be seen to be one fairly continuous strand of white glass that is actually being viewed through a different color.

The "early" and "late" varieties may have been contemporary for a time during the 1930s. The early type was

Akro Agate Spirals, grouped by type. Top: Multicolor Opaque Spirals in opaque body glass; single-color Opaque Spirals in transparent body glass. Center: Single and multicolor Opaque Spirals in translucent body glass. Bottom: Single-color Opaque Spirals in opaque body glass; multicolored Opaque Spirals in transparent body glass. Spirals are a descendent of the Swirl design

and Akro Agate is the only company known to have made them. Early Spirals were sold in a box labled "Aces" and were often called Aces. Later multicolored Spirals in a box with the comic character Popeye on the cover were called Popeyes. The most recent name for spirals is Corkscrew. From the collections of Lawrence Chapman, J. Fred Early, Laurie A. Mackie, Robert Payton, and Dennis Webb.

produced by the M. F. Christensen and Son Glass Company from 1902 through 1917, when the company went out of business. Akro Agate began producing this type in 1914 upon relocation to West Virginia. The Christensen Agate Company, in business from 1925 to 1933, produced this type as well. A late producer (after 1939) of the early type was the Heaton Agate Company, but since the type was no longer that popular, it was not produced for long.

The late variety was produced by Alox Manufacturing Company, Bogard, Champion Agate, Heaton Agate,

Ravenswood Novelty Works, and perhaps Akro Agate. An interesting revival of this design dubbed the Whirlwind was introduced in 1983 by Champion Agate and produced in Transparent only.

The variety with two different colors of striping did not appear until much later than the single-colored striping, sometime between the mid-1930s and the late 1940s.

The Transparent and Translucent Swirls were very popular for a long period of time. The randomly swirling pattern itself may have been the natural result of the limitations of the early machines. That is, the hand-dipping aspect of the production naturally lent itself to a twisting motion; the swirling pattern is the result. In fact, it would have been hard to produce any other pattern at all during the pre-1925 period, with the exception of Clears or Solids.

Opaque Swirl or Slag: This marble can be described exactly like the related Transparents and Translucents, except that it is opaque. In the 1920s the Opaque Slags with a reddish (brick) color body glass were called Immics in the Chicago area.[10] Recently they have been given a new name—Bricks.[11]

The Opaque is more common than the Transparent Swirls and was made over a longer period of time, lasting well into the 1940s, and enjoying a revival in 1977 and again in 1983. The earlier production types of the 1920s and 1930s are most commonly two-colored marbles but are also seen in three colors. Champion Agate's Bicentennial Special Pack included a red, white, and blue Opaque Swirl produced exclusively for that event. Champion Agate also made a four-colored type sometime after 1938. Gladding-Vitro's 1977 Opaque Swirls exhibit four colors also, as well as a five-colored variety.

Champion again revived this type in 1984, with its Old Fashioneds, acknowledging by the name that they are reproductions of an earlier style and are nearly indistinguishable from their Ravenswood antecedents. The Old Fashioneds have either two or three colors per marble.

Within the Opaque Swirl type are many separate designs, made by many companies over a long period of time.

Makers of Opaque Swirls

Akro Agate	Heaton Agate
Alley	Jackson Marble
Alox	Kokomo Opalescent Glass
Cairo Novelty	Marble King
Champion Agate	Peltier
Christensen Agate Co.	Ravenswood Novelty
M. F. Christensen and Son	Vitro Agate

Spirals: The descendant of the Swirl design, Spirals occur in all degrees of opacity; the Opaque variety is characterized by two equal-sized interlocking spirals of glass roughly forming an S-shape as they curve around the marble, usually making one complete revolution. In the Opaques it is hard to define which is body glass and which is striping, since the marble is simply made of two or more colors of glass, having the same form.

In the Transparent and Translucent varieties, the colored striping is always in a colorless or milky white body glass, and the striping is smaller than the body glass. The striping in the Transparents and Translucents sometimes makes two complete revolutions around the marble.

There are some major changes that occur in the Spirals that are unlike most marbles that came before this type. These differences are the result of the move toward total mechanization of the manufacturing process, beginning with the Freese patents of 1925 and continuing through the late 1920s. Most significant among these changes was that the marbles were of a consistent size and the colors in marbles of any single batch were mixed in exactly the same proportions every time. In other words, every marble coming off the rolls looked just like every other marble of that batch. Formerly, variation resulted from the gatherer's hand-mixing the colors of each marble, and judging the size of the gob by eye.

An equally significant change was that now more than two colors could be included in a single marble. This was a result of the Freese apparatus, which allowed several colors to be worked at once and combined into a single marble. Spirals occur in two, three, and four colors.

The Spiral is a very distinctive type, representing a landmark in marble manufacturing. The Akro-named Spiral has also been called True S Sigma by Bourque (*Marble-Mania*, Vol. 31, July 1983), Corkscrew by Castle and Peterson, and Barberpole by some marble players and collectors. Spirals are only known to have been produced by Akro Agate. The Spiral was made by using an attachment designed by John F. Early for his patented machine; the attachment itself was not patented. Some of this equipment was protected by patent; since it was well known that a patent does not truly prevent someone from copying a piece of machinery, other machinery was protected by secrecy. Akro Agate quit producing marbles in 1950; while it is not known for certain when they stopped making the Spirals, it is safe to assume that the type was made through the 1930s and possibly into the 1940s. In general, World War II interrupted production of luxuries like toys, but this was not the case with marbles. Following the war, however, the sharp decline in demand for toy marbles finished Akro, and it is not known what types they produced during the late 1940s.

Spirals occur in a full range of sizes from small ($\frac{5}{8}$ inch) to larger than $1\frac{1}{16}$ inches, in $\frac{1}{16}$-inch increments. As mentioned before, all degrees of opacity occur, although Opaque and Transparent are much more common than Translucent. Two- and three-colored examples are found in all three opacities. In the four-colored examples, clear is always one of the colors, technically making all four-colored varieties Transparents.

The color range seen in Spirals is much greater than in any earlier types. In many earlier types, such as the Swirl, it was unusual not to have white in a marble. But in the Spirals, white is by no means a required color, even though it is still a common color in this type.

The Opaque bi-color variety occurs in more than fifteen color combinations, including the expected black and white, as well as the more unusual red and purple or green and orange. Since the other Spirals are more scarce, a complete color listing is not possible; it is, however, safe to say that just about any colors in any combinations can be found in the Spirals.

1"Chinese Checkers," *Popular Science*, Vol. 133 (September 1938), p. 56.

2Lewis L. Moore, former manager, Vitro Agate Corporation, Parkersburg, W.Va.

3Lewis L. Moore, ibid.

4Albert Christian Revi, *Nineteenth Century Glass*, 1959, p. 253.

5Charles D. Gibson, personal communication.

6Stewart Rosenbaum, NASA News Room, Washington, D.C., September 29, 1983, personal communication.

7Stanley Snider and Vivian C. McLaughlin, Director, Resource and Research Center for Beaver County and Local History, Beaver Falls, Pa., personal correspondence.

8Jerry Needham, "Kids Go For All the Marbles as Game Makes Comeback," *The Dallas Times Herald*, June 23, 1991, A-19 and A-21.

9Thelma Shull, *Victorian Antiques* (Rutland, Vt.: Charles E. Tuttle Company, 1963), p. 243.

10William H. Carhart, personal correspondence.

11Larry Castle and Marlow Peterson, *Collectible Machine-Made Marbles*, (Ogden, Utah: Utah Marble Connection, not dated but copyright date of 1989), pp. 8 and 9.

Chapter VI

• • •

Marbles of Other Materials

The early Greeks called the sphere the most perfect form. It has been said that a marble is a sphere, but all spheres are not marbles. Children from the earliest times used any sphere to play the oldest game in history—starting with stone, progressing to clay, and to the glass of the industrial iron age and beyond.

STEEL MARBLES

When we think of metal marbles, most of us think of ball bearings. Before the industrial revolution brought us ball bearings, children probably used molded bullets when they wanted a metal marble. Joseph Strutt[1] says that "small metal balls" were used around 1780 in a game called "Bumble-puppy" in England.

Since the latter part of the nineteenth century, ball bearings have been the most common metal objects used as marbles. But for a very short time, there were some true marbles made of steel. "Ottumwa" steel marbles were advertised in the October 1909 *Playthings* catalog. The ad shows Johnston & Sharp Manufacturing Company, Ottumwa, Iowa, as the manufacturer and George Borgfeldt & Company as distributor. The ad continues, "These marbles this season [for 1909–1910] are given an extra finish and are more accurate and smoother than the product of past years" and asserts that "they will not bend, chip or break." Their hollow steel marbles were patented and "all bright or in assorted colors." Four sizes were available—$\frac{9}{16}$ inch, $\frac{5}{8}$ inch, and $\frac{3}{4}$ inch in regular weight; and $\frac{5}{8}$ inch in extra-heavy weight.[2] (The patent for these marbles is Patent No. 812,135 filed March 3, 1905 and granted to A. Johnston under the title of "Manufacture of Hollow Metallic Balls from Sheet Metal." The patent describes in great detail the method of making a hollow marble from a square sheet of metal, and the final step shows a completed marble with the distinguishing "X" or fold mark.)

Hollow steel marbles in "Size 1" ($\frac{11}{16}$ inch) were offered in the 1910 Butler Brothers catalog. In their 1914 catalog, City Products Corporation offered hollow metal marbles right beside ball

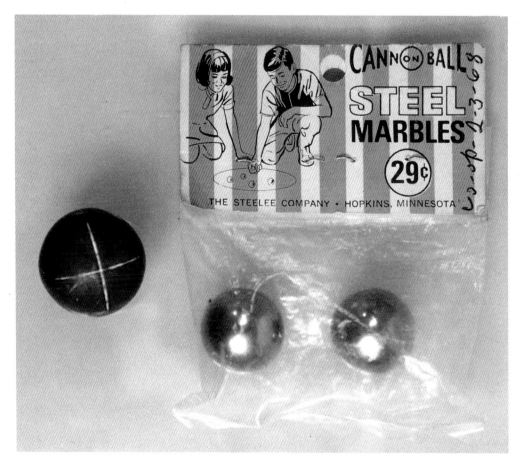

At left, a hollow Steelie from the author's collection. The "X" mark characteristic of hollow steel marbles has been highlighted in chalk. At right, solid Cannon Ball (Steelie) marbles by the Steelee Company of Hopkins, Minnesota. Christine McMillan Collection.

Carole A. Bowen of Oregon continues to delight collectors with her machine-ground marbles of glass fiber-optic cable. The shimmering bands around the circumference of these marbles are caused by the

numerous filaments in the cladding or coating on the outside of the cable. The marble at left in this photo is made of fiber-optic cable; the one at right is made of flint. Photo by Dennis Webb.

bearing marbles. The hollow Steelies of 1914 were ⅝ inch in diameter.

The March 1927 Butler Brothers 50th Anniversary Sale catalog advertised marbles of solid steel in assorted colors, two hundred in a box at 55 cents per hundred. According to Ferretti,[3] "Steeleys" (solid metal ball bearings) were popular as shooters during World War II. However, marble players remember that Steelies were never popular with players because of their devastating effect on glass marbles. Steelies were taboo in most games, and the introduction of a Steelie into a game without prior agreement among the players caused controversy and conflict. Use of a steel marble by contestants in National Marble Tournaments is not allowed.

At a much later date, The Steelee Company of Hopkins, Minnesota, offered "Cannonball Steel Marbles" in a polyethylene pack with a paper label. Judging from the style of dress on the boy and girl shown on the label, the package is from the early 1960s. The marbles are solid steel ball bearings, two for 29 cents. The disdain of marble players for Steelies is apparent in the rarity of such packages and the extremely rare instances of commercial offerings of steel balls for use as marbles.

The hollow Steelie, like the solid steel bearing, did not enjoy the popularity of the handmade glass or stone marble and is not highly collectible due to its short life. The application and patent dates serve as a dating tool for the antique dealer and marble collector. As of this date, there are no known examples of these marbles in assorted colors. Colored Steelies would be a prized addition to a marble collection.

With the advent of the space age came the metal "magnetic marble" which was probably prompted by the magnetic marbles used in experiments aboard the 1985 Discovery Shuttle Mission. The marbles, which consist of tiny magnets hidden inside a plastic shell, were designed and used by NASA astronauts for experiments in zero gravity. Subsequently, this novel marble became an instant hit with children as well as marble collectors. This type is advertised extensively in several leading catalogs.

OTHER MATERIALS

Besides glass, ceramic, stone, and metal, other materials have been used for marbles and marblelike objects. Of these other materials, the most common are plastic and wood, but ivory is occasionally seen in collections. These ivory balls are probably balls made for use with roulette wheels rather than true marbles.

Plastic toys were common by the late 1950s, and plastic balls appeared in many children's toys, particularly as noisemakers or eye-catchers in moving toys for babies. The light weight of plastics limits its use in marbles, but the plastic balls from roll-on deodorant dispensers are sometimes seen in marble collections.

In the 1970s there were rumors and unconfirmed information that Sulphide marbles were being produced in plastic. In 1990, "Rad Rollers—Collectible Action Marbles" appeared at novelty stores. At present they are available in cardboard containers with six figures such as Teenage Mutant Ninja Turtles, Batman, and The Simpsons. The figures are not made of clay (Sulphide) and are implanted in acrylic. Although this item looks like a Sulphide, it belongs in the category of a novel collectible instead. The display board for these items contains a three-sentence description of a "Circle Shoot" game. Patent is pending on this unique sphere.

Wood, like plastic, is too light for marbles used in traditional games, although a 1946 magazine article mentions that wooden marbles might have been used in the past.[4] Wood has been used for larger game balls such as croquet, and croquet balls are sometimes seen in collections along with ceramic carpet bowls. Smaller wooden balls, down to the size of traditional marbles, appear in wood craft kits. It is also reported that some marble-stoppered bottles used wooden balls.

An extraordinarily beautiful machine-made marble appeared in 1989, thanks to advances in communications technology. In 1970 Corning Glass Company scientists produced a working optical fiber to carry a laser beam in a glass filament. In 1988 AT&T perfected a commercial lightwave system using glass fiber two-thirds the thickness of a human hair; the fibers were compressed into a solid cable. The cable consists of an ultra-pure glass core to carry the light and a glass cladding or coating with a highly reflective index to keep the light from leaking out.

To make the marble, a section is cut from the solid cable, ground down into a preform, and then ground into a sphere on a machine. The glass cladding produces an amazingly wide aura of reflective color on the girth of the sphere; its intense beauty far surpasses that of the tiger's-eye. Also, the many threads or filaments cause the aura to shift as the marble is rotated. The inner core of the cable, now the inner core of the marble, appears as two translucent poles or "windows." If you hold the marble up to your eye, you cannot see through it; however, if you place the marble on top of print, you can read the print with ease.[5]

Thanks to modern technology, this beautiful modern marble is worthy of display in any glass collection.

Carole A. Bowen of Bend, Oregon, is the first person known to the authors to make this exotic marble. Examples of her craft were displayed at the 1989 and 1990 Buckeye Marble Collectors Club meet in Columbus, Ohio.

Since the introduction of this spectacular beauty by Bowen, there have been reports that other craftsmen are making marbles out of fiber-optic cable.

[1]Joseph Strutt, *The Sports and Pastimes of the People of England* (Methuen and Co., 1903; reissued Detroit: Singing Tree Press, 1968), p. 222.

[2]James H. Davis, personal conversation.

[3]Fred Ferretti, *The Great American Marble Book* (New York: Workman, 1973), p. 53.

[4]"That's Marbles, Son," *The Saturday Evening Post*, Vol. 219 (July 13, 1946), p. 69.

[5]Dennis Webb, "Favorite Pieces—Fiber Optic Marbles," *Glass Collector's Digest* Vol. IV, No. 6 (April/May 1991), p. 80.

Chapter VII

● ● ●

Game Boards & Other Miscellaneous Items

Frequently, a love of marbles inspires a love of marble-related items, such as games that use marbles for playing pieces or postcards bearing pictures of marbles or marble players. In recent years, as the hobby of collecting marbles themselves has gained in popularity, so has collecting marble games and memorabilia. Games and gizmos that once sat forgotten in the attic now command premium prices at marble meets and flea markets across the nation. This chapter describes a few of the more popular and outstanding types of marble memorabilia.

CHINESE CHECKER GAME BOARDS

One of the most familiar marble games, Chinese Checkers, has been produced since the 1930s in a multitude of designs. The early types showed more elaborate, traditional designs incorporating Oriental themes. The pattern of the playing field is usually a six-pointed star; however, there are rare examples of four-pointed playing fields. Boards with the original packages (cardboard boxes) and original marbles command the highest prices. It is often impossible, however, to be positive that the marbles in a Chinese Checkers game are the originals, since most opaque single-colored marbles made since the 1930s are difficult to distinguish from those made today. Thus, it would be easy for someone to find a board, add some modern marbles, and claim that it is a complete original set. The best advice is not to pay much premium for the idea that the marbles are the originals, unless the original box is present. It is much more likely that if the delicate cardboard box is still with the board after many years, the original marbles probably remain with the set as well.

Board games are highly sought after as marble memorabilia due to the variety of colorful designs. Avid marble collectors mount them on club room walls with marble posters and calendars.

Some significantly collectible Chinese Checkers boards are Chen Check Chinese Checkers, Ching-Ka-Chek, Hop Ching, Mah Tong, Man-Dar-In, San Lo, and Ting Tong Tan. The Alox Manufacturing Company sold Chinese Checkers boards, including one unusual four-sided board.

OTHER GAMES

The popular board game of solitaire has been attributed to an unfortunate French nobleman of the eighteenth century who was sentenced to solitary confinement in the Bastille. He whiled away his lonely hours on an improvised Fox and Goose (an early English game) board and developed an ingenious game for one person.

The game spread to England, where it inspired a craze during the Victorian era. The solitaire board, whether a simple wooden set or an elaborate creation of carved ivory, was a feature in every parlor.[1]

In America the game is called General Grant's Game because it reportedly came into being during the Civil

The Mah Tong Chinese Checker board was sold by the Alox Manufacturing Company.

Although most Chinese Checker boards have six sides, rare four-sided boards do surface from time to time.

Vitro Agate Company also made a solitaire game board.

MARBLELIKE OBJECTS AND MISCELLANEOUS ITEMS

When collecting or researching marbles, one comes across many objects that are not marbles but are similar to them. Some of these non-marbles were put to use as marbles, even though that was not their original intended use. The most common of these is the Steelie, the solid steel ball bearing from automobiles and other machinery (see Chapter VI). "Small metal balls" were used in games as early as 1780.[2] Also used in earlier days were marbles from marble-stopper bottles, obtained by smashing the necks of the bottles. A more recent example of non-marbles often offered for sale to marble collectors as "old" marbles are industrial ore-grinding balls and spherical glass ingots. The ore-grinding balls, after use by the mining and refining industry, look very much like large, old limestone marbles. However, they are much harder (almost unbreakable by any means).

Glass ingots, which are intended to be refined into fiberglass, are simply glass balls about 1 inch in diameter, crudely made and usually chipped. They look like battle-scarred old marbles. Their distinguishing characteristics are a greenish tint and an orange-peel surface that is usually marked by creases, fold marks, and chips.

The Czechoslovakian "Crystal Ball" is a transparent colorless or purple glass ball about 1 inch in diameter with thirty-two facets, numbered 0 and 00 to 30. These balls are sometimes called Fortune-Telling Marbles. The facet with the zero on it also says "Made in Czechoslovakia." The incised numbers and wording originally had white paint in them but this is often worn off from handling. Instructions for using the Crystal Ball and the answers to questions in the mind of the roller are contained in Volume 24, October 1981 of *Marble-Mania*.

Plastic balls have found many uses as toys and in industry, and as mentioned in Chapter VI, balls from roll-on deodorant have been seen among children's marbles or in collections. Plastic balls are also used in industry as filters, as bearings, and in the measurement of irregularly shaped volumes.

Semi-precious stones such as bloodstone, obsidian, petrified palm wood, rose quartz, and many others, as well as the old favorite, agate, are still being made into marbles. However, few of these are actually used as marbles and are simply made to appeal to marble collectors and mineral buffs.

Marbles made to resemble miniature pool balls may also be seen in collections.

The agate sphere was a favorite stone for a bauble or head of a hat pin many years ago. The agate was often cut off, becoming an instant marble. Rare examples are found in extensive agate collections; the cut-off point is obvious.

Berry Pink of Marble King would sometimes com-

War. A particularly collectible solitaire board is the General Grant Solitaire Game Board, a circular board with a cross pattern of holes for marbles and a groove near the outside edge. Truly antique boards command a rather high price compared to modern reproductions. Prices run upward from $250, which is not unreasonable if the full set of thirty-two genuine handmade Swirls is included. Flea market folklore has it that the original boards were accompanied by handmade glass Swirls, which is probable, since they were from the same period. However, collectors should be aware that the wooden boards can be reproduced by any competent woodworker today, and antique marbles added to form a "set." Many modern reproduction boards have been seen with antique marbles, and some old boards have been matched up with modern marbles. The caveat here is to make sure that antique marbles and an antique board are present before paying a high price. There is no way to be sure that the marbles and the board were originally part of the same set, if indeed the General Grant game was ever sold commercially in the past. It may simply have been a popular homemade game set.

A highly collectible modern solitaire set is the Precious Stone Solitaire Game (General Grant) sold by the Museum of Fine Arts, Boston. The marbles are hand-turned and the board is made of wood from Madagascar. Of note is the selection of a wide range of beautiful stones.

This game was called Fortification Solitaire in James T. Edson's patent 47,491 dated April 25, 1865. The patent was for improvements upon an existing board. It consisted of a series of semi-spherical recesses around the edge, with a hole allowing a "ball" to drop into a tray underneath, which also served as a storage area. The

A handmade cherry solitaire board featuring the game known as General Grant's Game, which reportedly evolved during the Civil War. The game is shown here with amber Clearies. The board is hollow, providing storage for the marbles.

pliment a tournament player with a present of a genuine agate marble made in Germany—a highly prized shooter. Another of Pink's marble gifts that opened many doors was a present to the secretary guarding the office; this was a special plastic jewelry box with an agate marble inside and "Berry Pink" in gold lettering inscribed on top. Many sales were made using this unique and rare calling card.

Award-Winning Art: Marbles play a never-ending part in our lives, particularly in art and advertising. Don Grzybowski, an artist painting professionally in his home studio in Colorado Springs, Colorado, has held many one-man shows sponsored privately by art collectors, corporations, and museums. He uses handmade and machine-made marbles in some of his award-winning pastels to highlight his still lifes, seascapes, and landscapes. A particularly outstanding piece named "Buckaroos Roundup" shows a wooden cowboy and a shadow of a real cowboy trying to lasso a spray of luminous marbles.[3]

Big Blue Marble: Roger W. Howdyshell's classic imprinted Big Blue Marble appeared again nearly a decade later, but in giant size. A water tower in the shape

of a sphere was constructed on the Montgomery County College campus in Germantown, Maryland, in 1980. At the outset, there was a choice to build either an esthetic tank (or tanks) hidden from view, or to build something more showy. The decision was to build a "big blue marble" resembling earth as seen from outer space. The tank is spherical, 108 feet high by 96 feet wide, and stores up to two million gallons of water. The cost of painting the tank in blue and white (Slag-like) and light brown representing land was approximately $140,000, roughly twice the cost of painting the traditional light green, silver, or rust used on ordinary water towers. Locally, it is called "The Big Blue Marble." It enjoyed considerable attention in the February 1990 issue of *Washingtonian* magazine and was recently featured in "Ripley's Believe It Or Not" as the world's biggest marble. The tower painting is signed at the base "Peter S. Freudenberg 1980." The engineering firm was Greely and Hansen.[4]

Candy Kiss: The Candy Kiss, made by Charles Gibson and recently shown at the 1992 Buckeye Marble Collector's Club, is unique and colorful. The "candy" part is a marble similar to a round peppermint candy, using

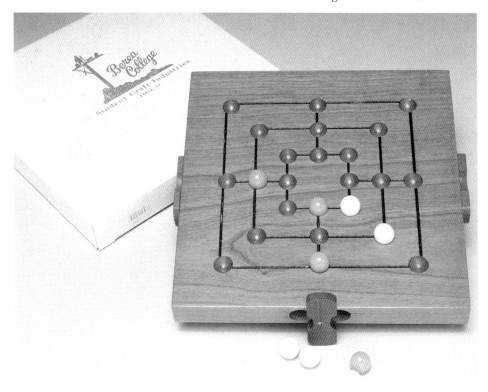

Square cherrywood Nine Men's Morris game made by Student Craft Industries of Berea College in Berea, Kentucky. Note the storage area inside the board, and the butterfly closure.

other miscellaneous objects to include reflectors for automobile fenders. The inventor is Henry Arthur (Art) Fisher of Vitro Agate, but the two patents indicate the name as Henry A. Fischer. The term of the design patent is seven years, so the trays with Patent No. 99,857 would have been marked between June 2, 1936 and the date when Patent No. 2,094,529 was granted. However, some trays were fabricated prior to the granting of the design patent. Ironically, the title of the design patent is "Design for a Tray," and the title for the patent is "Ornamental Assembly and Method of Manufacturing the Same." The tray was more commonly called "Jewel Tray" around the Vitro Agate factory, since Art Fisher was not a user of tobacco products. Despite this label, the smaller tray was actually used as an ash tray.

Marbles of various colors were used from the Vitro Agate stock and mounted around a circular body of brass in two sizes with either a smooth or a grainy texture. The smaller 3-inch type had a "gold" surface, and the larger 5-inch size had a chromium color. All or no markings appear on the bottom. The rarest of all is the 1939 New York World's Fair special edition, which featured an illustration of a gigantic perisphere (globe) and a trylon (slim column) symbolizing the fair theme of "The World of Tomorrow." *The New York Times* called it "Ball and Tack."

Of the four types of this tray, the three rarest in descending order are the New York World's Fair Tray with no markings; the same tray containing just the design number; and the "Fisher-Master-Jewelry Tray," showing both design and patent number. Some New York Worlds Fair Trays do not have a bottom portion, and some do, with both patent and design numbers shown. There are two types of this rarity. One shows "Fisher Jewel Tray Pat 2094529 Des 99857"; and the other shows "Jewel Tray Pat 99857." The first is the earlier type.

Recently it was learned that a tray was made containing the image of Babe Ruth; however, it may be an elusive collectible, as there are no known examples.

The Jewel Tray has become a marble collectible due to the variety of marbles used, the two known sizes, different markings, and a known pedigree and registered markings.

A fourth, rarer type of tray marked "Fisher-Master-Jewel Tray" and containing both patent and design numbers is valued at $75. All identifying markings are on the underside of each tray.

Jigsaw Puzzle: Interest in marbles and marble-related items continues to grow by leaps and bounds. For example, a jigsaw puzzle featuring a collage of various types of modern machine-made marbles of five hundred interlocking pieces recently appeared for sale in a leading

various colors, and the twisted glass ends, representing a candy wrapper, are of clear glass.

Chocolate Covered Marbles: The Brock Candy Company of Chattanooga, Tennessee, produced and sold chocolate-covered marbles in 1935. The box contained 120 of these candies and the lid depicted three boys playing the marble game of ringer. This box is considered very rare.[5]

Dixie Cup: Heilemann's Ice Cream Company of Jefferson, Wisconsin, offered a unique premium on the lid of its ice cream cup: "Bag of 50 Marbles. Rainbow colored. ⅝ diameter. Glass Marble King marbles. Send any 1 Dixie Cup lid and 25 cents (coin)." The offer expired August 31, 1963. The lid displays what appears to be a bag of marbles in plastic with a header, but no lettering on the header. There are no known examples of this type of package.[6]

Hydroponic Plant Growing Kit: Vitro Agate introduced its "Vitro Grow" kit to plant and flower nurseries in 1989, three years before it ceased production of marbles. The kit contains 350 pieces of 9/16-inch clear glass marbles (seedy type), ¼ ounce Vitro Grow plant food, and one instruction booklet. The marbles hold the roots and plant in place, and the plant food, with water and sunshine, completes nature's wonder. The kit is contained in an attractive clear plastic tub with a cover. This was another do-it-yourself project with marbles A variety of colored Clearies was available; the aqua blue was especially attractive.

Jewel Tray (Ash Tray): There are four known types of these trays with marbles mounted around the edges. The two patents pertaining to this beautiful tray are Design Patent No. 99,857 (applied for October 21, 1935; patent granted June 2, 1936) and Patent No. 2,094,529 (applied for September 20, 1935; granted September 28, 1937). The latter patent addressed the fabrication of the tray and

card and stationery store. The title of the puzzle is "Marbles" and the box is marked "An authentic Springbok jigsaw puzzle 20" x 20" Marbles." Apparently, the photographer took certain liberties, since several of the more colorful "marbles" are made of rubber and are used in the game of jacks.

The **"Marblescope"** (kaleidoscope) is a contemporary design created from marbles by Carolyn Bennett and is an exclusive advertised in the Summer 1986 catalog of the Smithsonian Institution. A subsequent exclusive (featured in the Fall 1987 Smithsonian catalog) is a Marble Kaleidoscope handcrafted by Keyworth Metal Studio. A handblown marble by Jody Fine rests in a cradle for a removable marble to form the kaleidoscope picture. A novel feature of this toy is that the marble may be removed and one with a different design may be placed in front of the viewer, giving the viewer a wide range of color. (Various craftspeople are now making similar items.) Other marble items in this catalog include a Chinese Checkers game with precious stone marbles.

Marble Whimsy: Webster defines "whimsy or whimsey" as a fanciful or fantastic device, object, or creation. Serious marble collectors may now add a marble whimsy to their collection. A contemporary maker of marble whimsies is Laurie A. Mackie, who creates wooden objects with

marbles exposed in a cage-like structure. Mackie's best-known whimsy is a school teacher's pointer with marbles contained in the handle. There is a legend pertaining to this particular design—the marbles in the handle are a very obvious message to the students that the teacher has not "lost her marbles."

Postcards: Another sideline of the marble hobby is collecting postcards depicting marble-playing scenes. Bertram M. Cohen recognized the historical significance of postcards and added them as memorabilia to his extensive marble collection.[7] A fine example of the use of postcards promoting an industry is the Master Marble postcard that was available at the Master Marbles Shop at the Chicago World's Fair in 1933. The souvenir mailing card carries a printed promotional ad; cost of mailing at the time was one cent. Master Marble Company is the only known marble factory to use a postcard to promote marbles.

Stereoscopic Cards: Stereoscopic cards were quite popular several decades ago as parlor entertainment for all age groups. The collection of Bertram M. Cohen contains a great variety of these cards depicting marble players. Of note are the background scenes, which provide historical details of the era between 1850–1890. These cards are a valuable addition to a marble memorabilia collection.

Two examples of the highly collectible marble Jewel Tray. At left, brass tray with white Opaque marbles bears the stamp "Design Patent No. 99,857" on its underside. At right, the rare 1939 New York World's Fair Jewel Tray with Opaque dark blue marbles. The trays were patented by Art Fisher of Vitro Agate Company. Vitro Agate used a variety of marbles in its Jewel Trays. This marble-related item first appeared in the first edition of this book. Laurie A. Mackie and Lewis L. Moore collections.

Razor Blade Sharpener: This device was designed for sharpening safety razor blades, and was sold in dime stores during the Great Depression years. This unique tool was manufactured by Wonder Specialties Company, 18 West 65th Street, New York City, and sold for 25 cents. The following directions accompanied the gadget: "Moisten sharpener, hold sharpener level, draw blade straight down between the crystal balls very lightly; do this several times until smooth and sharp."[8]

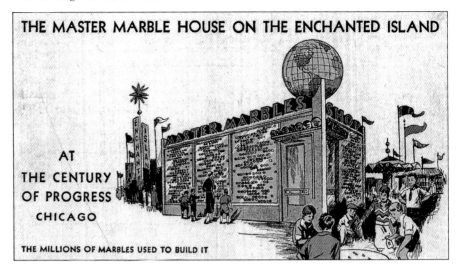

The Master Marble postcard was sold as a souvenir at the Master Marble House at the Chicago World's Fair in 1933. Bertram M. Cohen Collection.

[1]Francois Poulet, general manager of retail operations, Museum of Fine Arts, Boston, personal correspondence.

[2]Joseph Strutt, *The Sports and Pastimes of the People of England* (Methuen and Co., 1903; reissued Detroit: Singing Tree Press, 1968), p. 222.

[3]Bertram Cohen, personal correspondence.

[4]"The Big Blue Marble," *The Paper*, (Germantown, Md., Campus of Montgomery County College, October 26, 1979), pp. 6-7; and Rita Shumaker, Facilities Office, Montgomery County College, personal correspondence.

[5]Roy D. Katskee, "Marbles in Original Boxes," *Collector's Showcase*, Vol. 12, No. 11 (November 1992) pp. 32-35.

[6]James "Jim" H. Davis, Louisiana, personal correspondence.

[7]Cohen, ibid.

[8]*Marble Collectors Unlimited*, Issue 45 (Fall 1992), p. 2.

Chapter VIII

• • •

Marbles in Catalogs

An entertaining and informative source of data on early marbles is the toy section of department store or specialty store catalogs. The marble listings in catalogs correspond with the popularity of marbles as children's toys. While marbles were a basic toy in children's play, beginning with the earliest European settlements in America, catalogs themselves did not appear until much later. Marbles were first seen in catalogs of the late 1870s and continued through the mid-1930s. The disappearance of marble listings in the late 1930s corresponded with the decline in demand for marbles as toys that continues through the present.

The Sears, Roebuck and Company catalogs furnished a continuous source of listings from 1903 through 1935. Other catalogs from smaller companies provided interesting additions, but these were fewer and farther between. Few libraries carry complete collections of the catalogs of the more obscure City Products Corporation, or *Our Traveler*, or the Baltimore Bargain House.

In almost all cases, whether the company was large or small, the listings were accompanied by illustrations. Quite often these illustrations were very good, and distinct types of late nineteenth century marbles are distinguishable. Usually, but not always, the illustrations matched the product advertised. With the advent of widely available machine-made glass marbles around the 1910s and 1920s, the illustrations became stock designs that did not change from year to year, but simply showed a marble—and not necessarily the marble offered.

William Croft and Sons of Toronto, Canada (established 1855), lists and illustrates several types of marbles in its 1912 trade catalog. Type names apparently have changed through time. Among other marbles, the Croft catalog listing includes Fluffy Allies (now known as Latticino Cores), Fine Allies (unusual cores—solid divided, also Lutz marbles and Opaques), Flag Allies, in the colors of the Union Jack (now Peppermint Swirls), Brandied Glass Allies (Micas), Opal Threads Allies (Clambroths), Figured Glass Allies (Sulphides), Crystal Gold Band Allies (Lutz type), China Ballots (Ballot marbles), Flint Stone Marbles (now "Flinties," made of chalcedony), Brown/Blue Agates (Benningtons), and Fine Onyx Allies (M. F. Christensen and Son's brown, green, or blue glass Slags).[1]

An interesting marble called Klondyke appeared in a 1912–1913 Canadian catalog, perhaps named after the Klondike Gold Rush at the turn of the century. This marble appears to be what is now called Onionskin Lutz.[2]

The following is a listing of catalogs carrying marbles, the dates the marbles were offered, and how the marbles were described in the catalogs.

CATALOG LISTINGS OF MARBLES
1876–1935

Clay Marbles
1886: Montgomery Ward, listed as "clay."
1895: City Products, listed as "clay."
1914: City Products, listed as "painted clay."
1916, 1919: Sears Roebuck, listed as "painted clay."
1917: Simmons Hardware Company, St. Louis, Missouri, listed as "clay marbles."
1917–1928: Sears Roebuck, listed as "clay."
1918: *Little Folks* (a magazine for toy retailers), listed as "American Painted Marbles."

Steel Marbles
1909: *Playthings*, listed as "Ottumwa" Steelie marbles.
1914: City Products, listed as "American Steelie Hollow Steel."
1914: City Products, listed as "Approximately Solid Steelie."
1917: Simmons Hardware Company, St. Louis, Missouri, listed as "Steelie."
1927: Butler Brothers, listed as "solid steel."

Stone Marbles
Agate
1894–1895, 1903: Montgomery Ward, listed as "agate."
1903: Our Traveler, listed as "Cornelian Agates."
1903: Sears Roebuck, listed as "agate."
1903: Sears Roebuck, listed as "Blood Carnelian."
1907–1910: H. H. Tammen Curio Company, lists agate marbles from pure agate and handsomely marked, striped red carnelian and striped Black Onyx Agate. Large "Cabinet Pieces" ranging from 2 to 3 inches were also available.
1912: Wm. Croft & Sons, listed as "Stone Marbles and Flint Stone."
1914: City Products, listed as "Genuine Carnelian."
1914: City Products, listed as "agate."
1927: Butler Brothers, listed as "Prima Agates" and "Cornelians."

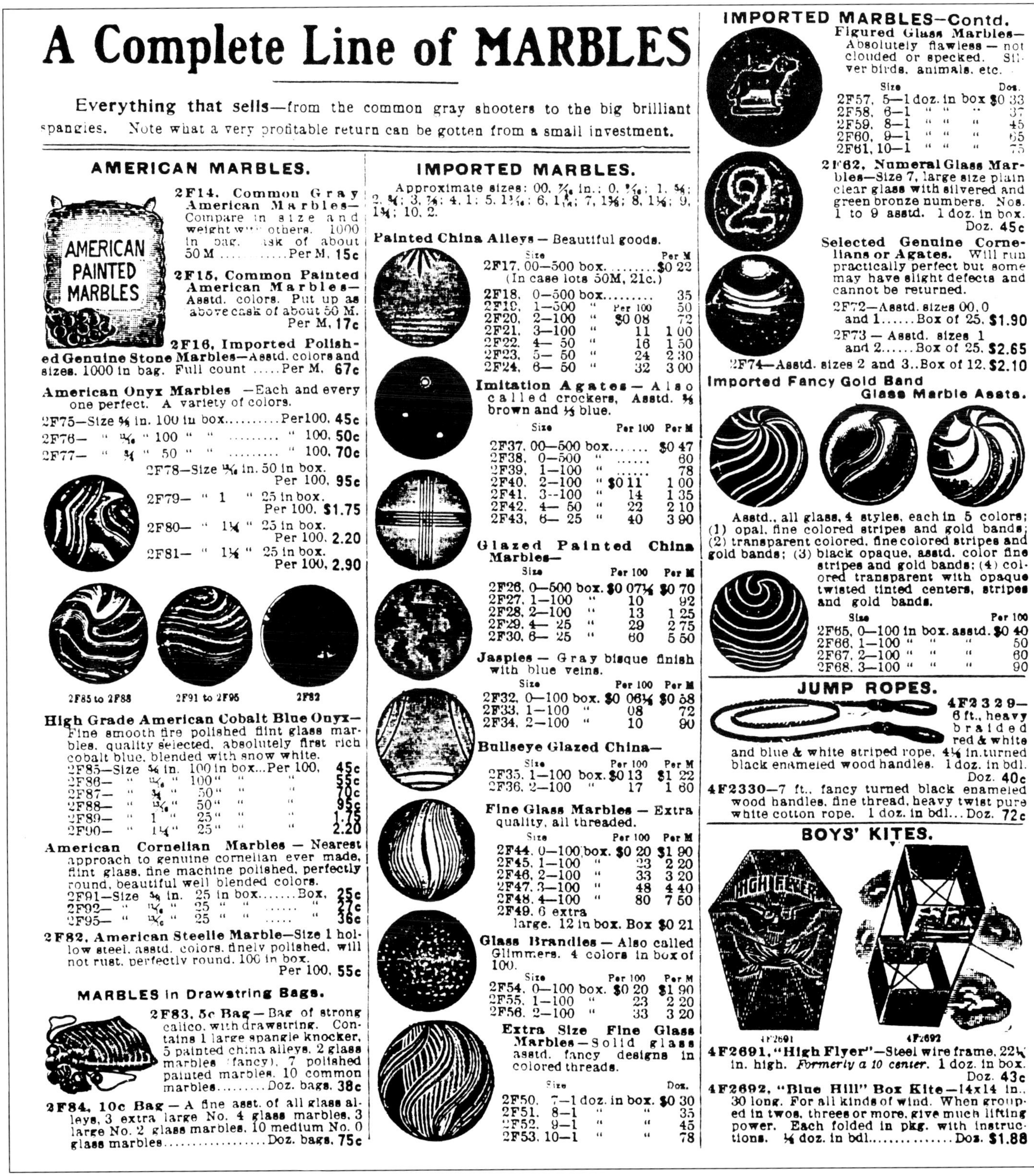

A Complete Line of MARBLES

Everything that sells—from the common gray shooters to the big brilliant spangles. Note what a very profitable return can be gotten from a small investment.

AMERICAN MARBLES.

AMERICAN PAINTED MARBLES

2F14. Common Gray American Marbles—Compare in size and weight with others. 1000 in bag. Cask of about 50 M.........Per M, **15c**

2F15, Common Painted American Marbles—Asstd. colors. Put up as above cask of about 50 M. Per M, **17c**

2F16, Imported Polished Genuine Stone Marbles—Asstd. colors and sizes. 1000 in bag. Full count .....Per M, **67c**

American Onyx Marbles —Each and every one perfect. A variety of colors.

2F75—Size 5/8 in. 100 in box.........Per100, **45c**
2F76— " 11/16 " 100 " " .... " 100, **50c**
2F77— " 3/4 " 50 " " .... " 100, **70c**
2F78—Size 13/16 in. 50 in box. Per 100, **95c**
2F79— " 1 " 25 in box. Per 100, **$1.75**
2F80— " 1 1/4 " 25 in box. Per 100, **2.20**
2F81— " 1 1/2 " 25 in box. Per 100, **2.90**

2F85 to 2F88 — 2F91 to 2F95 — 2F82

High Grade American Cobalt Blue Onyx—Fine smooth fire polished flint glass marbles, quality selected, absolutely first rich cobalt blue, blended with snow white.

2F85—Size 5/8 in. 100 in box...Per 100, **45c**
2F86— " 11/16 " 100 " " " **55c**
2F87— " 3/4 " 50 " " " **70c**
2F88— " 13/16 " 50 " " " **95c**
2F89— " 1 " 25 " " " **1.75**
2F90— " 1 1/4 " 25 " " " **2.20**

American Cornelian Marbles — Nearest approach to genuine cornelian ever made, flint glass, fine machine polished, perfectly round, beautiful well blended colors.

2F91—Size 5/8 in. 25 in box.......Box, **25c**
2F92— " 11/16 " 25 " " ...... " **27c**
2F95— " 13/16 " 25 " " ...... " **36c**

2F82, American Steelie Marble—Size 1 hollow steel, asstd. colors, finely polished, will not rust, perfectly round, 100 in box. Per 100, **55c**

MARBLES in Drawstring Bags.

2F83, 5c Bag—Bag of strong calico, with drawstring. Contains 1 large spangle knocker, 5 painted china alleys, 2 glass marbles (fancy), 7 polished painted marbles, 10 common marbles.........Doz. bags, **38c**

2F84, 10c Bag — A fine asst. of all glass alleys, 3 extra large No. 4 glass marbles, 3 large No. 2 glass marbles, 10 medium No. 0 glass marbles.................Doz. bags, **75c**

IMPORTED MARBLES.

Approximate sizes: 00, 7/16 in.; 0, 9/16; 1, 5/8; 2, 3/4; 3, 7/8; 4, 1; 5, 1 1/16; 6, 1 1/8; 7, 1 3/8; 8, 1 1/2; 9, 1 3/4; 10, 2.

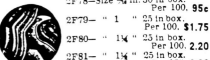

Painted China Alleys — Beautiful goods.

Size		Per 100	Per M
2F17. 00—500 box.........			$0 22
(In case lots 50M, 21c.)			
2F18. 0—500 box.........			35
2F19. 1—500	"		50
2F20. 2—100	"	$0 08	72
2F21. 3—100	"	11	1 00
2F22. 4— 50	"	16	1 50
2F23. 5— 50	"	24	2 30
2F24. 6— 50	"	32	3 00

Imitation Agates — Also called crockers. Asstd. 1/2 brown and 1/2 blue.

Size		Per 100	Per M
2F37. 00—500 box.......			$0 47
2F38. 0—500	"	......	60
2F39. 1—100	"	......	78
2F40. 2—100	"	$0 11	1 00
2F41. 3—100	"	14	1 35
2F42. 4— 50	"	22	2 10
2F43. 6— 25	"	40	3 90

Glazed Painted China Marbles—

Size		Per 100	Per M
2F26. 0—500 box.		$0 07 1/2	$0 70
2F27. 1—100	"	10	92
2F28. 2—100	"	13	1 25
2F29. 4— 25	"	29	2 75
2F30. 6— 25	"	60	5 50

Jaspies — Gray bisque finish with blue veins.

Size		Per 100	Per M
2F32. 0—100 box.		$0 06 1/2	$0 58
2F33. 1—100	"	08	72
2F34. 2—100	"	10	90

Bullseye Glazed China—

Size		Per 100	Per M
2F35. 1—100 box.		$0 13	$1 22
2F36. 2—100	"	17	1 60

Fine Glass Marbles — Extra quality, all threaded.

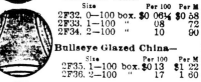

Size		Per 100	Per M
2F44. 0—100 box.		$0 20	$1 90
2F45. 1—100	"	23	2 20
2F46. 2—100	"	33	3 20
2F47. 3—100	"	48	4 40
2F48. 4—100	"	80	7 50

2F49. 6 extra large. 12 in box. Box $0 21

Glass Brandies — Also called Glimmers. 4 colors in box of 100.

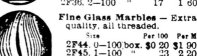

Size		Per 100	Per M
2F54. 0—100 box.		$0 20	$1 90
2F55. 1—100	"	23	2 20
2F56. 2—100	"	33	3 20

Extra Size Fine Glass Marbles — Solid glass asstd. fancy designs in colored threads.

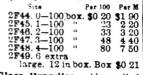

Size				Doz.
2F50. 7—1 doz. in box.				$0 30
2F51. 8—1	"	"		35
2F52. 9—1	"	"		45
2F53. 10—1	"	"		78

IMPORTED MARBLES—Contd.

Figured Glass Marbles—Absolutely flawless — not clouded or specked. Silver birds, animals, etc.

Size				Doz.
2F57. 5—1 doz. in box				$0 33
2F58. 6—1	"	"	"	37
2F59. 8—1	"	"	"	45
2F60. 9—1	"	"	"	65
2F61. 10—1	"	"	"	75

2F62, Numeral Glass Marbles—Size 7, large size plain clear glass with silvered and green bronze numbers. Nos. 1 to 9 asstd. 1 doz. in box. Doz. **45c**

Selected Genuine Cornelians or Agates. Will run practically perfect but some may have slight defects and cannot be returned.

2F72—Asstd. sizes 00, 0 and 1......Box of 25, **$1.90**
2F73 — Asstd. sizes 1 and 2......Box of 25, **$2.65**
2F74—Asstd. sizes 2 and 3..Box of 12, **$2.10**

Imported Fancy Gold Band Glass Marble Assts.

Asstd., all glass, 4 styles, each in 5 colors; (1) opal, fine colored stripes and gold bands; (2) transparent colored, fine colored stripes and gold bands; (3) black opaque, asstd. color fine stripes and gold bands; (4) colored transparent with opaque twisted tinted centers, stripes and gold bands.

Size				Per 100
2F65. 0—100 in box. asstd.				$0 40
2F66. 1—100	"	"	"	50
2F67. 2—100	"	"	"	60
2F68. 3—100	"	"	"	90

JUMP ROPES.

4F2329—6 ft., heavy braided red & white and blue & white striped rope, 4 1/2 in. turned black enameled wood handles. 1 doz. in bdl. Doz. **40c**

4F2330—7 ft., fancy turned black enameled wood handles, fine thread, heavy twist pure white cotton rope. 1 doz. in bdl... Doz. **72c**

BOYS' KITES.

HIGH FLYER

4F2691 — 4F2692

4F2691, "High Flyer"—Steel wire frame, 22 1/2 in. high. *Formerly a 10 center.* 1 doz. in box. Doz. **43c**

4F2692, "Blue Hill" Box Kite—14x14 in., 30 long. For all kinds of wind. When grouped in twos, threes or more, give much lifting power. Each folded in pkg. with instructions. 1/4 doz. in bdl...............Doz. **$1.88**

Onyx
1886: Montgomery Ward.
1895: City Products.
1903: Sears Roebuck, listed as "Black Onyx."
Limestone
1903: Sears Roebuck, listed as "Unpolished Imported."
1903: Sears Roebuck, listed as "Polished Imported."
1914: City Products, listed as "Polished Imported."
1927: Butler Brothers, listed as "polished stone" and "colored stone."

Porcelain Marbles
1886, 1894–1895: Montgomery Ward.
1895: City Products.
1895: Montgomery Ward, listed as "American Majolica Marbles" (white).

Goal Keepers' Leg Guards

No. 1/275—Men's size, made from selected Sheepskin, seven strong canes, extra padding. Size 10in. x 14½in., splendid value

Doz. prs..............$44.00
Retails............ $2.75 pair

No. 2/350—Men's size, made of heavy canvas. Size 11in. x 29in. Good value.

Doz. prs.............$56.00
Retails............ $3.50 pair

1/275   2/350

Skate Straps

20 in. Split Leather, 1 doz. pair in package. Doz pr..........$1.60

20 in. Russett Grain, 1 doz. pair in package. Doz. pr..........$2.20

24 in. Russett Grain, 1 doz. pair in package. Doz. pr......... $2.50

20 in. Black Grain Leather, 1 doz. pair in package. Doz. pr..........$2.40

24 in. Black Grain Leather, 1 doz. pair in package. Doz. pr..........$3.00

27 in. Black Grain Leather, 1 doz. pair in package. Doz. pr..........$3.50

Stone Marbles

	Bag
Grey, 1000 in Bag	$ .70
Polished, 1000 in Bag	.90

Flint Stone Marbles

Grey   Polished

	Grey
Grey, 1000 in Bag	$1.00
Polished, 1000 in Bag	1.20

China Ballots

	Per 100
White, 100 in Box	$ .50
Black, 100 in Box	.50

Fluffy Allies

No. 0—100 in Box. Per 100..........$ .90
1—100 " " 1.00
2—100 " " 1.40
3—100 " " 1.80
4— 50 " " 2.80
5— 50 " " 4.00
6—1 doz. in Box. Per doz. .70
7—1 " " .80

Stone Bowlers

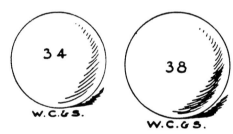

34   38
W.C.&S.   W.C.&S.
Polished   Grey

	Bag
No. 34—Polished, 100 in bag	$1.50
38—Grey, 100 in bag	1.50

Fine Allies

No. 8.   No. 6.   No 4.   No 2.

No. 0—100 in Box. Per 100..........$ .50
1—100 " " .60
2—100 " " .80
3—100 " " 1.10
4— 50 " " 1.50
5— 50 " " 2.40
6—1 doz. in Box. Per doz. .60
8—1 " " .80
10—1 " " 1.50

Crystal Gold Band Allies

No 1   No 2   No 3   No 4   No 5

0—100 in Box. Per 100..........$ .50
1—100 " " .60
2—100 " " .80
3—100 " " 1.10
4— 50 " " 1.80
5— 50 " " 2.40

Flag Allies

No 1   No 2   No 3

No. 0—100 in Box. Per 100..........$ .90
1—100 " " 1.00
2—100 " " 1.40
3—100 " " 1.80

1903: Our Traveler, listed as "Jaspies" or "Cloudies," "Bisque" or "Glazed" (white with blue veins).

1903: Our Traveler, listed as "Painted China."

1903: Sears Roebuck, listed as "Glazed China."

1903: Sears Roebuck, listed as "Glazed Bull's-eyes."

1903: Sears Roebuck, listed as "Glazed Jaspers."

1903: Our Traveler, listed as "Patent Agates" or "Potteries" (blue or brown).

1905: Butler Brothers, listed as "Painted China Alleys," "Glazed China Marbles," "Bull's-Eye Glazed Chinas," or "Jaspers."

Handmade Glass Marbles

(Type Unknown)

1886, 1894–1895: Montgomery Ward.

1903: City Products.

1903: Our Traveler.

1912: Wm. Croft & Sons, listed as "China Ballots," "Painted Glazed Chinas," "Bull's Eyes Disc," "brown or blue Agates," and "Flamed Agates."

1912, 1914–1915: Sears Roebuck.

1914: City Products, listed as "Imported Hand Made."

1927: Butler Brothers, "Fine glass" marbles; illustration indicates handmade Swirls, but this is rather late for handmade glass types, so the marbles sold may have been machine-made.

Handmade Glass Marbles

(Known Types)

1894–1895: Montgomery Ward, listed as Sulphides or "Figured Glass."

1894–95: Montgomery Ward, listed as "Ballot Marbles."

1895, 1914: City Products, listed as Sulphides or "Figured Glass."

1903: Our Traveler, listed as Sulphides or "Figured Glass."

1903: Our Traveler, listed as "Brandies" or "Glimmers" (Mica).

1903: Sears Roebuck, listed as "Brandies" or "Glimmers" (Mica).

1903: Sears Roebuck, listed as "Threaded glass" (Swirls).

1903: Sears Roebuck, listed as "Tipple and Threaded."

1905: Butler Brothers, listed as "Fine Glass Marbles," "Glass Brandies," "Glass Cornelians," "Glass Tigers," "Imitation Onyx Glass Agates," "Fancy Figured Glass Marbles" (Sulphides), "Numeral Glass Marbles" (Sulphides), "Glass Spangles." Also lists assorted marbles in drawstring bags.

1912: Wm. Croft & Sons, listed as "Crystal Gold Band Allies," "Fine Allies and Fluffy Allies," "Flag Allies," "Opal Threads-Allies," "Figured Glass Allies," and "Brandied Glass Allies."

1914: City Products, listed as "Fancy Gold Band Glass" (Lutz-like).

1921–1923: Sears Roebuck, listing reads "Imported Glass (similar to the glass marbles sold before the war, with bright colored streamers through the center)."

(Type Not Certain)

1903: Our Traveler, listed as "Imitation Onyx."

1905: Butler Brothers, listed as "Common Gray Marbles," "Common Painted Marbles," or "Imitation Agates."

1910: Sears Roebuck, listed as "National Onyx."

1915: Sears Roebuck, listed as "onyx." Catalog illustration indicates handmade glass.

Machine-Made Glass Marbles

1912: Sears Roebuck, type unknown.

1913: Sears Roebuck, listed as "Glass Onyx."

1914: Sears Roebuck, listed as "Onyx Imitation Agates." Catalog shows machine-made swirled variety.

1914: Sears Roebuck, listed as "Imitation Agates."

1914: Sears Roebuck, listed as "Jade."

1914: Sears Roebuck, listed as "Turquoise."

1914: Sears Roebuck, listed as "Imitation Cornelians."

1914: City Products, listed as "American Onyx."

1914: City Products, listed as "High Grade Cobalt Blue Onyx."

1914: City Products, listed as "Oriental Jade."

1914: City Products, listed as "Persian Turquoise."

1914: City Products, listed as "American Cornelians."

1914–1918: Sears Roebuck, listed as "Onyx." Catalog illustration shows machine-made swirled type.

1915–1918: Sears Roebuck, listed as "Onyx Imitation Agates," but with no illustration.

1917: Simmons Hardware Company, St. Louis, Missouri, listed as "American carnelian, cobalt blue-onyx, and striped onyx."

1917–1918: Sears Roebuck, listed as "Onyx," with no illustration.

1919–1928: Sears Roebuck, listed as "Imitation Onyx."

1926–1928: Sears Roebuck, listed as "Imitation Carnelias."

1927: Butler Brothers, listed as "onyx."

Note: Other Sears Roebuck ads offering "Genuine Akro Agates" went on to specify different types:

1929–1930: "Red Imitation Cornelians."

1929–1930: "Assorted colored."

1929–1930, 1932: "Moonie."

1929–1930: "Cardinal."

1931: "Akro Agates." Illustration shows machine-made Spiral.

1932: "Cardinal Reds."

1932: "Flinties."

1932: "Imperials."

1933–1935: Sears Roebuck, listed as "Genuine Akro Agates."

[1]Craig Gamache, Canadian Marble Collectors Association and *Swirls*, Volume 1, No. 4 (December 1990), newsletter of the Canadian club.

[2]Craig Gamache, personal correspondence.

Chapter IX

• • •

Containers and Packages

Early Akro Agate packages and marbles, circa 1910–20. Lawrence M. Chapman Collection.

The containers in which marbles were shipped were often as distinctive as the marbles themselves. The overall design of containers and packages has changed more dramatically than marbles have in the more than one hundred years that such containers have been in use.

Before the machine revolution in marble making in the early twentieth century, marbles were sold to children in cloth bags or boxes of wood or cardboard from catalogs, or they were sold loose in retail stores. Up until the early 1910s, the normal package was an open box set on a store counter from which the customer selected individual marbles. This custom was among several aspects of the marble business that The Akro Agate Company changed. In Akro's earliest marketing efforts, between 1910 and 1914, the company took a new approach to the traditional method of packaging. Rather than the open bulk packages, Akro packaged five marbles in individual cellophane tubes. Despite a slightly higher price, the new idea was a resounding success; and while the older bulk display methods hung on for many years, the new standard was prepackaging.[1]

By 1915 United States marbles were being offered in sets of five to twenty-five marbles in cardboard boxes. Later, as the packages became more sophisticated, the number of marbles for sale in a single package increased

Old and new Marble King packages. At left, the "Tournament Assortment," containing 228 marbles, is an example of the cloth bag, one of the earliest types of container. At right, when Marble King replaced the cloth bag with a plastic one in 1950, the boy's clothing was modernized, too.

This collection of marbles, packaged in a handsome wooden box, is marketed by the Museum of Fine Arts, Boston. Proceeds from the sale of these marbles support educational activities at the museum.

up to one hundred. The larger boxes included either a bag (leather or chamois) to keep the marbles in or a knuckle-pad. Bright colors on the boxes were the rule; a favorite design in early boxes was a cutout pattern, which allowed glimpses of the marbles within.

Cardboard boxes had been used by German marble makers probably as early as the late 1890s, but these were for shipping to the customer from catalog offerings, rather than for fancy counter-display units.

The cutout covers on domestic cardboard boxes sometimes formed a playing board, as in the Alox Manufacturing Company's Tit-Tat-Toe box. Cutout cardboard boxes continued in use up into the 1940s. Other boxes included a cardboard playing surface inside, as in Akro's "Solitary (Chinese) Checkers" game.[2]

Master Marble and Master Glass both used a red, white, and blue cutout cover containing the circular triple "M" logo and lettering "Master Made Marbles." Master Marble included its Clarksburg, West Virginia, mailing address. The identifying information about the company that made the marbles in the package is found on the edge of the box.

Master Marble's Chicago World's Fair (1933) special packages included velour-like cardboard boxes with elaborate illustrations of fair buildings.

Another cardboard package was Akro's large box that served as a retail display as in the earlier bulk packages.

The difference was that along with the marbles, the box held an equal number of sticks of gum. To get a free marble, you bought a stick of gum for one cent. The buyer of the last stick received the single large shooter, free.[3]

Bags of various types were a favorite container from the earliest catalog offerings of the 1880s and were frequently part of the illustrations in marbles sections of catalogs. Cheaper types of marbles, such as clays and common stones, were sold in cloth drawstring bags of one thousand marbles; more expensive types were offered in calico drawstring bags in quantities of twenty or twenty-five.[4]

By 1914 net bags with drawstrings were in the catalogs, and the quantities of marbles had changed, with the new machine-made glass marbles being offered in quantities of fifty or seventy-five per bag.[5] Even so, the cloth bags of a thousand common clay or stone marbles were still offered up into the 1920s, and as late as the mid-1950s major American marble companies were still packaging marbles in cloth bags.

In 1937 Clinton F. Israel patented and assigned to the Master Marble Company a net bag with a rigid cardboard back for marbles (Pat. 2,085,365).

In the mid-1950s Marble King replaced their cloth bag with a polyethylene bag; the illustration of a boy playing marbles was changed only to modernize his style of dress from the 1930s to the 1950s.

Tin boxes appeared during the 1930s. The covers of the

boxes were painted and in some cases illustrated with whole scenarios of groups of children playing marbles.

Polyethylene see-through bags became the standard package in the 1950s and remain a common package type today, although cotton mesh net bags persisted for many years. By the 1980s, the cotton mesh had largely been replaced by plastic mesh bags, which are still frequently used by foreign marble makers in domestic markets.

In the mid-1970s the rigid plastic "bubble pack" with a cardboard back appeared. This package is currently a common packages offered at the retail level. Among American makers, it is used only by Marble King, but it is common among foreign makers.

Wood boxes with a sliding top containing collector assortments of various marble types and designs of unnamed origin, and solitaire games with precious stone marbles are now appearing for sale in several prestigious mail order and gift catalogs, such as Eddie Bauer, the Smithsonian Institution, the Metropolitan Museum of Art and the Museum of Fine Arts, Boston.

Even space-age magnetic marbles are advertised, a clear indication that marbles are recognized as collectibles. Vitro Agate Company in Anacortes, Washington, introduced an attractive container in the form of a plastic canister or tub, which has considerable utility as a shipping, storage, and display container. The canister is of durable clear plastic with an opaque white screw-on lid. The factory label and logo are pasted on top of the lid, making it an attractive and collectible marbles container. The main interest in this container is that it is an ideal way to display a marble collection.

Loose marbles are often sold in bulk. Marble King, Inc., for instance, advertises 25 and 50 pounds of boxed marbles in various sizes.[6]

25# Standard Bulk Packs
1-inch 500 pieces
$7/8$-inch 800 pieces
$3/4$-inch 1,300 pieces
$5/8$-inch 2,100 pieces
$9/16$-inch 3,000 pieces

50# Standard Bulk Packs
1-inch 1,000 pieces
$7/8$-inch 1,500 pieces
$3/4$-inch 2,500 pieces
$5/8$-inch 4,000 pieces

There is such a wide variety of packaged materials available for collectors that it is impossible to list them all. In general, regardless of which maker, the earlier packages are more sought after, and consequently are higher priced. Prices range from $5 for packages from the 1970s up to very high prices for others.

Generally speaking, the early cloth mesh bags are quite scarce due to their short period of use and the fact that they deteriorate. Serious collectors store and display the bags in plastic zip-lock freezer bags. Despite this scarcity, the cardboard packages, particularly those with factory design and name, command higher prices. The reported prices for certain individual marble packages are listed by manufacturer in Chapter XVI.

[1]*The Akro Agate Gem*, Newsletter of the Akro Agate Art Association, Box 758, Salem, NH 03079, Vol. 1, p. 5.

[2]Gene Florence, *The Collectors Encyclopedia of Akro Agate Glassware*, Collector Books, 1975, p. 9.

[3]Florence, p. 9.

[4]*Our Traveler* catalog, 1903.

[5]*City Products* catalog, 1914.

[6]Roger W. Howdyshell, personal conversation.

Chapter X

● ● ●

Glass Machine-Made Marble Production

In *All About Marbles and Rules of the Game*, author Sam McCarthy repeats this account of early English glass marble production: "The local factory uses scrap glass for raw material which is fed into an oil-fired furnace which can generate a temperature of 1,200 degrees C (2,192 degrees F). The glass emerges in liquid form from a valve which has been adjusted in relation to the size of the marbles required. The liquid silver is cut as it descends from the furnace and the globules fall into a water-revolving drum. The rolling and cooling result in the globules contracting into spheres and in doing so, the marbles are formed. There are two ways to produce the traditional coloring. For the opaque marbles the coloring agent is placed in the furnace with the scrap glass, or for the internal coloring, the melted coloring agent is streamed into the liquid glass as it emerges from the furnace."[1]

As this passage illustrates, the production aspect of the marble industry is complicated and challenging. Although the technology has changed somewhat since this account was given, there are still a number of steps that must be executed with precision. The process begins with the making of glass cullet.

A day tank once used at the Vitro Agate Corporation. This was the main melting tank for the glass. Photo by Dennis Webb.

THE GLASS RECIPE

In producing glassware of any kind, the maker's first decision is whether to create new glass or to reuse existing glass. New glass is referred to by marble makers as formula glass and is made according to a recipe. When melted and broken into workable chunks for melting, it is called cullet. Scrap glass such as broken bottles may also be used, alone or with cullet.

Some factories make their own formula glass, and others have a special standing order with another factory to make colored glass according to specific formula, thereby maintaining consistent color. Some factories use a combination of both formula and scrap glass. Recently, scrap glass has been used more than in the past because of the rising cost of ingredients.

Glass is not an easy material to work with and is appropriately described as "finicky." The two main ingredients of glass are silica and an alkali. To obtain variations in color, other substances are added. The exact proportions of coloring agents are developed over years of trial and experimentation; they are sometimes in measures as small as 2½ ounces in a batch of glass that weighs 865 pounds. In the heyday of the American marble industry, well-guarded color recipes were the keys to success.

Some agents used to produce color in glass may seem surprising. An early agent in ruby or pink glass was gold—a $20 "double eagle" gold coin was tossed into the melting tank with the glass—but selenium and cadmium sulphide have long since replaced gold. One of the more unusual additives was uranium oxide for a yellow or straw color. (For more about glass formulas, see Chapter XI.)

The dry ingredients for a given batch are weighed and mixed by hand in a flat wooden crib box before they are dumped in the melting tank. Since the advent of modern marble machines, the ingredients are placed in a cylindrical drum mixer with a power source for mixing. To turn this raw mix into glass requires high temperatures that vary according to the color of the glass being prepared. Chunks of solid cullet of various size are placed on top of the dry recipe to hold down the powdery ingredients during the melting process. Besides sealing the batch to assure the complete melting, the addition of the cullet also lowers the melting temperature.

The standard temperature is 2,400 degrees Fahrenheit but can vary to as low as 1,850 degrees for blue or azure glass. Ruby or pink glass is the most difficult of all colors to produce; 2,740 degrees Fahrenheit is standard for this color, but if the temperature is exceeded, the color becomes dark. A "seedy" condition will occur if the glass is not cooked properly or long enough. Seedy glass is that which contains many small gaseous bubbles.

Melting time is about eighteen hours, but this depends upon the size of the melting tank and the type of glass. Maintenance of a steady temperature is critical for a "run" of any color. The term run refers to the production of a particular batch of glass. Natural gas is used to heat furnaces to melt the ingredients and to keep the glass in a "plastic" state for working. It was the availability of natural gas and a high grade of sand that brought the marble makers to West Virginia, making it the focus of the marble industry in the United States. At present propane gas is also used.

In its first year of operation, about 1914–1915, the Akro Agate Company had stationary melting furnaces made of Cohart fire clay blocks, which contained four pots where the glass batch was melted. The molten glass was then transferred by ladle to the small gathering pots used by marble workers. The melting pots were replaced in the mid-1920s by day tanks, which had a capacity of one to five tons of batch. In addition to the above melting furnaces, another furnace called a monkey furnace was used to preheat the melting pots or gathering pots. These pots were made of fire clay and had to be preheated to avoid breakage when the molten glass was placed in them.

On-site cullet was made by ladling molten glass into cast-iron kettles filled with water, which caused the glass to fracture. The kettles were on three wheels and when filled could be moved to the cullet storage area and dumped. The cullet was broken into small chunks for future melting.

The occurrence of seedy glass, mentioned earlier, was a problem in the earlier days of marble production. Due to the density of the glass and the small size of the air bubbles, the bubbles would remain in the molten glass and become part of the marbles. In the mid-1920s, Arnold Fiedler, an ingenious chemist who worked at Akro Agate, solved the problem with a potato. He

The all-steel cullet wagon moves large volumes of cullet, scrap glass, or other glass used for making marbles. Photo by Dennis Webb.

stuck a potato on a metal rod and pushed it through the molten glass to the bottom of the melting tank. The heat of the molten glass caused the potato to give off bubbles of gas, and as these larger bubbles rose to the surface of the tank, they absorbed or lifted to the top the smaller bubbles, eliminating the problem.

Lewis L. Moore, of Vitro Agate, described another old method, wherein a two-by-four pine board was used in the same manner as the potato. Modern recipes incorporate borax to keep bubbles from forming. Variations in the quantity of borax can affect the color of the glass. Constant maintenance of a working level of

The all-steel kettle is used to transport molten glass or to prepare cullet. To prepare cullet, water is poured into the kettle; then molten glass is added. The water causes the glass to cool and fracture. Photo by Dennis Webb.

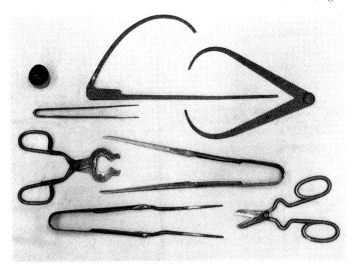

A collection of glassmaking tools on display at The Art of Fire at Savage, Maryland. In the bottom row are, left to right, a pair of pincers and shears, used for cutting glass. In the middle row are footsetting shears and another pair of pincers. In the next row up are a pair of jacks, the basic tool for handling glass, and two pairs of calipers; the right calipers measures the diameter of a bowl; the one at left measures both diameter and depth. At top left is a wild-cherry wood bowl for forming spheres. Photo by Dennis E. Webb.

Glassworkers' tools—the blowpipe, at left; and the punty, right. The punty was used through the mid-1920s. Courtesy of Jack Bogard.

molten glass in the tank also helps prevent bubbles. In more recent times these tiny bubbles have been considered attractive in clear marbles and have been purposely left in the finished product. An exception is the Cat Eye type, however, in which absolutely clear glass is desired.

MAKING MARBLES

Once the glass recipe is prepared, the challenge is to produce small, solid spheres from a molten substance. Machine-assisted production of glass marbles was first developed by Martin F. Christensen of M. F. Christensen and Son Glass Company, in Akron, Ohio, who patented his invention in 1905. His was the first mechanical aid beyond the punty, which had been used from the very earliest handmaking period. As noted earlier, the punty was the primary tool for handling molten glass.

Christensen's machine used a pair of oppositely arranged wheels much like an automobile, but much smaller. The wheels, which each had a single, continuous semi-circular groove on the rim, turned toward each other, thus shaping a gob of molten glass into a sphere at their meeting point.

As developed by Christensen, the machine required three men to operate it—one called the gatherer, who dipped the molten glass out of a striping pot with a punty; a cutoff man, who used shears to cut off the proper amount of teardrop-shaped, dripping glass from the punty; and a man to turn the rollers. After it was cut from the punty, the gob of glass then dropped into the groove of the forming wheels. When the marble was perfectly formed, the wheels automatically spread apart, allowing the new marble to drop into a bucket below (see Chapter XII on patents).

The marble-making operation began with about twenty-five pounds of molten glass ladled with a cast-iron dipper from the main melting pot into the gatherer's pot. The gatherer then dipped the preheated head of the punty iron into the molten glass. A quantity of the glass would adhere to the rod, which was then withdrawn from the pot so that the cutoff man could shear off the prescribed amount. For two-colored marbles, the body glass was normally opaque white or colored transparent glass that was ladled in first, then the striping (the design color) was ladled in on top of the body glass.

Normally, different types or colors of glass float at different levels in the pot and will not mix because of their different densities. They will mix only if stirred together while in the molten, plastic state. Dipping the preheated punty head through the glass to the juncture between the two colors provided only enough mixing action to cause a small quantity of each color of molten glass to adhere to the punty's head. The relative amounts of body glass and striping glass desired were what determined the depth of the insertion.

Because the gatherer had to draw the punty head back through the upper color, it was impossible to produce marbles with more than two colors by this method. Three-colored swirling patterns did not appear until an automated method of feeding the glass was developed in the mid-1920s.

The gatherer's skills in judging the depth of insertion of the punty, and the twisting of his hands, provided beautifully intricate swirls and individual patterns in the glass. No two marbles were ever exactly alike. The popularity of this style of marble was enormous, which was demonstrated by the fact that in 1924, Akro Agate had eighteen hand-operated machines working at one time.

Progress was inevitable; by 1912, with Horace C. Hill's invention (granted a patent in 1915), modifications were made whereby the gatherer would trip an air-operated cutoff shear with his punty. This eliminated the cutoff man's job. Hill's patent also replaced the forming wheels with grooved cylindrical rolls, which were mechanically powered also, eliminating the job of the man who turned the rollers. Even with these mechanical aids, gatherers continued to handle the hot glass with the punty through the mid-1920s.

MODERN METHODS

By the mid-1920s the fully mechanized age of marble-making had arrived. Mechanical feeding/shearing devices that measured out and cut off the molten glass and then dropped the measured amount through the funnel or trough into the rollers had been improved to the point that glass was no longer hand-fed by the gatherer. Even the more exacting part of the art, mixing the colors in multicolored marbles, was mechanized in 1925. The melting unit of a modern marble machine consists of a main melting tank for body glass of a single color; it may include a separate striping tank for each color other than the body glass color. Striping tanks are contained within or outside the main tank. There are advantages and disadvantages to each tank design. Fuel may be saved if the striping tanks are within the main tank, but problems are presented if repairs or maintenance are required. Conversely, fuel costs are higher if the striping tanks are located outside the main tank, but repairs and maintenance are easier.

Bringing a tank full of recipe glass to a molten state is expensive. Thereafter, maintaining a constant temperature is mandatory. A sudden loss of fuel is a catastrophe for a marble manufacturer. The molten glass inside the tank solidifies, and chipping it out is an impossible task. The best and quickest—and most expensive—solution is to tear down the tank, remove the glass, and start all over again.

Glass color may be changed without completely draining the tank and shutting off the fuel supply. Molten glass is allowed to drain to as low a level as possible without causing the tank to overheat and melt down. Intermingling of colors occurs until the original glass has flowed through the orifice at the bottom of the tank. This transition period results in aberrant marbles. However, they are mixed with existing loose stock and appear on the market, resulting in unusual marble names given by collectors and not recognized by the marble factory. Some beautiful aberrations appear in the vanes of a Cat Eye, such as a light orange or red in the yellow vanes or azure on white opaque vanes. Aberrations also occur in other design types.

Some factories do not practice the above shortcut but allow a run to be completed before changing colors. A run is completed by allowing all molten glass to drain, and it is at this time and not before that the heating fuel is cut off.

A new run may then begin with refiring and using the same or different color glass either in the main tank or striping tanks.

MULTICOLORED MARBLES

When manufacturers started using machines instead of men to shape their marbles, they had to find a way for the machines to reproduce the colorful variations once imparted by talented gatherers. Machines patented by Ira Freese included a main elevated feeder that had inside it several compartments to handle different colors of glass, keeping them all separate. The patent (Patent 1,529,947, granted March 17, 1925) also featured a specially designed nozzle with different inlets that could blend or fold two or more distinct colors in consistent proportions, rather than the earlier variations produced by the gatherer's hand-dipping and twisting method.

The glass feeders used in connection with the Freese patented method of glass-making were called Steimer feeders, after their inventor, Thomas Steimer (Patent 1,564,909). The machines were supplied to marble makers by the Hartford Empire Company, which is named in the patent. Hartford charged an initial fee of $2,500 per machine and an additional rental fee of three cents per thousand marbles produced. Some of the machines, however, were fraught with mechanical problems, and Hartford was not quick enough in repairing them to suit some of the marble makers. This costly dilemma prompted some of the makers to duplicate the patented feeders to meet their production demands.

SHEARING

At about the same time as the advent of Freese patents, which made it possible to produce variegated glass by machine, inventors were also busy improving other aspects of marble production. Many of these efforts focused on "shearing," which is literally the cutting off of the marble from the stream of molten glass. One method that was developed was the "hot shear," which involves some rolling or preforming of the glass gob before it drops into the funnel and onto the rollers. When used on multicolored marbles, hot shearing produces variegated glass. The quality of color in hot sheared marbles is considered better than the "cold shear" (see below). With the hot shear method, the interior striping color of an opaque marble is lost. The hot shear method also requires more heat.

The cold shear method, developed after the hot shear, involved a simple cutoff of a measured amount of glass with no manipulation before the gob hit the rollers. This method produces striping only on the outside of multicolored marbles. Subsequently, the cold shear was modified into a method called "veneering," which is the placement of 1/64 inch of color coating or striping on the entire surface of the marble.

In the cold shear and veneering methods, when the molten glass colors are flowing from the

After the marble is sheared it drops into a partially open hollow tube, which feeds it into the grooves of the rollers. The marbles, one in each groove, rotate constantly as they are formed into completed marbles. This machine is at JABO, Inc. Photo by Dennis Webb.

flow tanks into the orifice, the body glass flows in the center while the striping flows on the outside of the bi-colored stream surrounding the body glass. Production by cold shear or veneering is less expensive than some other methods. Since the interior of the marble no longer has to contain more expensive colored glass, almost any type of recycled glass can be used for the body, and the colored striping glass is required only on the surface.

The two methods, hot and cold shearing, have been used concurrently in the same plants; the determining factor is what equipment is at hand and what marbles are being produced.

A unique application of the cold shear method in the United States was developed in early 1955 by Marble King, which was then located at St. Marys, West Virginia. This was the Japanese-style Cat Eye, with the body glass on the outside and the "X" striping for the "eye" in the center. A hollow tube was injected down through the tank holding the molten body glass. This tube sat directly above and inside the orifice ring where the molten stream of glass exited the tank. Molten striping glass flowed through the hollow tube and was injected into the center

of the stream of body glass. It came out in a particular shape because of the design of the hollow tube, somewhat like the tip on a cake decorator's tool. Two streams of glass (clear and colored) were sheared off into a gob after flowing through the orifices of the melting tanks above.

Marble King's Rainbow is made using a similar method, but with the body glass in the center and the single- or multiple-colored striping glass on the outside—an arrangement similar to veneering.

CONTEMPORARY MARBLE PRODUCTION

The production phase, whether by hand or by machine, has changed relatively little since the 1920s. A typical modern marble rig consists of two main components—a stationary melting tank which is built on grade; and the rollers, which are located at one end of and underneath the tank. Scrap glass or cullet is fed into the tank from the opposite end. The rollers are mounted on a movable frame, which allows removal for repair and maintenance. The rate of flow out of the tank is controlled by the size of the orifice cup, which fits into the orifice ring at the bottom

A JABO marble machine operator is poised with tongs to remove possible rejects or aberrations. Photo by Dennis Webb.

of the tank. Molten glass flows by gravity through the orifice cup. There are two cup sizes—3/4 inch for marbles up to $^{11}/_{16}$ inch and $1\frac{1}{4}$ inches for all larger marbles. Actual size is controlled by minor adjustments to the feeder. Each machine has sliding panel cutters to cut the flowing stream of molten glass into a gob. Shears and feeders are located between the orifice cup and rollers. The shears cut off a set amount of molten glass, which drops into the feeder. The feeder guides the molten gob into the grooves of the rollers.

There are two general types of feeders. One is the "traveling" or oscillatory guide that delivers the gob to the rollers by funnels; the other is a stationary feeder that directs the gob into the groove of the rollers. JABO, Inc., developed and uses a fabricated stationary tubular trough that guides the molten gob directly into the groove of the rollers; the trough is partially open to allow continual observation by the operator. Some preforming occurs as the gob travels down the circular tube. This method speeds up the forming of the gob into a marble.

A change in the diameter of a marble may be made by changing the orifice cup, switching the rollers to a larger

or smaller size, or by fine adjustments to the shears. The speed of the rollers, shears, and feeders is synchronized. The turning action of the rolls spins the glass in different directions, producing the spherical shape as it travels to the end of the rolls. Blueprints of the L. E. Alley duplex marble machine motor in use at the St. Mary's factory shows a "40 RPM-1200 RPM" capacity. This machine also had a safety bar between the two inside rollers, which rolled downward.

A "double feed" machine was fabricated for use at the Cairo Novelty Company, which operated from 1948 to 1950. This machine was intended to double production while the rolls continued to turn at the same rate of speed as on a single feed machine. According to the patent application (Patent 2,422,413 granted 1947), this machine offered to increase production "materially," using "tiltable chutes to distribute the globules to the respective sets of rollers of the rolling machine so as not to permit contact of the marbles with each other during the rolling action." However, due to continued mechanical difficulties, the machine was never very successful, and it was not used after the 1950 flood that ended the Cairo enterprise. The

A duplex-type marble machine at Mid-Atlantic of West Virginia, Inc., in Ellenboro, West Virginia. Photo by Dennis Webb.

term "double feed" should not be confused with the term "duplex," which designates more recent machines that use a double pair of rolls. Few modern operations use a single feed mechanism, in which only one gob of glass is cut off and dropped onto a set of rollers at one time.

The manufacturing procedures are monitored by the machine operator. One of his duties is to watch for defective gobs on the rolls, which he quickly plucks out of the rollers with tongs. This operation has been automated at Marble King. Constant attention and adjustments of the feeder are necessary to maintain the correct size of gob. The operator also must assure that the grooves of the rolls are kept clean and smooth. Smooth grooves mean smooth marbles. Many modern foreign-made marbles exhibit a rough orange-peel surface as a result of pitted grooves.

Similarly pitted surfaces can be seen on the spherical glass ingots produced for spinning fiberglass. A smooth surface finish on these ingots is not as critical as it is for marbles used in play and for certain other industrial uses.

The speed of all rollers and shears is timed by one drive. Rejects may result when the gob is not hitting the groove in the rolls; this is corrected by adjusting the funnel. Some unusually shaped and grotesquely beautiful objects are produced when this occurs, but these are relegated back to the melting tank or to the outside dump. Gobs of glass that were too large for the rolls' grooves are forced into a shape called a watermelon, which is an elongated form with two teats on opposite ends. If the glass is too cool, the sphere forms too rapidly and will have smooth depressions of swirled lines or pockets. If the glass is too hot, the sphere will assume grotesque shapes. Foreign objects may appear in some transparent or translucent rejects.

Roll marks occur when the molten glass hits the slides, funnels, or the edge of the roll before hitting the grooves and therefore does not roll out into a sphere. When marbles are too small, they are usually crushed. If the shears are not centered and the marbles are larger on one side, or the marbles are too large for the rolls, a "string of pearls" can result—several glass gobs stuck together in a string, somewhat resembling a segmented caterpillar. These forms are also thrown away or remelted.

Rejects are not normally found in a marble collection. However, a well-rounded collection may contain various examples of reject types. The plus side to collecting rejects of any type is that they do show various colors used, but do not depict the actual design desired by the factory. Foreign objects, including small bits of gravel contained in contaminated scrap glass, have resulted in a transparent marble reject now called a Pet Rock Sulphide. This is not a real Sulphide but a marble collector's conversation piece.

As marbles are moving along the rolls, they are also annealing and hardening as they cool. It is essential to properly anneal glass. If the glass is cooled too quickly, it becomes brittle and will shatter. Annealing gives glass a degree of hardness equal to that of steel.

The metal rolls absorb some of the heat of the glass, but the marbles, though no longer plastic, are still hot when they reach the end of the rolls and drop into a trough. Akro Agate used a trough made of angle iron about 10–12 feet long with a 2-inch decline, which transported the marble to a heated metal bucket, called a lehr, where it continued its gradual cooling.

Master Marble improved the annealing process by using a worm gear to move marbles from the rolls to the metal bucket. The time taken for the marble to travel along the trough or worm gear is a planned part of the cooling process. The worm gear saved floor space in the working area. The metal of the worm gear also helped retain the heat of the glass. Most current makers, however, use U-shaped troughs.

When the lehr is full, its contents are dumped into large metal bins for more cooling. Marble lore has it that the bins full of cooling marbles provided a unique place for members of the night crew to take a cat nap.[2]

Documentation is lacking about the annealing process of early handmade marbles and marbles made on machines before the advent of the Hill and Early patented machines. It is obvious that earlier marble types chipped rather easily, indicating a defect in annealing, whereas modern machine-made marbles can withstand rigorous play and even bounce without chipping when dropped on a concrete floor. This advantage may be because there is more annealing during the forming process on the long rollers, and subsequent annealing in metal containers and bins, as compared to the short time period of rolling on two wheels on an M. F. Christensen machine

After cooling, the marbles are removed from the production area, or the "hot end," and are taken to the sorting and packaging area, a short distance from the hot end. According to O. K. Griffith, in the Ravenswood plant back in the 1940s and early 1950s, the marbles were moved from the production area to the sorting and packaging area via metal guttering and drain pipes. This was a very effective but noisy operation.

In the sorting and packaging area, marbles are inspected again to catch any defectives such as those containing foreign objects, off-round shapes, and marbles with roll marks. These defectives are removed to be remelted or discarded.

In the sorting system used by Akro Agate the cooled marbles rolled by gravity over a wooden table, while the defective marbles were manually removed by girls employed as sorters.

Akro's sorting for size was accomplished by a metal grater with various sizes of holes through which the marbles would drop. Another more recent method is the use of a set of smooth rollers coming at a 90-degree angle from below the end of the forming rolls. The rollers have a small space between them which gradually widens toward the other end. As marbles of various sizes fall onto these sorting rollers and travel along, the smaller-sized marbles drop out first, then larger and larger marbles gradually drop through. Metal buckets are placed in a row under these rollers to catch the newly formed marbles. This method is very exact and is used when a close tolerance on the diameter is required by the purchaser. In the manufacture of playing marbles, the above grading method is not necessary. Even so, diameters are closely monitored during production by the operator, who periodically measures the marbles with calipers and makes fine adjustments to the feeding mechanism.

The standard numbering system used in the early days of machine-made marbles was based on increments of $1/16$ inch and began with the size designated as "000," which was $1/2$ inch in diameter. Akro Agate's production documents indicate the following sizes:[3]

000	$1/2$ inch
00	$9/16$ inch
0	$5/8$ inch
1	$11/16$ inch
2	$3/4$ inch
3	$13/16$ inch
4	$7/8$ inch
5	$15/16$ inch
6	1 inch
7	1 $1/16$ inch
8	1 $1/8$ inch

Recently, sizes 9 and 10 have been added to the above list in light of the 1¼-inch and 1½-inch marbles produced by Marble King.[4]

At the marble factories, large wooden bins hold thousands of marbles sorted according to type, size, or color for short- or long-term storage.

Excess marbles or overruns are stored away and kept for sale later. Occasionally these stored marbles will be forgotten and later discovered, to be brought out for sale to individual marble salesmen or other marble makers to enhance some of their promotional packaged items.

The marbles are finally packaged in bulk or smaller packets with the manufacturer's logo or the logo of the purchaser and the marbles' names. Packaging machines vary from factory to factory and reflect the imagination, individuality, and ingenuity of the marble makers. They are individually designed and are fabricated by local machinists. They reflect a high degree of craftsmanship and pride of work.

Despite the name given to a marble type by the manufacturer, children at local or regional levels develop their own favorite descriptive names. For instance, Marble King's name for one of their brands of marbles is "Rainbow," but two color combinations are internationally known as the Cub Scout (blue and gold), Bumble Bee (black and yellow), and Black Widow (black and red).

Orders for marbles are of course dictated by demand and promotion of the product. Berry Pink, who was the original "Marble King," and was most active in the 1920s and 1930s, had an ingenious method for determining the

When the newly formed marbles come off the rollers, they fall onto another set of sorting rollers. The space between these rollers gradually widens, allowing the smallest marbles to drop out first, slightly larger ones next, etc., into the waiting buckets. Photo by Dennis Webb. Courtesy of Jack Bogard.

Fabricated steel bucket at end of chute and rollers. Photo by Dennis Webb. Courtesy of JABO, Inc.

type and color of marbles to produce and in what quantity. Pink sponsored and attended many marble tournaments, beginning in 1922 and continuing for many years. At the tournaments, he would offer a double handful of assorted marbles and ask a player to select ten

or so marbles of his choice. Using this method with several players, Pink could tell with a fair degree of accuracy the current type and color demand among the real marble users. The color red was normally chosen over all other colors.

[1]Sam McCarthy, *All About Marbles and Rules of the Game.* Printed by Tolly's Marble Promotions for the British Marbles Board of Control, circa 1988, p. 2.

[2]Naomi A. Sellers, personal conversation.

[3]Joseph A. A. Bourque, Sr., *Marble-Mania*, newsletter of the Marble Collectors Society of America, Trumbull, Ct., Vol. 7, p. 4.

[4]Roger Howdyshell, personal conversation.

Chapter XI

• • •

Glass Marble Formulas and Recipes

There is nothing in the world like glass, especially a glass marble with spectacular and fantastic designs and color. The same beautiful glass that was used to make pressware and other glass novelty items was also used to make marbles; thus, collectors of glassware are now also collecting marbles.

Historical references show that glass was first made in Sumeria more than two thousand years ago. Little is known about the production of glass at the time, but Mesopotamian cuneiform tablets record some recipes indicating that it was a difficult and secret undertaking. For centuries the recipes were a closely guarded secret. Glass objects were reserved for royalty and the very rich. A recipe deciphered in the Summer of 1993 shows that it takes "60 parts sand, 180 parts ashes from sea plants, 5 parts chalk."[1]

Pliny the Elder, an early Roman historian, gives the following account of the origin of glass:

"The story is that a ship, laden with niter, being moored upon the spot (Syria), the merchants, while preparing their repast upon the shore, finding no stones at hand for supporting their cauldrons, employed for the purpose some lumps of niter which they had taken from the vessel. Upon its being subjected to the action of the fire, in combination with the sand of the seashore, they beheld transparent streams flowing forth of a liquid hitherto unknown; that, it is said, was the origin of glass."

After some time, refinements were made, and various types of silica and alkali came into use. Silica used included sand, quartz, flint, chert, chalcedony, fluorspar, and feldspar. Alkali included potash, soda ash, and calcium carbonate, which gives stability and resistance to glass. Pure silica can be melted and used on its own, but in practice this needs very high heat; the addition of the alkali causes the material to fuse at a more manageable heat. Component parts of a recipe other than silica and alkali included coloring agents, fining agents, a clarifier or decolorizer, flux, fix, and in some cases an oxidizing agent. These components are addressed separately below.

MID-EIGHTEENTH CENTURY COLORING AGENTS

Red:	Gold, iron, copper, magnesia, and antimony
Blue:	Zaffer (oxide of cobalt) and copper
Yellow:	Silver, iron, antimony, and magnesia with tartar
Green:	Copper, Bohemian granate [garnet] and those which produce yellow or blue
Purple:	All such as will produce red and blue
Orange:	Antimony, and all those that will produce red and yellow
Black:	Zaffer, magnesia, copper and iron, in various combinations

COLORS AND METALLIC SALTS

Color	Metallic Salt
Violet	Nickel or manganese silicates
Blue	Cobalt or cupric silicates (the copper color is greenish-blue)
Green	Chromium or ferrous silicates
Yellow	Ferric or cerium silicates. Uranium compound also gives a greenish fluorescence
Amber	Iron and manganese silicates in conjunction with other chemicals
Gray or smoked	Manganese, iron, and copper silicates in certain proportions, or copper and nickel silicates
Black	High manganese content with some cobalt, copper, or ferric silicates, or alternately chromium and ferric silicates

Normally, a coloring agent is a metallic oxide or metallic salt, which might be added to give the glass color, to remove color, or to make the glass opaque. See the accompanying chart comparing some early recipes.

In addition, an opaque white glass could be made with the addition of calcined tin (known as *putty*), calcined antimony, arsenic, calcined hartshorn or bones, and sometimes common salt.[2]

Combinations of coloring agents could produce other colors. Also, increasing or decreasing the amount of coloring agents could alter colors. For instance, varying the amount of gold or selenium-cadmium sulphide could produce colors ranging from light pink to deep ruby red. Likewise, varying the amount of cobalt would result in colors from a deep Bristol blue to azure.

Glass containing manganese turns an amethyst color when exposed to the sun; the depth or degree of color depends upon the length or time of exposure. For dating purposes, it is useful to note that manganese was eliminated from glass formulas in 1915 due to its scarcity and conversion to the war effort.

Using metallic salts to produce various colors was an important technological advance. Some colors are obtained by the combination of two or more colored salts, a method that allows for an unlimited variety of shades. Colors produced by some oxides vary greatly with the composition of the glass.

Uranium oxide gave the glass a light straw to dark-brownish color, depending upon the amount in the formula. It was used in clear transparent and colored body glass, and the resulting product was called uranium glass. Marbles made with uranium give a slight reading on a Geiger counter and display a vivid green under ultra-violet ("black") light. Uranium oxide was at one time used by several American marble makers; it has recently been eliminated due to recent government health and safety restrictions.

Red or ruby glass has an interesting history and evolution. The earliest coloring agent was almost pure gold; the color was called gold ruby. Only a small amount is necessary, such as one part by weight to 10,000 parts of glass; even one part per 50,000 produces a fine ruby color. The best glass for producing gold ruby is lead crystal. The characteristics in melting are unique since the first melting gives a colorless or, at the most, straw yellow or amber glass. Reheating at a dull red heat causes the ruby color to appear. The next type of ruby glass is copper ruby glass; its recipe calls for cuprous oxide or cuprous sulphide. However, some reducing agent such as potassium bitartrate, stannous oxide, or ferrosoferric oxide must also be added to the batch. Selenium ruby glass is a recent entry; its agents are selenium and cadmium sulphide. One well-known mix is $1\frac{1}{4}$ pounds of selenium for fourteen pounds of cadmium sulphide.

Cranberry color is an old recipe using gold as a coloring agent and is often seen in the small threads and narrow bands of early hand-made marbles. In contrast, darker red design features are seen in later machine-made marbles, when selenium-cadmium sulphide replaced the costly gold oxide or gold.

However, in recent years little use is made of selenium-cadmium sulphide due to a rise in price. Selenium now costs $8 per pound, and marble makers are reluctant to include red in their designs.

Gold is no longer used in making marbles. However, it continues to be used in some glass houses to make the renowned "cranberry" glass.

A commonly held belief that the color of goldstone glass is derived from gold or finely ground copper makes the recipe a matter of controversy. An early recipe by Fremy and Clemandot shows that it was made by using three hundred parts of pounded glass, forty parts of copper scales, and eighty parts of iron scales; it is then "cooked" for twelve hours and slowly cooled. The operative word "scales" is not understood and could mean an oxide of the metal.[3]

Agents other than the basic ingredients are part of a recipe. The important ones are listed below.

Fining Agents: Sometimes called "sweeping," the fining of a batch of glass in the melting stage is a process by which condensation of "seed" into larger bubbles rising to the surface allows them to escape. An old and fairly effective method is the use of organic materials such as potatoes, beets, pieces of moist wood, and so forth. When plunged into the molten glass, the material rapidly turns into gas, leaving little residue; the gases so formed, chiefly water vapor, effectively "bubble" the glass. As a final step, the froth on top is skimmed off, as in making fruit jelly. The skimming process may be called "plowing." Recently, chemicals such as ammonium nitrate and arsenious oxide have been used. Arsenious oxide may be used as a fining agent, flux, and colorizer.

Clarifier or decolorizer: Also called glassmaker's soap in early years, this is an ingredient that when added to the batch "washes out" discolorations caused by undesirable agents, particularly iron, in the sand. Arsenic was used until the early 1950s. The larger glass factories use cobalt or selenium to clear the glass. It works just like in the old days when one used bluing in the wash so the clothes would come out white instead of gray.

Flux: An alkaline substance, such as potash or soda, this ingredient aids the fusion of the silica; it produces a rapid chemical activity, causing the batch to melt together. Potassium oxide also acts as a flux.

Fix: This agent is used in most glass batches to hold or "fix" the color and is most often used in red, yellow, ruby, and orange. Sulfur is the key agent.

Oxidizing Agent: This ingredient liberates oxygen and prevents discoloration of glass, and it may also prevent it from being easily reduced. Sodium and potassium nitrates, red lead, manganese dioxide, and less commonly, barium peroxide, may be used as the agent.

Before mixing a batch, the glassmaker strives to have on hand high-quality ingredients, particularly iron-free sand. Precise measuring, weighing, and mixing of the ingredients, whether by hand or mechanical means, is also critical, as is the appropriate melting temperature and time to produce a desired metal (molten glass). Last but most important is the constant attention and care of the craftsman, with his "feel" and his glass knowledge, which are hardly ever recorded. All of this makes glass into a treasured artifact and desirable collectible. Local and national museums, especially the Corning Glass Museum in Corning, New York, display their glass with pride.

Once a formula has been developed, the company will usually stick with a proven recipe and use it for many years. However, experimentation to obtain new or exotic colors not in use by other factories is a continuing effort. Glass formulas are jealously guarded, but one may refer to technical manuals and journals for basic recipes and information. The glass craftsman can recognize a certain feel to glass in the molten state and notice any slight variance in color.[4]

A formula may be deceiving. An old story tells how a master marble batch maker died and his successor inherited the written formula. However, the colors subsequently achieved were not quite the same. It was

later discovered that the former batch maker was a user of chewing tobacco, and the batch mixing box was his big cuspidor. This "secret" ingredient was not in the formula.[5]

There are over 100,000 known recipes for glass, says Bob Harris, a fabricator of scientific glass at NASA Goddard Space Flight Center in Greenbelt, Maryland.[6]

The following are recipes used by Akro Agate and Master Marble. Note that some coloring agents are in ounces and other main ingredients are in pounds, necessitating thorough mixing. Various company names generally describe the color, which may have been adopted by serious marble collectors and writers. For instance, some of the Alabaster marbles have recently been named after fruit drinks by some authors.

Recipes for Opal Glass

Opal Ivory
Sand	500 lbs.
Soda	213 lbs.
Feldspar	300 lbs.
Sodium Silica Fluoride	90 lbs.
Zinc	20 lbs.
Nitrate of Soda	23 lbs.
Uranium [Oxide]	2 1/2 lbs.
Selenium	1 1/2 lbs.

Opal Green
Sand	500 lbs.
Soda	213 lbs.
Feldspar	300 lbs.
Fluorspar	90 lbs.
Sodium Silica Fluoride	90 lbs.
Zinc	20 lbs.
Nitrate of Soda	23 lbs.
Bicarbonate of Potash	4 lbs.
Black Copper Oxide	2 1/4 lbs.

Opal Yellow
Sand	500 lbs.
Soda Ash	213 lbs.
Feldspar	300 lbs.
Fluorspar	90 lbs.
Sodium Silica Fluoride	90 lbs.
Zinc	20 lbs.
Cadmium Sulfide	10 lbs.

Opal Blue
Sand	500 lbs.
Soda Ash	213 lbs.
Feldspar	300 lbs.
Fluorspar	90 lbs.
Sodium Silica Fluoride	90 lbs.
Zinc	20 lbs.
Nitrate of Soda	23 lbs.
Cobalt Oxide	5 1/2 oz.
Black Copper Oxide	2 1/2 lbs.
Borax	2 1/2 lbs.

Opal Red (for Striping)
Sand	300 lbs.
Soda Ash	100 lbs.
Feldspar	150 lbs.
Zinc	30 lbs.
Fluorspar	36 lbs.
Sodium Silica Fluoride	50 lbs.
Bone Ash	11 lbs.
Barium Carbonate	8 lbs.
Borax	8 lbs.
Antimony Oxide	1 1/2 lbs.
Cadmium Sulfide	5 lbs.
Selenium	1 1/2 lbs.

Opal White
Sand	1,000 lbs.
Soda Ash	380 lbs.
Feldspar	430 lbs.
Fluorspar	170 lbs.
Sodium Silica Fluoride	190 lbs.
Nitrate of Soda	40 lbs.
Borax	10 lbs.

Recipes for Alabaster Glass (Meteor and Cloudy)

Alabaster White
Sand	500 lbs.
Soda	216 Lbs.
Feldspar	200 lbs.
Fluorspar	40 lbs.
Bone Ash	14 1/4 lbs.
Nitrate of Soda	17 3/4 lbs.
Salt	24 lbs.
Aluminum Hydrate	67 lbs.
Zinc Oxide	17 1/4 lbs.

Alabaster Green
Sand	500 lbs.
Soda	216 lbs.
Feldspar	200 lbs.
Fluorspar	40 lbs.
Bone Ash	15 1/4 lbs.
Nitrate of Soda	17 3/4 lbs.
Salt	24 lbs.
Aluminum Hydrate	67 lbs.
Zinc Oxide	7 1/4 lbs.
Bicarbonate of Potash	2 lbs.
Black Copper Oxide	1 lb.

Alabaster Purple
Sand	500 lbs.
Soda Ash	216 lbs.
Feldspar	200 lbs.
Fluorspar	40 lbs.
Bone Ash	15 1/4 lbs.
Nitrate of Soda	17 3/4 lbs.
Salt	24 lbs.
Aluminum Hydrate	67 lbs.
Zinc Oxide	7 1/2 lbs.
Manganese	5 lbs.

Recipes for Miscellaneous Glass

Tiger Eye
Sand	500 lbs.
Soda Ash	195 lbs.
Barium	10 lbs.
Borax	10 lbs.
Fluorspar	5 lbs.
Cadmium Sulfide	5 lbs.
Selenium	$3^1/_2$ lbs.
Carbon	8 oz.
Zinc	50 lbs.
Bicarbonate of Potash	1 oz.
Black Copper Oxide	$2^1/_2$ lbs.

Striping Black for Alabaster (Black)
Sand	400 lbs.
Soda Ash	175 lbs.
Feldspar	150 lbs.
Limestone	40 lbs.*
Nitrate of Soda	15 lbs.
Manganese	9 lbs.
Cobalt	8 oz.
Bicarbonate of Potash	$2^1/_2$ lbs.
Nickel Oxide	1 lb.

Original formula indicated 40, which may have meant that limestone was at one time used but was deleted at a later date.

Striping Green for Alabaster
Sand	500 lbs.
Soda Ash	213 lbs.
Feldspar	200 lbs.
Fluorspar	40 lbs.
Bone Ash	$15^1/_4$ lbs.
Nitrate of Soda	$17^3/_4$ lbs.
Salt	24 lbs.
Aluminum Hydrate	67 lbs.
Zinc Oxide	$7^1/_4$ lbs.
Bicarbonate of Potash	4 lbs.
Black Copper Oxide	$2^1/_4$ lbs.

Striping Blue for Alabaster (Alabaster Blue—A)
Sand	500 lbs.
Soda Ash	216 lbs.
Feldspar	200 lbs.
Fluorspar	40 lbs.
Bone Ash	$15^1/_4$ lbs.
Nitrate of Soda	$17^3/_4$ lbs.
Salt	24 lbs.
Aluminum Hydrate	67 lbs.
Zinc Oxide	$6^1/_4$ lbs.
Cobalt Oxide	$5^1/_2$ oz.
Black Copper Oxide	$5^1/_2$ lbs.

Striping Blue for White (Special Blue B-1/2 for Striping White)
Sand	500 lbs.
Soda Ash	200 lbs.
Feldspar	100 lbs.
Zinc	60 lbs.
Fluorspar	20 lbs.
Sodium Silica Fluoride	10 lbs.
Bone Ash	22 lbs.
Barium	10 lbs.
Borax	15 lbs.
Copper Oxide	$2^1/_2$ lbs.
Cobalt	66 oz.

Note: *The recipes for striping could also be used to make a single-colored design. Variance in recipe for alabaster and white is noted; possibly the variance is to highlight the striping for that particular color of body glass. Akro Agate was the first marble factory to use common table salt to make alabaster. It was only natural that Master Marble would also use this same ingredient to make its alabaster since it was the brainchild of John F. Early, who worked for both companies.*

Flintie
Sand	375 lbs.
Soda Ash	120 lbs.
Feldspar	162 lbs.
Fluorspar	42 lbs.
Sodium Silica Fluoride	60 lbs.
Zinc	50 lbs.
Red Lead	22 lbs.
Bone Ash	8 lbs.
Cadmium Sulfide	$7^1/_2$ lbs.
Selenium	$3^7/_8$ lbs.
Antimony	$3^1/_2$ lbs.
Carbon	$2^1/_2$ oz.

Alabaster Blue
Sand	500 lbs
Soda Ash	216 lbs.
Feldspar (300)	200 lbs.
Fluorspar	40 lbs.
Bone Ash	$15^1/_4$ lbs.
Nitrate of Soda	$17^3/_4$ lbs.
Salt	24 lbs.
Aluminum Hydrate	67 lbs.
Zinc Oxide	$7^1/_4$ lbs.
Black Copper Oxide	14 oz.
Cobalt Oxide	$1^3/_4$ oz.

Alabaster Red
Sand	600 lbs.
Soda Ash	200 lbs.
Feldspar	300 lbs.
Fluorspar	50 lbs.
Sodium Silica Fluoride	65 lbs.
Zinc Oxide	60 lbs.
Barium (20)	16 lbs.
Borax	8 lbs
Bone Ash (25)	22 lbs.
Potash Carb. Hyd.	54 lbs.
Antimony	3 lbs.
Cadmium Sulfide	10 lbs.
Selenium	3 lbs.

Recipes for Clearie Glass (Clearie and Litho)

Crystal		Yellow or Canary			
Sand	1,100 lbs.	Sand	1,100 lbs.	Potash Carb. Hyd.	18 lbs.
Soda Ash	495 lbs.	Soda Ash	495 lbs.	Barium	5 lbs.
Feldspar	100 lbs.	Borax	5 lbs.	Borax	10 lbs.
Nitrate of Soda	50 lbs.	Barium	5 lbs.	Cadmium Sulfide	5 lbs.
Limestone	140 lbs.	Limestone	140 lbs.	Fluorspar	5 lbs.
Fluorspar	5 lbs.	Nitrate of Soda	50 lbs.	Antimony	5 lbs.
Arsenic	2$\frac{1}{2}$ lbs.	Uranium Oxide	10 lbs.	Selenium	2$\frac{1}{4}$ lbs.
				Carbon	8 oz.
				Zinc	45 lbs.

Green		Amethyst		Red	
Sand	1,100 lbs.	Sand	1,100 lbs.		
Soda Ash	500 lbs.	Soda Ash	495 lbs.	Sand	500 lbs.
Limestone	135 lbs.	Borax	5 lbs.	Soda Ash	212 lbs.
Nitrate of Soda	55 lbs.	Barium	5 lbs.	Potash Carb. Hyd.	18 lbs.
Borax	2$\frac{1}{2}$ lbs.	Limestone	135 lbs.	Barium	5 lbs.
Barium	5 lbs.	Nitrate of Soda	50 lbs.	Borax	10 lbs.
Uranium Oxide	5$\frac{5}{8}$ lbs.	Feldspar	100 lbs.	Cadmium Sulfide	5 lbs.
Black Copper		Manganese	7 lbs.	Fluorspar	5 lbs.
Oxide	1$\frac{1}{2}$ lbs.			Antimony	5 lbs.
Bicarbonate of		**Azure**		Selenium	2$\frac{1}{4}$ lbs.
Potash	7$\frac{1}{2}$ oz.	Sand	500 lbs.	Carbon	8 oz.
		Soda Ash	212 lbs.	Zinc	45 lbs.

Assistance for this chapter came from personal conversations and correspondence with glassmen too numerous to mention. J. Fred Early graciously provided a copy of the personal hip-pocket notebook of his father, John F. Early, which contained recipes used at Akro Agate and Master Marble.

[1] William S. Ellis, "Glass," *National Geographic,* December 1993, p. 44.

[2] Geoffrey Wills, *The Collector's Book of Glass* (New York: Hawthorne Books, 1966), p. 28.

[3] T. H. Gibbs-Smith, *The Great Exhibition of 1851, A Commemorative Album* (London: Victoria and Albert Museum, 1950), p. 17.

[4] Roger W. Howdyshell, personal conversation.

[5] R. Foster Holcombe, master glassman at the Art of Fire at Savage Mill, Md., personal conversation.

[6] Maurice Martin, "Glass Action," *The Washington (D.C.) Post Magazine,* April 11, 1993, p. 5.

Chapter XII

• • •

Patents Related to the Marble-Making Industry

Significant patents issued during the years 1892–1957 provide a historic tour of advances in the automation of the marble-making industry. Inventions that would later be important in marble making began appearing in the mid-1800s; these were not designed for marble-related functions but for other uses. Patents for machines that produced "spherical bodies" (in this case pills) and procedures for making "variegated glass" (marbleized tiles) were well known long before they were applied to making marbles.

Matthew Lang of East Akron, Ohio, applied for a patent in November 1891 (which was granted in November 1892), for a "Machine for Molding Marbles or Other Articles from Clay, &c." As significant as it might have been had it been developed earlier, Lang's invention came too late in the life of the clay marble industry, which never again equaled the popularity it had enjoyed in the waning years of the nineteenth century.

Christian C. Hill of Chicago designed a machine in 1897 having a pair of "cylindrical roller-dies" with grooved surfaces for "simultaneously forming a series of balls." He meant his invention for the manufacture of metal ball bearings, but it could have been easily modified for use in making marbles. However, this possibility was apparently not noticed or used by the fledgling American marble-making industry, as the inventions of the next decade never recognized his particular combination of mechanics. This oversight is demonstrated by a patent six years later than Hill's that included a pair of hand-held tongs with molds for forming marbles, which would have been much less productive than Hill's patent. This invention never caught on either.

Martin F. Christensen of Akron, Ohio, designed a marble-making machine in 1902 that was patented in 1905. Basically, his machine was similar to Christian Hill's machine but produced only one marble at a time, where Hill's would have produced several.

It was not until Horace C. Hill's 1915 patent (applied for in 1912) that essentially the same mechanics as Christian Hill's 1898 patent were used in the commercial production of marbles.

Since the 1905 Christensen patent, improvements have continued. Some of these "improvements" were experiments that did not succeed, but others were genuine advances that are still in use today.

Patent numbers are assigned by the U.S. Patent Office sequentially, according not to the application date but to the date granted. They are listed below in numerical order. It is important to remember that in the period covered, there was sometimes a gap of several years between the time an inventor applied for a patent and the date it was granted. Therefore, an inventor had probably been using his machine for quite some time prior to the date of the patent. The application dates as well as the patent (grant) dates are given.

Since patents, including specifications and detailed illustrations of equipment, are open to public access, all secrecy is lost when a patent is granted. Even though a patent grant is supposed to protect the inventor's rights, patent infringement suits can be in court for years before resolution (see Patent Suits chapter). During that time a competitor might have been using the original inventor's own designs in competition against him. Obviously, it was not always in the best interest of the inventor to make public his new designs by applying for a patent; some inventors chose not to patent but to use their inventions without patent, relying on secrecy for protection.

GLASS MARBLE PATENTS

Patent 600,532 (March 15, 1898) for "Machine for rolling balls"; applied for May 15, 1897, by Christian C. Hill, Chicago, Illinois.

This patent involved the combination of a pair of grooved cylindrical roller-dies and guides for holding the balls in position while the rolling operations continued. The device was meant for making ball bearings but was very similar to later grooved roller machines used in the marble industry.

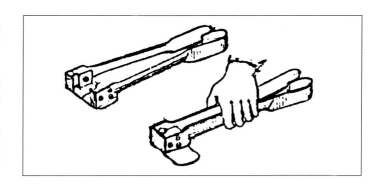

The Leiter Patent, No. 733,013, a tool for making marbles.

Patent 733,013 (July 7, 1903) for "Tool for making marbles"; applied for April 7, 1903, by Jeremiah J. Leiter, Canton, Ohio, and assigned to Emile P. Converse, Massillon, Ohio.

In this device, jaws were secured to handle members; the jaws had semicircular grooves with cutting blades.

This device may have been an improvement over the prior handmade methods used in marble making, but it produced only one marble at a time and was a technological generation behind the Christensen 1905 patent (see below).

Patent 802,495 (October 24, 1905) for "Machine for making spherical bodies or balls"; applied for December 1902 by Martin F. Christensen of Akron, Ohio. Used by the M. F. Christensen Glass Company.

This machine used a pair of wheels with semi-circular grooves on their edges. The wheels turned so that the rolls moved in opposite directions at their "working point" (the edge where they almost met). A gob of molten glass was dropped onto the wheels at the working point, and their turning worked the glass into a spherical shape as it cooled and hardened. When the gob of glass had been rounded and was hard, the wheels were levered apart and the marble dropped from the working wheels. This machine produced only one marble at a time.

Patent 1,164,718 (December 21, 1915) for "Machine for making spherical bodies"; applied for September 19, 1912, by Horace C. Hill of Akron, Ohio. Assigned to and used by the Akro Agate Company.

Hill's machine was similar to Christensen's except that it replaced the two wheels with a pair of cylinders with "helical peripheral grooves" arranged so that the grooves (also called "leads") of the two cylinders were exactly opposite each other at their working point. This arrangement allowed a gob of glass to automatically move away from the beginning point, rounding and cooling as it moved toward the other end. In this way, additional marbles could begin forming while the previous ones were still working.

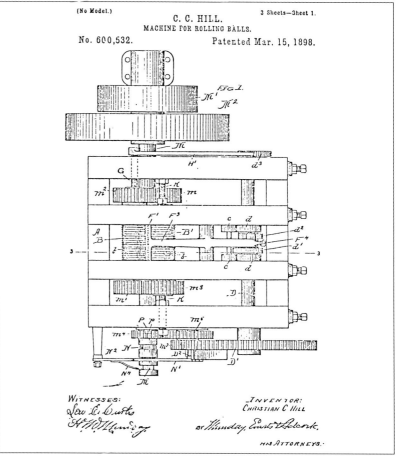

This machine provided a significant increase in the quantity of marbles that could be produced by the same number of workers and machines in the same amount of time. The final length of the grooves was widened and deepened so that the finished marble automatically dropped off the cylinders; the cylinders no longer had to be levered apart by hand.

Patent 1,226,313 (May 15, 1917) for "Marble machine"; applied for March 15, 1917, by George Joseph Cook of Fairmont, West Virginia.

This device employed a horizontally rotating plate with a spiral groove working against an overhead spirally

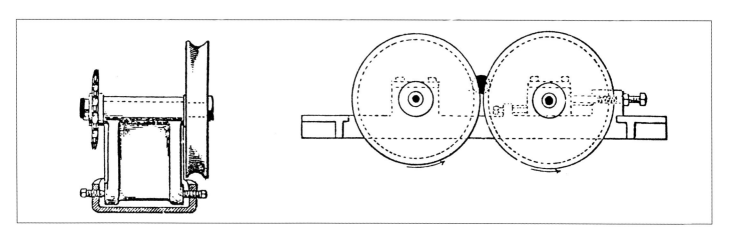

M. F. Christensen 802,495, Oct. 24, 1905

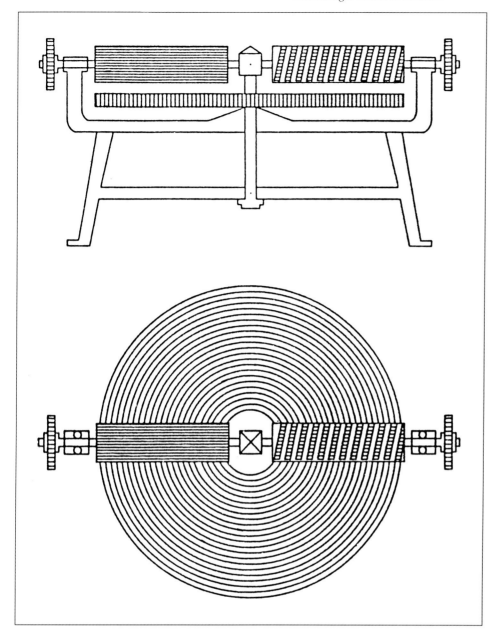

G. J. Cook, marble machine. Patent No. 1,226,313, May 15, 1917.

applied for on April 15, 1922, by Ira H. Freese of Clarksburg, West Virginia. The machine was used by the Akro Agate Company.

Freese used a main melting tank for clear glass with a number of smaller tanks within the main furnace, each of the smaller tanks having a nozzle designed to inject a stream of colored glass into the center of the clear glass stream as the glass was discharged from the melting tanks toward the marble-making machine.

Patent 1,564,909 (December 8, 1925) for "Glass-Feeding Mechanism"; applied for February 12, 1910, by Theodore C. Steimer of Pittsburgh, Pennsylvania; assigned to the Hartford-Empire Company of Delaware.

This machine was not designed specifically for marbles but could have been applied to them fifteen years earlier than it actually was, had the patent been granted when originally applied for. The death of the inventor may have had something to do with the delay; the patent was re-submitted by his executor, Charles M. Steimer.

Simply put, the Steimer invention allowed a constant size of "charge" to be delivered from the melting furnace to the mold or press by way of a regulating chamber and plunger. It was used by various companies beginning in the late 1920s on a rental basis from the Hartford-Empire Company.

Patent 1,601,699 (September 28, 1926) for "Machine for manufacturing marbles and similar articles"; applied for December 12, 1924, by William J. Miller of Swissvale, Pennsylvania, and assigned to Victor J. Greene, Pittsburgh, Pennsylvania. Used by the Nivison-Weiskopf Company of Cincinnati from 1921–1924 and later by the Peltier Glass Company of Ottawa, Illinois.

This machine was nearly identical to the Christensen patent of 1905, except for the replacement of the two wheels with grooved cylinders and minor differences in the arrangements of the rollers.

Patent 1,761,623 (June 3, 1930) for "Machine for making spherical glass bodies"; applied for March 22, 1926, by John F. Early, of Clarksburg, West Virginia. The machine was assigned to and used by the Akro Agate Company.

Early's machine employed the same mechanics as its predecessor at Akro, Horace Hill's 1915 patent. But Early changed the alignment of the grooved cylinders so that the edges of the grooves did not coincide, but were offset a little. This offset improved the roundness of the marbles

grooved roller so that their meeting edges formed a spherical space; the molten gob began its journey at the outside of the disk and dropped through a hole in the center when finished. As with Hill's 1915 machine, several marbles could be working at the same time.

Patent 1,488,817 (April 1, 1924) for "Machine for forming spherical bodies"; applied for November 11, 1922, by Howard M. Jenkins of Pittsburgh, Pennsylvania.

Similar to Hill's 1915 machine, but this machine had eight pairs of grooved wheels and a mechanism to distribute gobs of glass to them; the machine was adjustable to make marbles of different diameters. When a marble in a pair of wheels was completed, one wheel was moved away from the other, dropping the finished marble off the forming machine.

Patents 1,529,947 and 1,529,948 (March 17, 1925) for apparatus and method for making variegated glass;

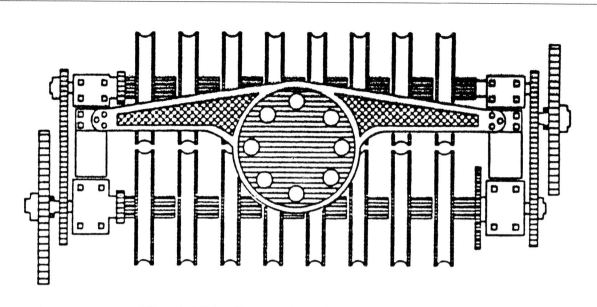

H. M. JENKINS   PATENT 1,488,817

MACHINE FOR FORMING SPHERICAL BODIES
(SIMPLIFIED ILLUSTRATION)
PATENTED APRIL 1, 1924
(APPLICATION FILED NOV. 11, 1922)

by causing them to rotate, constantly changing axes while forming and hardening. It was a decided improvement over the Hill 1915 patent.

Patent 1,880,916 (October 4, 1932) for "Machine for manufacturing spherical bodies"; applied for May 25, 1928, by John F. Early; assigned to and used by the Akro Agate Company.

This change added a second set of grooved cylinders to Early's 1930 patent, along with a guide for directing gobs of glass alternately into the grooves of either pair of cylinders. This "duplex" machine essentially doubled the output of each machine, since twice as many marbles could be working at the same time.

Patent 1,993,235 (March 5, 1935) for "Shearing machine for marble making machines or the like"; applied for February 27, 1933, by Russell U. Adams and Clyde Hibbs of Sistersville, West Virginia. The machine was assigned to and used by the Lawrence Glass Novelty Company.

This device cut gobs from a falling stream of molten glass and discharged them alternately along two different directions; for use with a two-paired cylinder machine like Early's 1932 patent.

Patent 2,422,413 (June 17, 1947) for a "Marble making machine"; applied for May 23, 1944, by Oris G. Hanlon, of Massillon, Ohio. Used by the Cairo Novelty Company.

Hanlon's patent claimed a "novel shearing mechanism" designed to increase production by the movement of a cutting blade over a series of holding cups. The multiple gobs of molten glass were then dropped alternately onto two pairs of grooved rollers as in the 1932 Early patent. This device was not very different from the Adams/Hibbs 1935 patent and did not work very well.

Patent 2,791,210 by N. E. Vogt and H. M. Randall, applied for January 4, 1955, and granted May 7, 1957.

Along with the above patents, various "marble shooters," designed to improve marble players' skill, were

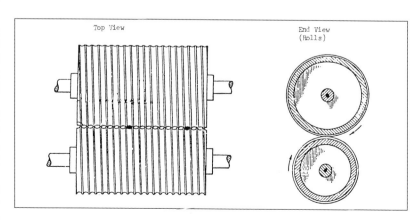

John F. Early. Patent No. 1,761,623, June 30, 1930.

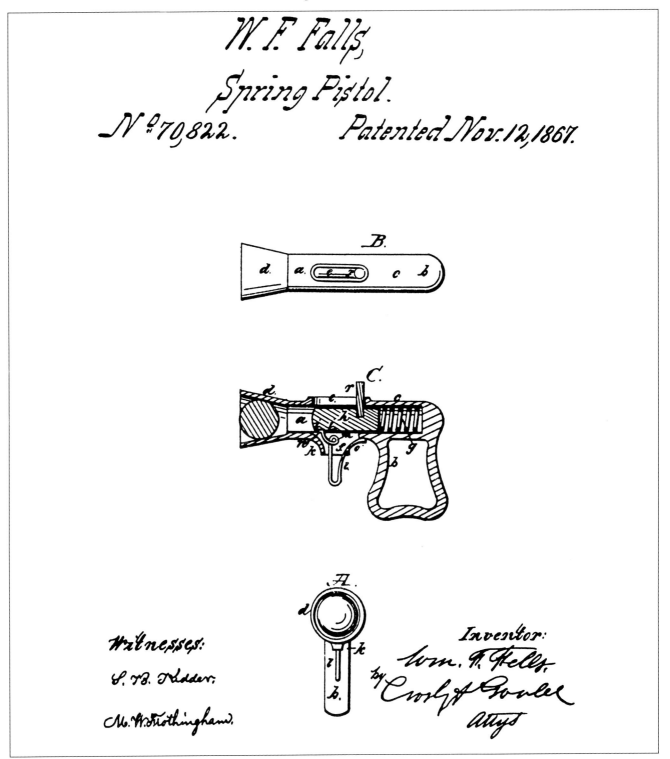

Patent No. 70,822, granted to W. F. Falls, November 12, 1867. "This is the first patented marble shooter containing the necessary functions of a pistol, trigger, barrel, and spring for propulsion."

invented and patented from the mid-1860s through the early 1950s.

CLAY MARBLE PATENTS

Several patents for making and coloring clay marbles were issued during the 1890s in Ohio and assigned to factories located there. Patents of note were issued to Samuel C. Dyke, Matthew Lang, and Henry Mishler. **Patent 431,454** granted July 1, 1890, for "Machine for Manufacturing Marbles" to Actaeon L. Dyke. Four "claims" describe this machine; it consists of a belt-driven set of spirally grooved rotating disks, which were automatically fed clay pellets cut from a bar of clay.

Apparently each clay pellet worked its way around the disks; by the time it reached the outer end of the disks, it was rounded into a marble. The basic idea of this patent is very similar to G. J. Cook's 1917 Patent 1,226,313, in that both had grooved disks, upon which a pliable material was worked and rounded, then automatically released. Dyke's machine used a full disk for the upper contact, while Cook's used two rolling pin-like cylinders.

Patent 439,031 granted May 5, 1890, to Actaeon L. Dyke of Akron, Ohio, for "Process of Coloring Marbles." The process indicates the rolling of marbles in a vessel having a limited amount of coloring matter, so as to partly color the marbles, and then placing them in another vessel, having a limited amount of a different coloring matter. The process described, particularly the "limited amount" and placing the marbles in a second vessel, would probably produce speckled, multicolored clay marbles. The patent states that "One man can color many bushels of marbles per day."

Patent 449,255 granted March 31, 1891, for "Die for the Manufacture of Marbles" to Matthew Lang of Akron, Ohio, Assignor, by Mesne Assignments, of One-Half to the East-End Marble Company of the same place. The die consists of an upper and lower die with cups. A plastic sheet of clay, which is thicker than the proposed marble, is placed on the lower die. The upper die is positioned over the lower die and then put under pressure. Surplus clay is forced through the issue and discharge openings. Any number of marbles may be produced at one time.

Patent 451,855 granted May 5, 1891, for "Machine for Molding Marbles" to Actaeon L. Dyke. This machine looks like a bicycle wheel laid on its side. The forming groove for the clay in this case is a groove around the periphery of the wheel, still like a bicycle wheel without the tire. The wheel turns the clay pellets against an opposing surface, which is grooved, and rounded forms result. A feeding mechanism, which includes a cutting knife, is also mentioned; at the end of the process, perhaps one time around the wheel, the rounded marbles are ejected.

Patent 463,418 granted November 17, 1891, for "Machine for Molding Marbles from Plastic Material" to Samuel C. Dyke. Dyke's idea was similar to the Dyke Patent 451,855 and Christensen Patent 802,495, in that a clay pellet was made to travel in a semi-circular groove until it was rounded, then ejected. In this patent, the track the pellets traveled in was a "grooved bed"; the pellets were

propelled by a belt that rolled them along in the grooves. Part way along the pellet's travel the grooves zigzagged for a short distance to change their direction of rotation, making them more rounded.

Patent 471,243 granted March 22, 1892, for "Machine for Making Playing Marbles" to Henry Mishler. The machine is designed with a continuous groove around the outer face of a cone; a charge of clay is placed within the groove. The rapid rotation of the cone causes the clay charge to roll from the upper end to the lower end of the groove and assume the form of a perfect sphere.

Patent 485,282 granted November 1, 1892, for "Machine for Molding Marbles or other Articles from Clay, &c" to Matthew Lang. The machine is designed for molding articles from "plastic" material. It incorporates a mixing receptacle, which is connected by a tube to a distributing hopper. There is a reciprocating plunger in the

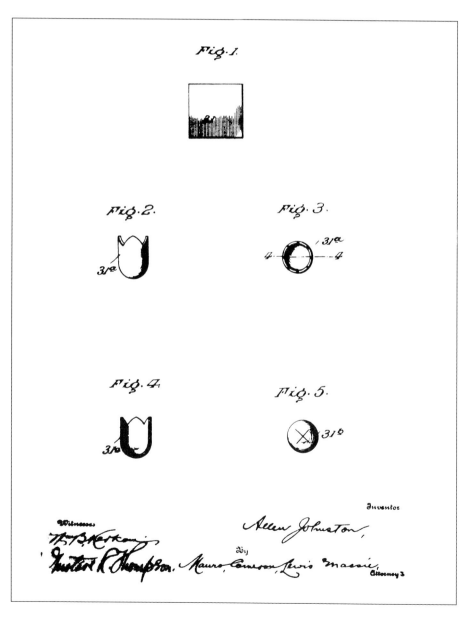

Patent No. 812,135, A. Johnston, Manufacture of Hollow Metallic Balls from Sheet Metal, February 6, 1906. Note the "X" mark on the completed metal ball, a distinguishing mark or signature for the marble collector.

distributing receptacle, a mold, a conveyor for the mold, and an elevator for the mold registering with the distributing receptacle. The patent shows two mold-halves that taper downward, each shaped to accommodate two halves of the molded object. One hundred marbles may be made at one time.

THE STEEL PATENT

Research disclosed only one patent pertaining to the manufacture of a steel marble. **Patent 812,135** was granted to Allen Johnston of Ottumwa, Iowa, on February 6, 1906. The process described in the patent addresses the use of a square sheet-metal blank and the stamping or drawing of the blank into the shape of a cup with a rounded bottom and a serrated rim.

An undated advertisement shows that Ottumwa marbles were being sold by Johnston & Sharp Manufacturing Company, Ottumwa, Iowa, as a "Steelie—Hollow steel marbles patented with all bright or assorted colors." The ad shows that three regular sizes of $\frac{9}{16}$-inch, $\frac{5}{8}$-inch, and $\frac{3}{4}$-inch diameter and an extra heavy weight in $\frac{5}{8}$-inch diameter were available from 1909 through 1910.

This Steelie is not too well known to marble collectors and is not often seen in major collections. The date of the patent indicates a unique marble design and material, making it a highly collectible marble. There is no known example of a colored Steelie.

Chapter XIII

• • •

Patent Suits in the Marble Industry

Two significant lawsuits regarding patents on sphere-making machinery involved many of the prominent people and inventors in the marble industry. The first was brought in 1929 by the Akro Agate Company against the Peltier Glass Company in U.S. District Court.

The Akro Agate Company vs. The Peltier Glass Company

The Akro claim was that Peltier's marble-making machine, invented by William J. Miller (Patent 1,601,699; September 28, 1926), infringed on certain parts of the Akro machine (Horace C. Hill's Patent 1,164,718; December 21, 1915). Specifically, and very importantly, Akro charged that Miller's use of helically grooved cylinders was an infringement of the Hill/Akro patent.

The basis for the Hill/Akro patent had been the addition of grooved cylinders to basic mechanisms employed in a previous marble-making machinery patent by Martin F. Christensen (Patent 802,495; 1905). The Christensen machine used a single pair of pulleylike wheels with grooves on their rims rather than the helical grooves along cylinders.

Christensen's 1905 patented machine included two wheels with a single groove around the periphery of each. The still-molten glass gob was kept between the opposing wheels until it was a finished marble. The Hill patent, on the other hand, used two cylinders with a helical groove on each. The turning cylinders pushed the glass gob from one end of the cylinders to the other, rotating it as it traveled to make it form a more perfect sphere. Several marbles could be in process on a Hill machine at one time, which improved productivity.

The original suit was decided in favor of the plaintiff (Akro) but was reversed on appeal by Peltier in the U.S. Circuit Court of Appeals. The appeals court, in reversing the earlier decision, found that while the use of helical grooves on cylinders (the basis for Hill's patent) was an advance over earlier marble-making patents (Christensen's in particular), Hill had not invented the helically grooved rolls, nor was he the first to use them for making "spherical bodies." Neither the Christensen nor the Hill machine was limited to the making of marbles; further, the court noted, the use of helical grooves in making spherical bodies appeared in at least three earlier patents—1888, 1901, and 1903.

The court found that the Miller machine was basically the same as the older Christensen machine and therefore not an infringement on any existing patent; the Christensen patent had expired and was in the public domain.

In essence, the appeals court decision invalidated the Hill/Akro patent, saying that all the mechanisms used in that machine were "old constructions," and part of the "prior art" of glassmaking. The mechanics and techniques employed had long been public knowledge, patented at least three times prior to this, but had just not been

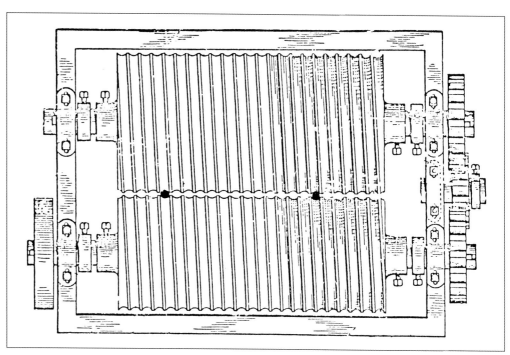

Top View Horace C. Hill, Patent No. 1,164,718, Dec. 21, 1915.

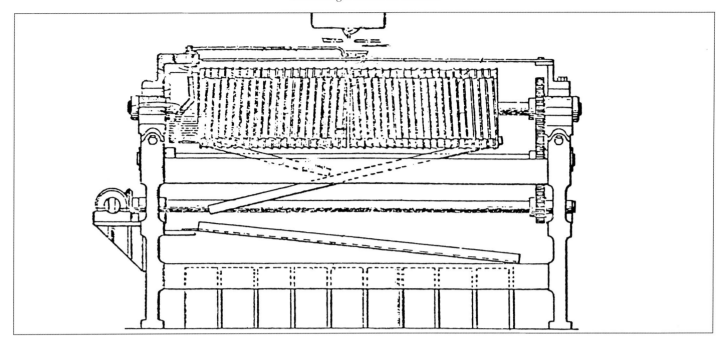

Side View John F. Early, Patent No. 1,880,916, Oct. 4, 1932.

employed in making marbles. The cylinders are in reality quite similar to the Archimedes screw, which was used to lift water from the Nile River before the birth of Christ. The use of known mechanics for a new product is not valid basis for a new patent. The appeals court decided therefore that the prior decision of the district court was in error, the case was dismissed, and a petition for a rehearing was denied. This decision meant that anyone could construct and commercially use a machine like that in use by Akro at the time.

This decision had economic and historical significance of the highest order for the marble-making business. It opened the opportunity for new marble companies to emerge. According to Donald Michels, of the Champion Agate Company, seven marble factories were soon in operation in Ritchie County, West Virginia. The late Roger Howdyshell, president of Marble King, said that the "breaking of the patent" was the most significant event in the history of the U.S. marble industry. It also set the stage for John F. Early to make significant refinements and modifications to the old technologies, seen in his patents of 1930 and 1932.

The Akro Agate Company vs.
The Master Marble Company, et al.

The second case was again initiated by Akro, in 1933, and was concluded in 1937, this time against the recently formed Master Marble Company and its "officers, directors and owners of the majority of the stock of Master." These included C. C. Grimmett, Clinton F. Israel, John F. Early, and John E. Moulton.

The suit charged that the marble-making machine used by Master Marble infringed on certain aspects of then-current patents for the Akro machine. (Patents 1,761,623,

June 1930; and 1,880,916, October 1932). Ironically, these patents were the invention of and had been applied for by one of the defendants, John F. Early, while he was still employed by Akro. They were assigned to Akro, but they were not granted by the Patent Office until after Early had resigned from Akro and had joined Master Marble.

The suit also charged that the Master Marble Company patent infringed upon Akro's patents for an apparatus and a method of mixing clear and colored glass (Patents 1,529,947 and 1,529,948; March 1925), issued to Ira Freese.

The charge against the officials of Master Marble Company was that they had conspired to enter into the marble business in competition against Akro while still employed at Akro.

The court's decision regarding the patent infringement was in favor of the defendant, Master Marble. It decided that the Early and Freese patent claims were invalid or void, due to the fact that they were not "novelties" (i.e., they were not anything new in the first place and should not have been granted a patent), and/or that Akro's suit claimed features not illustrated in the patent applications, and therefore not part of the patent as granted.

Further, the Court found that since the Miller/Peltier machine (Patent 1,601,699; September 1926) was in use in the marble industry prior to the Early/Akro patent 1,761,623, it "entirely defeats" that Akro patent.

Regarding the question of the four prior Akro officers who formed Master Marble, the court decided that they could not be held liable for infringement of Akro's patents, which had not been filed for or procured until after the defendants had already founded Master Marble Company and devised, installed, and used their own machines in production and sale of their own products. The entire case was decided in favor of the defendants.

Chapter XIV

● ● ●

United States Marble Companies

As we have noted earlier, machine-made glass marbles were first produced around 1902 by the M. F. Christensen and Son Glass Company in Akron, Ohio. The founder of the company, Martin F. Christensen, invented the device that made them, a "Machine for Making Spherical Bodies or Balls." Subsequent developments in marble-making technology, coupled with a growing passion for marbles among American children in the 1920s and 1930s, particularly during the Chinese Checkers craze, opened the market to more companies.

But the heyday of marbles was over almost as soon as it had begun. Foreign competition and changing tastes in toys put many marble companies out of business by the 1950s. Today, only six companies still produce toy marbles in the United States. Still, many of the old companies are remembered for the beautiful marbles they left behind.

Following is an alphabetical listing of American marble companies—past and present—and the marbles for which they are known.

THE AKRO AGATE COMPANY
Akron, Ohio, and Clarksburg, West Virginia

The Akro Agate Company was not the earliest major producer of machine-made marbles in the United States, but it was the most successful company of the early years, outlasting most of its predecessors and many companies that came later. Akro was a viable business for four decades, from 1910 to 1951, and the people at Akro were major contributors to innovations in marble design and production methods. By the mid-1920s Akro accounted for about three-fourths of all American marble production.

The Akro story began in 1910, when Horace C. Hill left the M. F. Christensen and Son Glass Company to begin his own business. Lacking adequate funds on his own, Hill invited Dr. George T. Rankin and Gilbert C. Marsh to join him as partners.

The new business was called the Akro Agate Company, taking "Akro" from Akron, where they began business. The trademark, which was granted in August 1911, was a crow flying through a large letter "A," holding a marble in its beak and two marbles in its claws. The Akro trademark was registered in Akron, Ohio, in 1911 by George T. Rankin and Gilbert C. Marsh prior to the company's move to Clarksburg, West Virginia, in 1914.[1] The slogan "Shoot Straight as A KRO Flies" appears on some Akro containers.

Working out of the Marsh and Wagner shoe store in Akron, the trio began their venture cautiously. Of the three, only Hill had any experience in the marble business, and they were not yet ready to commit to a full-blown marble factory. Beginning in 1910, they bought marbles wholesale from Hill's previous employer, the M. F. Christensen and Son Glass Company, for $3 per thousand and packaged them in cellophane tubes, five to a package. These packages sold for eight cents retail. Before this packaging innovation, machine-made glass marbles were sold in department stores six for eight cents—not packaged, but from loose stock. The cellophane packages proved to be a great success, and changed the way marbles were packaged and sold.[2]

The Akro Agate Company was incorporated in West Virginia on October 1, 1914, and moved its operations to Clarksburg, West Virginia, that same year to have better access to sand and natural gas supplies. Natural gas was inexpensive there, costing three cents per thousand cubic feet.[3] Akro leased and later purchased an existing plant that had been producing glass lenses for carbide automotive lamps.

In 1912 Hill applied for a patent on his hand-fed semi-automatic machine. The U.S. Patent Office rejected his original application in February 1914 because it was not significantly different from the prior Christensen patent. He resubmitted a slightly different claim, which was granted in December 1915 (Patent 1,164,718) and which was assigned to the Akro Agate Company as part of the partnership agreements.

Commercial production began during late 1914, and by July 1915 the company was selling sets of five of its own marbles in red, white, and blue cardboard boxes bearing the Akro trademark. The marbles produced were transparent with a white swirling stripe throughout; the exact design of this stripe was determined by the gatherer or "gathering boy." The gathering boys were actually

Recent photo of the Akro Agate Company. The prominent silo was built after Early's departure. After many years as the city of Clarksburg's public works garage, the building was vacated in 1992. Photo by Dennis Webb.

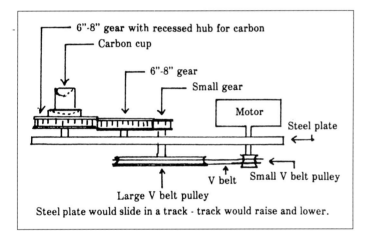

Adapter designed by John F. Early to produce Spiral marbles.

adult men, and were paid by piece work, per thousand marbles created. In one example of the skill of a gathering boy at Akro, the pattern of a perfect "2" was created in the swirling. According to J. Fred Early, the 2s were made by only one gathering boy for only one day. These marbles are quite rare. The only known examples are in Early's collection.

In 1916, before the company he had founded had really become financially successful, Horace Hill died suddenly.[4] In the following reorganization of the company, and in the face of great demand for their products, the Akro managers hired John F. Early from Akron, Ohio, as plant superintendent. Early's highest priority was to expand the factory and improve the production capacity of Hill's machines, which were in use at that time at Akro. A one-cylinder gas engine ran all the machines. From 1922 to 1924, an extension was built onto the building with individual motors for each marble machine.

Early's first significant design change came in 1924; his new machine used offset rollers. The grooves of the opposing rollers did not align with each other exactly, but one was offset just a little from the other. This change produced smoother marbles and eliminated roll marks by causing the marbles to change axes constantly. Early applied for a patent on this modified machine in March 1926; it was granted as Patent 1,761,623, in June 1930, and like the earlier Hill patent, was assigned to Akro.

The outdated Hill machines that were replaced with Early's new patented machine were sold as scrap to the Osborne Machine Company in Clarksburg, West Virginia. At a later date, one set was purchased from the machine company by Master Marble Company for experimental purposes, but it was never used commercially.

At the same time as the above patent application, Early also developed and used a conveyor screw to eliminate the long angle-iron trough that conveyed the formed marbles to the annealing can. The screw allowed the marbles to cool more slowly and saved space in the work area by eliminating the 10 to 12-foot-long trough, as well as producing "truer" marbles than the prior method. For reasons of secrecy, this conveyor screw was not patented, since drawings and specifications of the invention would have to be supplied to the U.S. Patent Office and would become public record, allowing other manufacturers access to the design. (Although the use of a patented piece of equipment in this manner would have been illegal, such use did occur nevertheless.)

Early applied for a second patent in May 1928, which was granted in October 1932 (Patent 1,880,916). This "duplex machine" consisted of two sets of cylinders arranged adjacent to each other and a dual feeding mechanism that more than doubled production on each machine. It eliminated hand feeding and produced more uniform gobs of glass. By 1932, when the patent was granted, Early had resigned from the company; the patent was assigned to Akro by a previous contract agreement.

In 1928 the Hartford Empire Company began supplying "feeders" to Akro, to be used in connection with Early's Patent 1,880,916. These feeders contained a clay orifice and clay plunger that regulated the flow of molten glass. The feeder was fluted, or channeled, allowing different colors of glass from different melting pots to be combined into a single marble in a consistent manner rather than by the gatherer's hand-directed method. The different flows of glass joined and were cut off by shears.

J. Fred Early, the son of John F. Early, furnished a description of an adaptor his father made to be used with his Patent 1,880,916. The purpose of the adaptor was to achieve a spiral design, imitating genuine stone agate marbles. On the marble-making machine, there was a space between the feeder orifice and the guide for shifting the gob of glass to a separate set of rolls. In this space, Early inserted a steel plate. A set of gears and pulleys powered by a small motor was mounted on the plate, and in the top of the final drive gear was a cup in which a piece of carbon was inserted. The top side of the carbon had another cup about $\frac{1}{2}$ inch deep with a groove or grooves cut inside it. A single groove provided a single spiral, and multiple grooves provided multiple color spirals to the body glass. Dating the Akro Agate Spiral is difficult, but a primary source states that the earliest, single spiral design was a single opaque wide spiral on opaque glass. The latest, multiple design was a multi-colored marble (transparent, translucent, or opaque) with fine to broad spirals on transparent body glass.

The whole assembly was on a steel plate that was mounted in a track, and was bolted to the feeder. The steel plate with its gears would slide under the gob of glass, raise to twist the gob, and then lower and retract out of the way of the cutoffs. The system was operated by a cam on one of the roll shafts and synchronized with the cutoffs. This adaptor was not patented, and therefore did not enter into the landmark infringement lawsuit later.

Marbles produced by the prior methods, by the gatherer, produced less uniform patterns, but the 1929 Early twisting modification gave the marbles a distinct and uniform spiral or twisting design. This distinctive design is easily recognizable as Akro and has not been duplicated by any other company.

Marbles were sometimes included with other products as prizes or premiums. Several marble companies over the years sold premium marbles to the manufacturers of cereals, bubble gum, Popsicles, and Cracker Jack. The Cracker Jack company included loose marbles in its boxes, but this method of packaging took an unexpected turn in 1928 when one unfortunate child allegedly swallowed the Akro Agate marble prize. Thereafter, the premiums were individually wrapped in waxed paper like saltwater taffy. A part-time employee of the company in 1928 recalls that "the machine had a roll of waxed paper two to three inches wide. As the paper was fed into the machine, a sleeve was formed and the marble inserted, the paper was cut and both ends were twisted as in a salt water taffy kiss." The machine, according to John F. Early's notes, was supplied by the Harvey Machine Company, Los Angeles, California.[5]

In the 1920s Akro sold millions of crystal marbles for use in the grinding of lithographic plates for the printing industry. Millions of ruby red marbles were also sold for use in reflectors and in road guardrail posts. These early industrial marbles were shipped loose in wooden boxes.[6]

In 1930, due to conflicts with president Gilbert Marsh's new manager, Willie Wetterau, several of the long-time employees—John F. Early, Claude C. Grimmett, Clinton F. Israel, and John E. Moulton—resigned from Akro. Grimmett, Early, and Moulton left effective May 1, 1930, and Israel resigned effective June 1, 1930.

In the case of John F. Early, there was also a problem with delivery of company stock that he had been promised as part of his employment and in return for assignment of his inventions to Akro. In 1922 he had entered into a ten-year contract with Akro; at the end of this time he was to receive 20 percent of the treasury stock of the company. In the meantime, however, the stock that should have been his was given to an attorney. This same attorney later accepted Early's resignation and cancelation of the contract. This cancelation released Early from the agreement that any future inventions he might develop would belong to Akro. Apparently the attorney was unaware of the significance of this release. When Gilbert Marsh learned of it, it was too late to resolve this significant problem.

Not long after leaving Akro, this cadre of master craftsmen formed their own company, the Master Marble Company, located in Anmoore, West Virginia.

By the mid-1930s the heyday of the marble industry had passed, and by the 1940s the surviving companies faced a serious decline in demand. Several fledgling marble companies came and went, and the surviving companies struggled with competition from each other and with the changing tastes in children's toys. After the mid-1940s, major retailers like Sears no longer listed marbles in their catalogs.

During World War II, Akro Agate produced masses of colorful toy dishes to replace imported toys from Japan. The going was slow at first, but American toy companies eventually enjoyed a boom, albeit a short-lived one. Formulas that were used to make marbles were used to make the toy line in an array of transparent, opaque, and marbleized glass toys. The most collectible is the Akro Agate Play-Time Set.[7]

Akro's other lines of glassware supported the company through the marble decline. After World War II, however, imports, returning use of metals, and the use of the newly discovered plastic for toys spelled the end for Akro.[8]

The Akro Agate Company was essentially out of business by mid-1950, and began selling off the stock of marbles on hand. The last of the company assets, including machinery, molds for other glasswares, and glass formulas, was sold at public auction on April 24, 1951, by Hetz Auction Sales, Inc., of Warren, Ohio. Berry Pink of Marble King bought all marble machines except one, which was sold to the Heaton Agate Company. Clinton F. Israel of the Master Glass Company bought all the formulas, accounts, and other records.[9]

The People at Akro

Lawrence E. Alley: Employed at Akro as a gathering boy, later went into business for himself.

Edmund Burroughs: Last president and treasurer.

John F. Early: Joined Akro in 1919; improved Hill's semi-automatic marble-making machine and designed the conveyor screw; credited with two patents; resigned 1930; partner in formation of the Master Marble Company.

Arnold Fiedler: This German-born and educated chemist was employed at Akro until about 1926; used potatoes to solve the problem of "seedy" glass. Fiedler also worked at the Christensen Agate Company and at the Cambridge Glass Company.

Claude C. Grimmett: Assistant secretary of Akro in 1916; later assistant agent and chief accounting officer, promoted to general manager 1926; resigned 1930; partner in formation of the Master Marble Company.

Ralph Heatherington: Key salesperson.

Henry Helmers: Employed 1922–1930 as chemist; along with Early, developed alabaster glass formula for Akro.

Horace C. Hill: Inventor of Akro's original marble-making machine in 1910; original founder and general manager; died 1916.

Clinton F. Israel: Joined Akro in July 1926 as draftsman; drew blueprints for John F. Early's patents; later in charge of packing department and assistant to John F. Early; resigned 1930; partner in formation of the Master Marble Company; later founded the Master Glass Company.

Gilbert C. Marsh: Original founder of Akro with Horace Hill and Dr. George T. Rankin; vice president 1910; president during Akro's lawsuits against Peltier and Master Marble; died 1948.[10]

E. E. McGalliard: Early minor shareholder; sold out to John Rowley, of the Akron Coal Company, in 1917.

John E. Moulton: Sales manager from about 1926 to 1930; resigned 1930; partner in the formation of the Master Marble Company.

George A. Pflueger: Became shareholder and secretary in 1916; managing agent 1921; Pflueger's marketing and promotion skills were significant to the success of Akro in the early years.[11]

Dr. George T. Rankin: Original founder of Akro with Horace Hill and Gilbert Marsh; became president 1910; died 1948.[12]

John M. Rowley: Early junior partner, bought out McGalliard in 1917 to become equal partner; manager of finances; also associated with the Akron Coal Company, Akron, Ohio; died 1924.

Willie Wetterau: Manager 1929–1930; the 1937 U.S. District Court trial transcript showing a decision in favor of Master Marble blamed his insulting management tactics as a major factor in the resignations of key personnel (Early, Grimmett, Israel, and Moulton) from Akro.

Marbles Produced by Akro Agate

Opaques: Akro, along with most of the other marble makers, produced millions of single-colored opaque marbles during the Chinese Checkers craze of the late 1930s and early 1940s. The typical set consisted of six colors of marbles, ten marbles each, sixty per box; colors were generally white, black, red, blue, yellow, and green. This type of marble was not used only in the Chinese Checkers game, but that was the most common usage. The exact span of time that Akro produced this type is unknown, but began before 1920.

Transparents: Akro's Transparents were called Glassies, and came in colors of red, crystal (clear), amethyst, azure, yellow, green, and amber;[13] Akro began producing Transparents before 1920.[14]

Translucents: Known as Vaseline, Custard, Alabaster glass, and Moonies or Moonstone, Akro's Translucents were in colors of white, purple, blue, red, green, and greenish-yellow.

Akro Agate did not designate a company name for the greenish-yellow color; however, at a later date it was combined with a red-brick color and the marble was called Lemonade and Oxblood, a rare name to describe a line of children's toys.[15] Subsequently, this same color combination was described as a "yellow-red combination."[16] There are two points of interest here—the first appearance of the color oxblood and the fact that the sources describe this color as rare. Marbles and pressware made using the lemonade and oxblood formula are scarce. They commanded a high price, particularly in the larger sizes.

The making of alabaster glass was a well-guarded secret, apparently known in Europe before the United States. Akro sent Henry Helmer and John F. Early to Europe in 1928 in an effort to learn how to produce this type of glass. This trip was a pretense, since the real purpose was to determine if certain German marble makers were using the Akro Agate patent. The suspicion was founded in the earlier discovery and ejection of an uninvited German national from the Akro Agate factory. The Germans did not allow entry into their factory. The trip was not successful, but Helmer and Early, with the help of the Corning Glass

Early Akro Agate marbles, which were made by machines with the assistance of men called "gatherers." Note the variety in the striping, due to the dexterity of the gatherer. The marble in the center, with black striping on the edge of the red, may be an aberration that occurred when the colors in the striping tank were changed. J. Fred Early Collection.

company, did develop the process that produced translucent or alabaster glass, beginning the same year (1928). The key ingredient in the recipe was common table salt. As much of a challenge as it may have been for a glassmaker, marbles of this type of glass in single colors were not popular and are fairly rare.

Recently, however, interest in this company-named color has grown. A canary stripe was added to a body glass of alabaster, and a light green stripe was added to a body glass of alabaster. These two marbles in particular are now quite collectible and are dubbed Lemonade and Limeade (see Chapter XI on glass formulas).

Patched Opaques and Patched Translucents: These were first made in the mid- to late 1920s, and were an extremely popular type during the 1930s; on white

Akro Agate Box Number 230 (cardboard), which is unique and scarce because the central figure is a girl. Normally, previous covers did not show girls—only boys. Robert Payton collection.

opaque or translucent bodies, patch colors included red, orange, green, blue, and yellow.[17] Patched Opaque colors include single colors of blue, red, orange, or green; double colors of green and red, green and yellow, green and orange, red and blue, burgundy and blue; triple colors of orange and yellow and brown, and four colors of blue and red and yellow and tan; all of the above marbles have white body glass.

The Translucent variety occurs in generally the same color combinations, except that the body glass is milky instead of Opaque white.

Brushed Opaques, Transparents, and Translucents: This type is so closely related in design to the Patched varieties above that the difference may be artificial. To the eye there are differences, but the two types may have come out of the same production run, some receiving a more well-defined patch of color than others. In any case, the colors used in the Brushed type are the same as the Patched types, with the exception that the Brushed types exhibit only one design color per marble. Also, the Brushed occurs in Transparent, although the Patched does not. The Brushed Transparent often occurs with a red body glass and a red brushed area.

The time span is the same as for the Patched type, mid- to late 1920s into the 1940s.

Transparent and Translucent Swirls or Slags: This type is most often identified with Akro, although it was not made exclusively by Akro. It was the earliest machine-made type, made by M. F. Christensen and Son prior to Akro. Akro, however, was the company that mass-produced this type in the late teens and early 1920s. An early favorite was known as Cerise Agate or Cardinal Red and had white striping in dark red body glass. Other body glass colors included clear, blue, green, purple, yellow, and amber; the striping was always white.

The popularity of this type of marble declined in the late 1920s. At that time Akro introduced the Transparent

and Translucent Spirals, which were Akro exclusives.

Opaque, Transparent, and Translucent Spirals: The mechanical advancements of the mid-1920s allowed Akro to develop and maintain a monopoly on these types. The two-colored Opaque variety is characterized by two interlocking spirals of different colors of glass. Since they are of the same size, it is difficult to say which is the body glass and which the design glass. In the Transparent and Translucent types, the body glass is always clear or milky.

In addition to appearing in the three degrees of opacity, the Spirals occur in two-, three-, and four-colored versions, with a single or double revolution of the spiral. The double revolution is the rarer type, as are the three- and four-colored types.

The color combinations are too numerous to list; suffice it to say that any combination of colors can be expected. The double-spiral and the three- and four-color types are not common enough to be certain, but it is a good guess that any colors found in the more common single-colored single-spiral marbles will be found in other types, as well.

As noted above, this type was made possible by the mechanical advances of the 1925–1928 period, and was probably produced into the 1940s. Because of their resemblance to marbles made from the mineral agate, these marbles were also called Aggies or agates.[18]

Spirals were first packaged in a box lettered "Aces" and are sometimes called by that name. A beautiful multicolored Spiral (transparent body glass) marble was packaged with the comic character Popeye on the box top. Some collectors call these marbles Popeyes because of their packaging. Recently, this outstanding spiral design has been mislabeled Sigma and Corkscrew, as well as Staircase and Barber Pole. The term Spiral is used in this book because it was used by the Akro Agate factory employees. One well-known collection contains ninety-two distinct design and color types of Akro Spirals.[19]

Akro Agates was the catch-all name often used in

catalogs beginning in the early 1930s, when marble users recognized that Akro's spiral designs were different. Some of the other marble names appearing in the 1932 Sears catalog are identifiable, and some are not: Flinties, Onyxes, and Imperials. Kids dubbed certain Akro marbles with their own names, such as Butterscotch Slag and Dark Hero.

On September 24, 1991, the City of Clarksburg placed a public notice in the local newspaper soliciting sealed bids until 2 p.m. on October 11, 1991, for "exclusive marble digging rights at the Clarksburg City Garage (old AKRO-AGATE MARBLE PLANT) #1 Dane Street, Clarksburg, West Virginia. Digging will be permitted only in designated areas at or near the site on property owned by the City of Clarksburg. The area must be restored to its original condition and appearance. A minimum bid of $5,000 will be required." This is the first known instance of a marble dump being advertised for bids to excavate marbles. The public notice may be faulty in that other types of glass material may have also been excavated, since Akro did produce other lines, such as pressware.

A primary source said that the dump would probably contain a lot of marble rejects; according to the patent infringement suit, Akro Agate tried to "doctor" the Early patents to match the Master Marble Company machines, which resulted in rejects.[20]

In an October 1991 newspaper interview, Frank Ferror, the Clarksburg city manager, reported that the only bid received to date (October 14, 1991) was $1,000, far below the $5,000 minimum bid. A subsequent meeting of the city council indicated that the city might abandon the idea of a dig, since a collector named Roger Hardy had been looking for marbles there since 1969.[21]

The minimum bid of $5,000 may have scared off potential bidders. The figure was based on the tentative offer of an Ohio man for exclusive rights; the man later changed his mind. An avid marble collector from Copley, Ohio, indicated that he might have paid that much at one time but was no longer interested because too much had already been carted off.

Roger Hardy's wife, Claudia, stated at the October council meeting that her husband was reiterating his offer of $500, and that digging rights were not worth $5,000 or even $1,000. The Hardys began collecting artifacts from the site in 1969, when permission was given by Sutter Roofing, which then owned the property.

The Akro property was purchased by the City of Clarksburg approximately eighteen years ago and was used for the city's public works garage. The dump area that was subject to bidding is a fairly deep hollow beside the plant; Akro had used it as a dump since 1930.[22]

The Akro Agate story does not seem to end. The building was vacated by the city in the spring of 1992 and remains empty, pending a decision regarding establishment of a glass museum or an Akro Agate Marbles Club. Certainly, the site should be considered for placement on a national historic register.

The collection of Roger and Claudia Hardy, consisting of Akro Agate pressware and marbles, is considered to be the best-known collection and has enjoyed considerable

notoriety at recent shows. It was featured in the February 1993 issue of *Mid-Atlantic Country*. The Hardys' book about Akro Agate is a valuable addition to a marble collector's library.

THE ALLEY AGATE COMPANY/ THE LAWRENCE GLASS NOVELTY COMPANY/ THE ALLEY GLASS MANUFACTURING COMPANY
Paden City, Sisterville, Pennsboro, and St. Marys, West Virginia

Lawrence E. Alley began his career in the marble business as a gatherer for the Akro Agate Company. He later left Akro to set up his own company in Paden City in the old Paul Wissmach Glass Company building, in 1929. In 1931 Berry Pink joined Alley, and the name of the company became the Lawrence Glass Novelty Company. Besides marbles, they made "moon balls"—large street lamp globes. The business was too large for the factory, so it moved to Sistersville in the summer of 1932. At the same time there were legal problems within the company, including a lawsuit. Berry Pink left the company and the marble business, but he would return some years later. The company moved again around 1934 to Pennsboro.

The company's marble-making machines were designed by Alley himself and were built in the Skagg Machine Shop in Sistersville. These machines produced 165 marbles per minute, a quantity not achieved by other machines of that time (about 1935). Alley did not patent the machines for reasons of secrecy. However, some Belgian businessmen proposed that Alley take his machines to Belgium and show them how to produce marbles. Alley declined, as he did not care for foreign travel, did not speak the language, and preferred to remain in the United States producing marbles at his own plant. Some of his machines were eventually sold to the Amherst Company of Pittsburgh, which later sent them to Belgium, enabling that country to enter the marble business after all.

A 1935 patent for a glass shearing mechanism for use in marble-making machines was granted to Russell Adams and Clyde Hibbs (see Patents chapter) and was assigned to The Lawrence Glass Novelty Company.

The company again needed more space and moved to St. Marys in 1937. The Pennsboro Glass Company moved into the vacated Alley building the following year and expanded the building in 1947 for production of a wide range of fine soda-lime crystalware of nearly two thousand design types. Employees have excavated Orphan Annie children's play tea sets from the Alley dump, indicating that Alley's marble line was extended to include the novelty items popular at that time.[23]

About the time of the move to St. Marys, Alley entered into an arrangement with J. Pressman and Company, Inc., a major New York toy company, whereby Pressman would market all of Alley's production. The entire output of the St. Marys facility went to Pressman for distribution in Europe.

Alley's fortunes in the marble business might have been much different except for a lucky incident involving mail delivery. Alley had an understanding with the local postmaster that the postmaster would cull out the "junk mail" before forwarding the mail to Alley. The initial letter from Pressman appeared to be unimportant promotional material and was almost thrown away with the junk, but something told the postmaster to keep it for Alley. That letter began a long-time business relationship and personal friendship between Alley and Pressman.

In the next few years Alley became one of the largest producers of marbles in the world. One of Pressman's marbles games was Hop Ching, its brand of Chinese Checkers, a new game in the late 1930s. The Pressman Chinese Checkers game board had an Oriental motif including dragons; the six triangles on the board were the same color as the marbles: red, turquoise, green, black, white, and purple.

Alley's Chinese Checkers marbles can be seen in an August 1940 article in *National Geographic Magazine* on West Virginia industry. Although Lawrence Alley was the person interviewed and the photograph was taken in Alley's St. Marys plant, Alley declined to be identified in the article; he was a modest person who did not like notoriety.

The hugely successful game of Chinese Checkers sold millions of marbles for Alley as well as other manufacturers during the late 1930s and 1940s. Alley shipped 14 million Chinese Checker marbles in six months.[24]

Some years after Alley had established his St. Marys plant, leaving Pennsboro, Champion Agate Company built a factory on Walnut Street, across from the former Alley marble factory.

At the height of production at the St. Mary's plant, Alley employed about 125 people. The plant was a busy place, with the activities of the batch makers, carry-in boys, machine workers, and women bagging the marbles. The cloth bags for the marbles were made in the sewing room upstairs.

In 1939 Lawrence Alley changed the name of the company to the Alley Glass Manufacturing Company and reorganized it as a family business, with several family members as officers. However, Naomi, one of Alley's daughters, was the only family member who was actually active besides Lawrence himself. Naomi worked in the plant as the secretary and ran the business when Lawrence was away. The plant manager during this period was "Pete" Oliver Roseman Hill.

In 1949, because of ill health, Alley sold the business to Berry Pink and Sellers H. Peltier. The name was changed to Marble King—another company that is still in the marble business.

Marbles Produced by Alley

Opaques: Black, orange, green, blue.
Opaque Swirls: Purple and blue, white and yellow, white and blue, white and red, blue and green, orange and white, brown and white, green and white.
Patched Opaque: Blue on white body.
Patched and Ribboned Opaque: Blue ribbon, yellow patch on white body.

The L. E. Alley marble factory in Pennsboro, West Virginia. Right and left wings of the main building were added after L. E. Alley left for St. Marys. The Pennsboro Glass Company now occupies the building. Photo by Dennis Webb.

Ribboned Opaque: Green and orange ribbons on 103 white body.
Transparents: Light green, clear, red, brown.
Transparent Swirls: White swirls in clear, white swirls in dark green.
Translucent Swirls: Brown swirls in white body.

These color combinations are not the complete range produced by Alley, but these are known from available examples. Sizes in these examples range from ½ inch to ¹³⁄₁₆ inch.

THE ALOX MANUFACTURING COMPANY
St. Louis, Missouri

The Alox Manufacturing Company was founded in 1919 by John Frier. Ownership passed to his son, Jack Frier, who closed the factory in 1989. As part of its toy line, Alox sold marbles that were purchased from West Virginia but decided to make its own marbles in the late 1930s. In addition to marbles, a large variety of Chinese Checker boards were sold, including a now rare four-sided playing board.[25]

Seven marble-making machines were purchased from a defunct West Virginia marble company, and two of the former employees were recruited to make marbles for Alox. Furnaces and tanks were originally heated by natural gas but were later converted to fuel oil.

The primary product was ⅝-inch Chinese Checkers; at the height of production, a half-million marbles were produced per day. The Alox Chinese Checker boards came in six- and four-sided varieties.

Transparent and Opaque Swirls in ⁹⁄₁₆-inch diameters were also produced and sold in red, white, and blue cut-out cardboard boxes. The box of the "TIT-TAT-TOE" set had circular cutouts in a checkerboard pattern to be used as the playing board.[26]

During World War II, marble production halted; it resumed after the war for only a short time. Due to difficulties in attracting workers, Alox ceased making

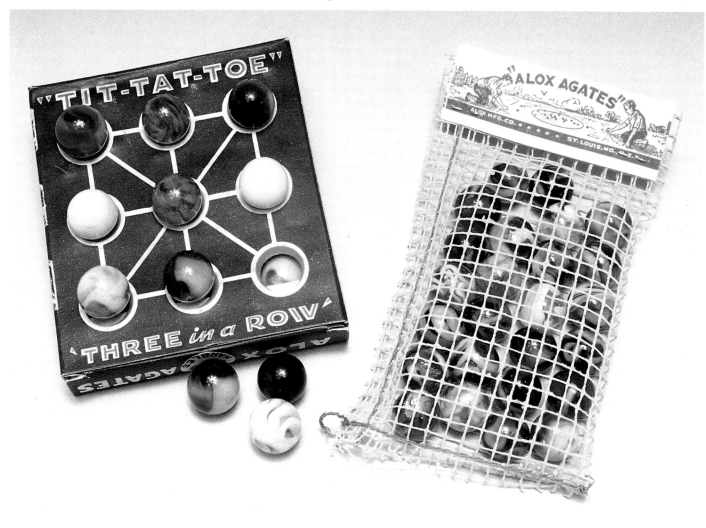

Alox Agates bag and box with "Tit-Tat-Toe" game.

marbles.[27] Alox continued selling its on-hand stock of marbles into the 1960s.[28]

The company's marble-making machines were scrapped in 1975, except for one machine that was sold to the Silver Dollar Amusement Park at Branson, Missouri, where it is part of an exhibit of machines used in glassmaking and other arts and crafts.[29]

C. E. BOGARD & SONS AGATE COMPANY/ THE BOGARD COMPANY
Cairo, West Virginia

In 1971 Clayton E. Bogard and his sons purchased the Heaton Agate Company in Cairo and changed the name to C. E. Bogard & Sons. Some time later Jack and Jerry Bogard and Tad Holipski became owners, and in July 1983, after Jack Bogard bought out the other partners, the name became the Bogard Company.

For a while after the purchase of the Heaton Agate facilities, Bogard sold excess Heaton packaged marbles with a C. E. Bogard & Sons label stapled over the original Heaton label.

During the period from 1971 to 1976, Bogard sold Cat Eyes from old Heaton Agate stock in color combinations of clear body glass with light red, white, blue, green, or yellow centers. C. E. Bogard made its own Cat Eyes for a short time, with four single-colored blades of powder blue, dark blue, purple, black, light green, and dark green. They also produced four-vaned Cat Eyes of two colors.

Bogard later produced a yellow Cat Eye, with yellow striping glass made by the Champion Agate Company and body glass made by Bogard. The intense yellow of this Cat Eye's yellow blades is attributed to the use of German cane for the blades; it has a lower melting point than the clear transparent body glass. Bogard produced a scarce and colorful package of Cat Eyes called "Mountaineer Shooters."

The company made a few pink Transparents using recipe glass from the Federal Glass Company in Columbus, Ohio; but even with recipe glass, the pink variety proved extremely difficult to perfect, and the design was discontinued. The cost of glass and possible nonacceptance of pink as a toy marble may have been factors. However, the pink seedy glass marble has now become a desired item for use in jewelry.

An interesting attempt to reproduce an early handmade design resulted in a marble very similar to Master Marble's Tiger Eye. Bogard's marble was a clear

Sample of marbles made by the Cairo Novelty Company in Cairo, West Virginia. They were recovered at the old plant site by West Virginia historian Dean Six. Courtesy of Dean Six.

Transparent with inner wisps of green, intended to duplicate the Onionskins of the nineteenth century. The striping of Bogard's variety, however, migrated toward the center of the marble and would not stay near the outside, as it should have in an Onionskin. This variety, like the pink Transparent, was made for only a short time.

Bogard produced single-color Opaques (Chinese Checkers) during the years 1971–1976; Opaque Swirls and non-industrial Transparents were produced as well.

In the mid-1970s, Bogard ceased production of all types but transparent single-colored industrial marbles in clear glass and light blue (azure). Jack Bogard had been the prime activist in convincing the aerosol can industry to try marbles instead of metal balls for the agitator balls in spray cans. Since that time, the aerosol can producers have been a major customer for industrial marbles. In early 1987 the factory was closed and all equipment moved to Reno, Ohio, under new name and leadership. A visit to the site in 1989 indicated abandonment and the appearance of disarray. Entrance into the plant area is blocked and posted "No Trespassing."

THE BOSTON AND SANDWICH GLASS COMPANY
Sandwich, Massachusetts

The Boston and Sandwich Glass Company, which was active from 1825 to 1888,[30] is famous among antique collectors for fine glasswares. Flea market folklore credits

Nicholas Lutz, who joined the company in 1869, with adding finely ground copper in swirling bands to marbles for the first time.[31] Marbles of this type are frequently called "Lutz" by collectors.

While Lutz may have pioneered the use of the copper/gold bands in marbles, it is certain that he was not the only glassworker who produced goldstone. Furthermore, correspondence with the Sandwich Glass Museum indicates that while "marbles were made at Sandwich by individual workmen . . . there is no evidence that any were made on a production basis except perhaps as enclosures for the cage-type bar stoppers."[32] Such production could not explain all of the goldstone-banded handmade marbles in existence; nor could End of Day personal gifts made by the workmen.

Since the goldstone technique in glassware was a centuries-old technique among European glass workers, it is safe to assume that many goldstone marbles were produced in Germany along with other types during the late 1800s.

THE CAIRO NOVELTY COMPANY
Cairo, West Virginia

On June 26, 1946, a corporate charter was granted to Dennis Farley, Oris G. Hanlon, and John Sandy, each residing at Cairo, West Virginia. They subscribed to 33⅓ shares each at $100 per share.

The Cairo Novelty Company's logo was a camel and

pyramid, alluding to Cairo, Egypt. The company produced marbles on a single machine—Hanlon's 1947 Patent 2,422,413.

According to one informant, the company did not produce marbles for play but for commercial use in the newer oil fields. *Oil Facts*, a petroleum publication, states that thousands of marbles are dropped into sluggish oil wells to help improve production. The marbles form a plug at the bottom, after which sand, chemicals, and water are pumped under pressure through the casing to loosen oil-bearing formations. However, a former employee says that the marbles made were mostly for play, in ⅝-inch and ½-inch sizes for Chinese Checkers, and a few ¾-inch diameters. One shipment of marbles was made for the oil fields.

Competition occurred in Cairo between the Heaton Agate Company and the Cairo Novelty Company. The check stub of an employee in 1947 shows that the employee was paid 40 cents an hour, and nearby Heaton Agate offered 50 cents an hour for performing the same task. The two companies also competed for the same supply of natural gas for their furnaces. When both the Cairo Novelty Company and the Heaton Agate Company were in operation, the pressure in the gas lines was not sufficient for two factories and slowed production in both.

Production seems to have spanned from 1946 to June 25, 1950, when a flood seriously crippled the factory, particularly the operations and machinery. However, the building remained intact and still stands. A recent site visit showed a building with wood sides, a brick floor, a metal roof, and a state of deterioration. The building is surrounded by second-growth trees and blackberries, tall ground cover, and weeds. The area is posted "No Trespassing," and a nearby resident stated that copperhead snakes and poison ivy are present. Despite the natural hazards, it was observed that the dump had been excavated.

After visiting the factory site, West Virginia historian Dean Six confirmed that the Cairo Novelty Company had indeed made marbles for play. Battered pieces of a cardboard box from the rafters of the building carried the name "Trap the Fox" and the inside of the lid carried the company name, address, date, and instructions for playing the game.

The local name for the general line of Cairo marbles is Clouds or Cloudy Days and Snakes. The company had not given specific names to different color designs. A sample of marbles recovered are:

½-Inch Slag-like Swirls: white opaque glass with a light green body.
⅝-Inch Slag-like Swirls: azure Swirls with white body glass, light green Swirls with white body glass, translucent light brick red with translucent white body glass.
¾-Inch Transparent Azure and White Body Glass, resembling earth from outer space—a beautiful design.

CHAMPION OF MARBLES

THE CHAMPION AGATE COMPANY
Pennsboro, West Virginia

The Champion Agate Company was founded in 1938 by Yucca Jones and Ralph Michels. By 1949 the company had been sold to Roy and Murphy Michels, who later sold it to Palmer Hill, who in turn sold the company in April 1965 to Donald G. Michels, nephew of Roy and Murphy. Michels incorporated the company in 1975. In 1983 Helen Michels became president and Dave McCullough became plant manager. In early June of 1991 Dave McCullough unexpectedly left the company to assume a corporate position with JABO, Inc., in Reno, Ohio. Dan Christian, the son-in-law of Donald and Helen Michels, became the plant manager. In early 1992 Donald G. Michels took over the management of Champion Agate once again.

Yucca Jones designed and built the marble-making machines that are still in use at Champion. The Champion machines were capable of turning out marbles in diameters as small as ⅜ inch. These tiny marbles were designed for hobby and decorative use.

Champion's storage operations are housed in an abandoned factory building located across the street from the Champion plant.

In 1938, the first year of operation, Champion produced Chinese Checkers and Clearies. Between 1938 and 1975, other types, including Opaque Swirls, Transparent Swirls, and Patched Opaques, were made.

By 1975 only Chinese Checkers were still being produced, but a special red, white, and blue randomly swirled design with an opaque

Prefabricated building recently erected by the Champion Agate Company in Pennsboro, West Virginia, to supplement their nearby factory. Piles of cullet and scrap glass are located nearby. Photo by Dennis Webb.

body was produced for the special 1976 Bicentennial Pack.

The Bicentennial Special Pack, produced and packaged by Champion, contained marbles made by Champion, C. E. Bogard & Sons, Heaton Agate, Jackson, Marble King, Master Glass, Peltier, and Ravenswood Novelty Works. This package was a wonderful collection of marbles made over a period of years by some of the foremost American marble makers.

Currently, Champion makes its own yellow and ruby glass from formula; other colors are recycled glass.

Chinese Checkers made by Champion were marketed by the Steven Manufacturing Company under the brand name Pixie. In 1982 the marbles industry benefited from the Pac-Man video game craze. The electronic game itself did not use marbles, but a spin-off Pac-Man board game that used Chinese Checkers-type marbles made by Champion and other manufacturers boosted the demand for this all-purpose design of game marble.

Champion produced the striping material used in yellow Cat Eye marbles made by C. E. Bogard & Sons. Bogard made the body, or basic clear portion, and put the final product together.

In 1983 and 1984 Champion produced two revivals of old designs: Whirlwinds and Old Fashioneds. The Old Fashioneds look like the Slags of the 1930s, while the Whirlwinds are a Transparent Swirl variety with a wispy white random inner design. The two types are reminiscent of marbles made by the Ravenswood Novelty Works and others during the 1930s and 1940s. These varieties are currently being sold in England, where they are very popular.

Another recent (1985) revival is the opalescent look of Champion's Pearls design, made in both Transparent and Opaque form.

Pearls was followed by another rare design. An unusual, exotic, and beautiful marble was born in 1988, when a machine operator unintentionally dropped a welding rod into a melting tank containing clear, transparent glass. The unique marbles produced from this accidental melding of metal and glass were attractive enough to prompt an effort to reproduce them deliberately by mechanical means. A small hole was drilled into the melting tank below the orifice ring. The operator then inserted a welding rod into the hole. By gently tapping the rod, he fed metal into the molten body glass as it left the machine, resulting in a fine black hairline design.

Champion Agate did not name this design, since it was produced only once as a special order and was not duplicated again due to labor costs. The costs could, however, be reduced by installing an adaptor to feed the rod. The marble itself resembles a colorless Clearie containing a wildly twisting trail of delicate black thread, making a continuous, random pattern within the glass orb.[33] This design should not be confused with the H. E. Hopf design now called Wirepull by Castle and Peterson. Collectors fortunate enough to have a specimen of this marble might classify it as a type of Wirepull, but a better name would be Backlash, since the design most closely

approximates a fly fisherman's silken line about to tangle hopelessly in midair.

THE CHRISTENSEN AGATE COMPANY
Cambridge, Ohio

Although incorporated in Akron in 1925, the Christensen Agate Company's plant was first established in Payne, Ohio. In 1927 a new facility was established in Cambridge in a small brick building behind the famous Cambridge Glass Company, on a spur of the B & O Railroad that served both companies.[34] The factory was under the management of H. M. Jenkins.[35] The company was reincorporated in 1927 by W. F. Jones, Robert C. Ryder, Beulah P. Hartman, H. H. Cupler, and Owen M. Roderick; it ceased operations around 1933.[36] This early marble factory was founded by Arnold Fiedler, whose name appears in the histories of several marble and glass companies. (Before working at Christensen, Fiedler had mixed glass for the nearby Cambridge Glass Company. After Christensen Agate closed, he moved to Clarksburg

The old Christensen Agate Company plant located on Bennett Avenue, Cambridge, Ohio. The building is now part of the Guernsey County Highway Department garage complex. Few if any scraps or rejects are on the ground site. Photo by Dennis Webb.

to work for the new Akro Agate Company.)

The Christensen Agate Company did not make its own recipe glass for marbles but bought scrap glass from the Cambridge Glass Company. Therefore, someone wishing to identify a marble color may refer to the several leading antique books covering the Cambridge Glass Company.[37]

Marbles were made by the manual method on one of the early marble machines typical of those used during that era; the factory did not use a fully automated modern machine until the last year of operation. In the early years, an estimated three thousand marbles were made per day. The marbles were sized using a screen with various-sized holes, and the smaller marbles dropped out first. The marble makers were paid only for the ones of the proper size; the ones not of the correct size, although perfect spheres, were relegated to a nearby dump.[38]

While this company's name is similar to the earlier M. F. Christensen Glass Company in Steubenville, Ohio, the original Christensen did not have any interest in the later company—a 1936 magazine article indicates that Martin F. Christensen died in 1920, five years before this company was founded.[39]

The son of the caretaker of the old Christensen warehouse recalls that many boxes of painted clay marbles were left there after the plant closed in 1933. The marbles were solid colors of blue, green, yellow, and red.[40] While Christensen may have sold clay marbles, it is doubtful that the company produced the clays in their glass marble factory, since the two manufacturing technologies are very different. However, it would not have been unusual for the company to sell clays that were produced by another company, perhaps a local Ohio company. Further, it is not surprising that a stock of clay marbles would have remained unsold, since by the time Christensen Agate closed, clay marbles had long been replaced in popularity by machine-made glass marbles.

Using antiquated machines, Christensen could make only thirty thousand marbles a day. The company ceased operations in 1933 due to competition on the part of the West Virginia factories, which used new, fully mechanical marble machines.

After Christensen Agate closed, glass specialist Arnold Fiedler moved on to Clarksburg to become an employee of the new Akro Agate Company. Thanks to Fiedler, the early Akro Agate colors have a striking resemblance to the Christensen Agate marbles.

Christensen Agate Company made Transparent and Translucent Swirls in green, white, honey, orange, and dark body glass with white striping; and Opaque Swirls in yellow and green, red and green, light blue and red, red and white, yellow and black, and black and white. These marbles were sold in square boxes of twenty-five, five marbles of five different colors per box. They were distributed by the Gropper Onyx Marble Company of New York City.[41]

Some, but not all, marble names were based on the Cambridge Glass Company colors. Typical names were Bloodies, made of beautiful ruby and white opaque glass; Blue Bells, light blue and opaque white; Blue Azurites; and Jennys. The red Jenny was named after an employee named Jennings.

During his time at Christensen, Fiedler is rumored to have made Sulphide marbles containing an eagle for one summer's run, sometime between 1927 and 1933.

A marble that has gained considerable notoriety due to its beauty and visibility is the Guinea, sold in a boxed set by Gropper. It has been alleged that no two are alike. The company name Guinea probably came from the white spots on the surface, resembling a guinea fowl. Body glass may be crystal, amber, or cobalt blue, with the color design on the surface.[42] When introduced, the colorful Guinea was not a popular marble; it shattered upon impact with another marble or object because of the way it was made. However, the Guinea gained considerable favor several years ago when marble collecting became popular.[43] There is some speculation that the Guinea may

be duplicated in the future, using the same technique that was employed in the making of Vacor de Mexico's Galactica or Confetti.

Christensen Agate's three most popular designs, in order of descending rarity, are the Guinea, the Flame (a beautiful orange-yellow Opaque), and the Jenny.

After the factory closed, the marble dump was often raided, and recovered marbles were used as missiles for boys' slingshots, aimed at targets in the nearby creek. Present-day efforts to recover them are fraught with danger due to quicksand.

Some years ago the Guernsey County Highway Maintenance Department took over the old Christensen Agate building. The agency scraped the yard area level for parking space, and covered the main dump with twelve feet of fill dirt to erect a storage shed.[44] In late July 1992 the area was posted "No Trespassing" to discourage marble-seekers.

THE M. F. CHRISTENSEN AND SON GLASS COMPANY
Steubenville, Ohio

On December 19, 1902, Martin F. Christensen applied for a patent on a "Machine for Making Spherical Bodies or Balls" of his own design. It was renewed March 29, 1905 (Serial No. 262,676), and patented October 24, 1905, No. 802,495. This patent is of historic interest, since it automated the marble-making process by taking the glass marble industry from hand production to machine production. (See Patents chapter.)

The factory was located at 453 to 459 Exchange Street, Akron, Ohio, and operation began on a full-time basis in 1903 by the founder and president Martin F. Christensen and his son Charles Frederick Christensen. M. F. Christensen died in 1915, and his son Charles assumed the presidency. For all intents and purposes, operations ceased in 1921 due to a dwindling supply of natural gas.

M. F. Christensen's introduction of true mechanical marble production proved successful in competition with the German handmade marble industry, whereas other United States companies, including the Navarre Glass Marble and Specialty Company, had failed. The glass marble industry shifted to the United States, with Akron, Ohio, as its center.

The machine patented by Christensen required a gatherer to gather a gob of glass on a punty, and another worker to cut off the gather of an appropriate mass, allowing it to drop into the grooves of the two rolls. (See Chapter XII.)

Horace C. Hill, a trusted key official, left the company under a cloud and became an official of the newly formed Akro Agate Company.[45] Allegedly, company secrets went with Hill to Akro Agate. At his new post, Hill obtained a patent for a new marble machine that was an improvement over the M. F. Christensen machine. The early marbles produced by Akro Agate bore a striking resemblance to the early marbles made at the M. F. Christensen and Son Company while Hill was employed there.[46] In particular, Akro Agate may have used the recipe to make the Cornelian (now known as Carnelian), which was purchased by M. F. Christensen from Harvey "Harry" James Layton, for one of its early colors. Layton's original idea was to duplicate the carnelian stone agate—a popular shooter at the time.

While located in Akron, Akro Agate bought marbles in bulk from the M. F. Christensen Company and sold them in its own packages.

M. F. Christensen and Son made both industrial and toy marbles, but it was the toy marbles that made history. Some of the glass marble brand names are Persian Turquoise, Oriental Jade, National Onyx, Royal Blue, American Cornelian, a limited production of Imperial Jade, and Moss Agate. Subsequently, new marbles were made of white onyx, purple onyx, and lavender (opaque). The two major marble designs are the American Cornelian and the National Onyx. The American Cornelian has variously colored stripes on reddish body glass; the National Onyx has white opaque striping on the following colors of body glass: white transparent, amber-brown, green, royal blue, purple, and the very rare black. Red or ruby colors were not included in this line.[47]

Color names similar to Christensen company brand names soon appeared at several other factories. Whatever the company's name for the two-color marbles, they have recently been designated by many different names.

A description of Christensen marbles is contained in *M.*

F. Christensen and the Perfect Glass Ball Machine by Michael C. Cohill. (The term "perfect glass ball" is misleading, since many of Christensen's marbles could be categorized as aberrations or rejects by today's standards. These marbles are now highly collectible; they are identified as "transitionals.")

THE DAVIS MARBLE WORKS
Pennsboro, West Virginia

The Davis Marble Works was founded in 1947, and production ended abruptly in 1948. The Davis enterprise was inspired by the Chinese Checkers craze and by the apparent success of several local marble factories in Ritchie County, West Virginia. After returning home from World War II in 1946, Wilson Davis entered into a partnership with his father and constructed a metal building on their farm property outside of Pennsboro. They first sought help from Roy and Murphy Michels of Champion Agate, but in vain. The Michels were afraid of competition. However, L. E. Alley, a well-known glassman making marbles at St. Marys, West Virginia, received Davis warmly and told him that he had sold a marble machine to Corning Glass for experimentation, and that it

Examples of the very early machine-made marbles called the National Onyx line by M. F. Christensen & Son of Akron, Ohio. The line consisted of white opaque striping with body glass of the following

colors: white transparent, amber-brown, green, royal blue, purple, and the very rare black. A body color of red or ruby was never used with this marble.

A selection of Heaton Agate Company marbles.

might be available. Davis located and rented a farm truck, drove to Corning, New York, purchased the machine, and returned to West Virginia at a total cost of $800.

The company's first production came in early 1947. Davis held a meeting with the "big" marble makers in the area in an attempt to sell his marbles. The effort was unsuccessful, and Davis decided to market his own marbles as an independent.

He placed an ad in the Sunday edition of the *New York Times*, soliciting business for the new company. It resulted in an estimated one hundred replies. With that response, Wilson Davis decided to go to New York during the Easter season of 1947 to follow up on the most likely prospects. An important toy producer took Davis to lunch and struck a deal with him. Marbles for the toy producer were shipped through Brooklyn, New York, to Puerto Rico, which received 99 percent of the total production. Davis employed two to three women to package the marbles in net bags; as the price competition stiffened, the company switched to cardboard boxes. Adding more financial strain, the price of glass cullet rose from $10 to roughly $110 a ton during the boom time that Davis practiced his craft.

Davis Marble Works made about fourteen million marbles, and its last eight-hour shift in the spring of 1948 produced eight five-gallon buckets of marbles. Competition was too keen to continue operation.

The building was subsequently used as a farm shed; it was destroyed by a rare West Virginia tornado in the 1980s. So ended the stormy history of one of several marble factories in Ritchie County.[48]

THE HEATON AGATE COMPANY
Cairo, West Virginia

Founded in 1939 by William Heaton, the Heaton Agate Company used a Pennsboro, West Virginia, mailing address, but its production facilities were located at Cairo.

Heaton produced a Cat Eye design in 1939 and 1940, more than a decade before the design was imported from Japan. Apparently William Heaton got the idea for his Cat Eye design from glass eyes produced in Mexico for stuffed animals. It was a case of an idea before its time. The design did not sell and was forgotten until the early 1950s, when the Cat Eye design imported from Japan caused a major change in children's preferences for marbles.

Heaton plant employees called marbles in the standard $5/8$-inch diameter size "game shooters" and the $3/4$-inch marbles "shooters."

In 1971 the plant and a quantity of packaged Heaton marbles were purchased by Clayton E. Bogard and his sons, and the name changed. (See section on C. E. Bogard & Son Agate Company.) The facility was in operation under the name of the Bogard Company until 1987.

Heaton produced Chinese Checkers from about 1939 to 1949, in colors of blue, light blue, white, green, and purple in ⁹/₁₆-inch diameters; they were sold in bags of sixty under the trade name Big Shot.

Other types produced were Marine Gems (Transparents), Translucents, an Opaque Solid striped variety, Transparent Swirls and Translucent Swirls, Opaque Swirls, Patched Opaques, and during the 1960s, Cat Eyes in white, light purple, light blue, dark blue, black, and light green.

IOWA CITY FLINT GLASS MANUFACTURING COMPANY
Iowa City, Iowa

The significance of this company, which is often called Iowa City Glass, is that as far as has been determined, it was the only documented American company to produce handmade glass marbles commercially during the nineteenth century. To be sure, there are isolated examples of End of Day marbles from other companies, but those were souvenirs, not regular products of the companies.

The Iowa City Flint Glass Manufacturing Company is rarely mentioned in antique references, partially due to its short life. All of the following information comes from two sources, Mariam Righter's *Iowa City Glass*, and Dr. J. W. Carberry's *Iowa City Flint Glass Manufacturing Company 1880-1882 Price Guide*, both published in 1982.

Incorporated on April 30, 1880, the plant was located at Kirkwood Avenue and Madison Lane in Iowa City. Iowa City was chosen because of its central geographical location, nearby sources of raw materials, and proximity to an expanding population of customers. The company began production about one year after incorporation, in the spring of 1881, and employed about 150 men. The plant superintendent was J. H. Leighton.

The company was founded to produce pressed glass, a popular item during that period. The production of marbles was apparently a minor sideline, and it is not known how many were produced. It is reported that the company made "glass marbles and that, inside some of the marbles, would be white birds and the like."[49] Those marbles pictured in Dr. Carberry's price guide are typical Latticino Swirls[50] and an End of Day marble.[51] The reported Sulphides are not pictured in either of the references cited.

The company closed in the early summer of 1882, having manufactured glass products for a little over a year, perhaps a year and a half. One of the main factors contributing to its demise may have been that the sand intended for use in the glass turned out to be unsuitable, leading to a lower quality product and much breakage. Rising freight rates and the lack of north-south freight lines through that part of the country also added to the problems of the ailing company. Competition from older and larger Eastern firms was a major factor as well. Righter reports that perhaps the most significant problem was the rough nature of the many workers imported to Iowa City from the East. Their heavy drinking, gambling, and brawling were a cause of concern for the general citizenry, eroding support of the "solid citizens" for the enterprise.[52]

After the glass factory closed, the plant itself was not occupied again for almost a decade, when it was used as a glove factory by E. F. Rate and Sons. The glove factory operated in the building until 1898, when a fire destroyed the facility. The site is currently occupied by a gasoline filling station.

JABO, INCORPORATED
Reno, Ohio

This marble factory was organized in early 1987 and is owned by a group of stockholders. JABO's machines are from the Bogard Company in Cairo, West Virginia; the machines were modified and have new chute feeders designed by one of the employees, who claims a 30 percent increase in productivity. JABO uses two larger-than-standard-size melting tanks. Each tank feeds two duplex machines, and each can hold enough glass to run for eighteen hours without refilling with cullet. Sensors to monitor melting temperatures are not installed in the tank; however, temperatures are maintained between 2,200 and 2,400 degrees Fahrenheit. Daily estimated production using two duplex machines is 1,250,000 marbles.

In early June 1991 there was a change in JABO's corporate structure. Jack Bogard became general manager; Dave McCullough, former plant manager at Champion Agate, was appointed vice president; Claude G. "Buck" Lamp was named factory maintenance supervisor; and Joanne L. Argabrite was made chief executive officer.

Although JABO began with industrial marbles, it has extended its line to include toy marbles. The combined expertise of Bogard and McCullough will no doubt result in some wonderful collectible marbles. The acquisition of marble machines from Vitro Agate, Anacortes, Washington, and that company's stock of marbles, together with the assets of JABO should make this factory a leading contender in the marble business. The stock of Vitro Agate, Anacortes, marbles—loose or packaged—is now considered highly collectible.

THE JACKSON MARBLE COMPANY
Tollgage, West Virginia

Carol Jackson, founder of the Jackson Marble Company, was a machine operator at Champion Agate and left there to start his own company about 1945. It was a bad time to start a new marble business, as the demand for marbles was on the decline. The new venture did not succeed and went out of business soon after its beginning.

The factory was located along old U.S. 50, near the outskirts of Pennsboro. It was on the east side of Number 7 tunnel of the abandoned B&O railroad at Tollgate, across the highway from the Pennsboro Apostolic Church. The original building was constructed of concrete block with a metal roof. When the factory closed, the building was expanded to accommodate a Ford Motor sales and repair venture. The abandoned building is owned by George Murphy of Pennsboro.[53]

Production of the Jackson Marble Company was limited to about two boxcar loads of marbles, which Jackson was not able to sell on the retail market. He did sell them to other marble makers, however, including

Champion Agate. Twenty-one years later, Champion included some of the Jackson marbles in its 1976 Bicentennial Pack, which included marbles made by many different American companies.

One known type of marble produced by Jackson was a conglomerate of clear body glass with one of six different colors of striping in a randomly swirled design, sometimes called Slag.

The marble collection of Bud Sweiger of Clarksburg, West Virginia, contains a fair sample of marbles made at Jackson. They appear to be quite similar to marbles made at Cairo Novelty Company in Cairo, West Virginia.

KOKOMO OPALESCENT GLASS COMPANY, INC.
Kokomo, Indiana

The Kokomo Opalescent Glass Company was established in 1888 and continues its operations at 1310 South Market Street, Kokomo, Indiana. The company's primary product is opalescent rolled sheet glass, which has found its way into lamps, domes, cathedral glass, and products of the famous Tiffany's. The company name is obviously derived from the city of Kokomo, which in turn was named in honor of a celebrated chieftain of the Miami Indians (Ko-ko-mo-ko), who was known for his many acts of kindness and humanity toward early white settlers.

In the late 1930s company officials faced a decision about how to dispose of some defective plate glass. Despite some uncertainty among the company officers, it was decided to use the rejected glass to produce marbles. All Kokomo glass is recipe glass, not recycled from prior uses, and is made using fine quartz sand from the famous sand pits in Ottawa, Illinois—also the source of sand for the Peltier Glass Company of Ottawa, Illinois.

Marbles were made directly from the rejected glass, and no remixing of colors was done to achieve a particular color for the marbles themselves. A single marble machine, typical in design and function to other marble-making machines of that period, was installed. It was capable of rolling out several different sizes of marbles; rollers of various diameter were kept in nearby racks.

Marbles made by the company were sold only by Kokomo, and not to other marble companies. They were packaged in mesh bags and boxes showing Chief Kokomo. A net bag of Kokomo marbles displayed for sale at the Marble Collectors Unlimited annual meet in Amana, Iowa, in 1989 depicts a bust of the chief in full feather headdress on each side of the label with the name "Kokomo" in the center. A Kokomo boxed item and sample of marbles made by the company are on display in the Elwood Haynes Museum in Kokomo.

A selection of marbles from the collection of Wallace C. Huffman, who was a member of the board of directors of the museum in the 1960s, showed a wide variety of colors but a limited number of designs.

Marbles appear to be from the latter period of marble production, the late 1930s or early 1940s, and are generally indistinguishable from similar marbles made by several other companies of that period. Comparison of marbles with known samples of Kokomo marbles is highly recommended for identification.

Marble production stopped before the end of World War II and the machine was sold to the Peltier Glass Company. Fortunate is the marble collector who has samples of these marbles, particularly in original packages, and especially the beautiful Ribboned Translucent featuring pumpkin orange on clear crystal.

Marbles Made by Kokomo Opalescent Glass Company

Opaque: Black.
Patched Opaques: Green on white; red on white; brown on white.
Ribboned Opaques: Orange on white; light blue on white; yellow on white; brown on white.
Patched Transparents: white and green on clear body; blue on dark blue body.
Patched and Ribboned Transparents: Red and white on light green; red and white on light blue.
Ribboned Transparents: White on dark blue.
Ribboned Translucents: Light blue on white; orange on clear crystal. (This orange is a particularly deep, rich color, unlike the reddish-yellow seen in many marbles.)[54] Several of the above designs contain seedy glass.

MARBLE KING, INCORPORATED/ BERRY PINK INDUSTRIES
St. Marys and Paden City, West Virginia

In 1949 Berry Pink and Sellers H. Peltier bought L. E. Alley's Alley Glass Manufacturing Company, which was then located near the intersection of Creel and 3rd Streets in St. Marys. Peltier was the son of Victor Peltier, founder of Peltier Glass. Pink owned 51 percent and Peltier 49 percent of the company. They named the new company Marble King, Inc.; Pink hired Roger Howdyshell as plant manager. Pink, located at corporate headquarters in New York City, managed the promotion and sales efforts of the company, while Howdyshell was in charge of day-to-day operations at the factory. Although Pink and Howdyshell are gone now, the company they built remains a vital part of the modern marble industry.

For the first few months, Marble King only sold marbles, it did not make them. Marbles produced by Peltier Glass Company of Ottawa, Illinois, were sold under the Marble King label until Marble King, Inc., became a producing company in July, 1949. Marble King continued operations in St. Marys until the plant was destroyed by fire in 1958. Howdyshell moved the company's machines to Paden City, and marble production resumed there within sixty days of the fire. The Paden City plant remains in operation today.

There is no doubt that it was the combined talents of Howdyshell and Pink that made Marble King an early leader in the industry. Pink, the more visible of the two, was a famous promoter in the 1930s; he became involved with marbles as early as 1922, sponsoring a marble tournament that year.[55]

Pink sponsored a Marble King Tournament at the site of the New York World's Fair in 1939 but disappeared from the marble scene for most of the 1940s. He reappeared in 1949 and lived the role of the "Marble King." Pink had no children, but he loved them and the game of marbles. He was often photographed playing marbles with children as part of his promotional efforts. Pink always wore a hat at these times because he was bald and did not want the youngsters to think he was too old to play. Pink's interest in the game was more than a publicity ploy. He was an excellent marble player. Karl Heim of the *New York Post* reported that Pink could stand six feet off and "plop a cats eye into the mouth of a recumbent milk bottle. He can also bust a glass bottle ten feet off."

As related earlier, the incursion of the Japanese Cat Eye design in 1950–1951 dealt an almost fatal blow to the already suffering domestic marble industry. The Japanese design was an immense success; American children lost interest in practically all other marble designs. United States marble makers, led by Marble King, attempted to curb the flow of imports by appeals to Congress for import duties, but their efforts were not successful.

In 1955 Howdyshell, Duncan V. Peltier, and Berry Pink made a trip to Japan in an attempt to buy a manufacturing plant there or to have the Japanese make Cat Eyes for Marble King. Their attempts failed, but on the trip they learned how to produce the design and put that knowledge to use on their return to West Virginia.

This extremely significant achievement bore fruit in early 1955, when Marble King produced the first American Cat Eye marbles. It was only the acquisition of this design that allowed Marble King (and other American marble makers) to survive. Marble King's Cat Eye design has not changed significantly in the three decades since its development and more closely resembles its Japanese ancestor than do other U.S. Cat Eye designs.

The new 1955 Cat Eye soon appeared as a promotional premium in Post Toasties cereal, a product of General Foods. The marbles were shipped in bulk and packaged in a clear cellophane tube. The tube contained six Cat Eyes that were typical of the four-blade single-color Cat Eye produced at that time; the colors were opaque white, azure, light red, and yellow. General foods in 1955–1956 placed a standing order with Marble King for one hundred million Cat Eyes. Pink, however, operating out of the main office in New York City, had overcommitted his factory, and it was necessary to defer some of the production to Vitro Agate Company.[56] A General Foods ad contained in *Life* magazine of March 28, 1955, shows the marbles loose in front of an empty box and not in a cellophane tube.

Beyond the Cat Eye coup, another significant development credited to Roger Howdyshell was a process called veneering. In veneering, a single-colored core of cheaper white opaque glass is covered with a thin layer or veneer of more expensive colored glass that forms the design. This production method was first used in the 1940s and continued until the mid-1950s. Subsequently transparent or translucent colored glass was used in the body.

Marbles produced by the veneering method are not easily identified; unfortunately for the marble collector, quite often the only way to determine if a marble is veneered is to break it. Certain designs, like Marble King's Rainbows, were produced by both veneered and non-veneered production methods. Most American companies have used veneering at some time.

The next significant development for the company came in 1963, when Howdyshell, Duncan V. (Don) Peltier, and Cornell Medley bought Marble King, Inc., and Berry Pink Industries.

In 1965 Berry Pink Industries was dissolved and became Berry Pink Industries Division of Marble King, Inc. Interestingly, for a time in 1967, marbles produced by Marble King were sold by the Peltier Glass Company.

In 1983 Howdyshell, who had been personally selected by Pink as plant manager in 1949, became the sole owner of the company. His reign as Marble King ended when he died on April 18, 1991. His wife, Jean, became president the following day and still serves in that capacity.

Continuing Pink's commitment to the national marbles scene, Marble King contributed to the annual National Marble Tournament in Wildwood, New Jersey, from 1968 to 1987. Creative Athletic Products and Services, Inc., of

The legendary Berry Pink, who did more than anyone to make marbles one of the most popular games in the U.S., and two of his youthful friends. Berry not only manufactured marbles but conducted hundreds of tournaments, awarding trophies and creating marble champs in almost every important city in the U.S. The photographer is unknown. Courtesy of the late Roger W. Howdyshell, President, Marble King, Inc.

The Spider-Man package is just one of a variety of Marble King blister packs valued by collectors. This one was produced in 1979, and comes with forty blue and red marbles and a nylon mesh bag and plastic carrier.

Howdyshell one of America's fifty-one "success stories."

Marbles Produced by Marble King

Toy and decorative marbles in Opaque and Transparent are produced in three body finishes—iridescent, frosted, and standard—in thirty-two color combinations. At present, marbles are sold in poly bags, mesh bags, and in bulk; other package options are available.

Cat Eyes: Marble King's design of Cat Eye is very similar to its ancestor, the Japanese-style Cat Eye, in that it has four very well-defined "X" blades that are joined in the center. The only difference between the two types is that in Marble King's Cat Eyes the blades are more wavy than the straight-vaned Japanese style, but this may vary slightly from marble to marble.

In early years, the Cat Eye was produced in one, two, and four colors within a single marble in sizes from 5/8 inch to 1½ inches. The single-colored type is seen in white, red, yellow, light bluish-white, blue, dark blue, green, dark green, and orange-yellow. The two-colored variety was made only a short time, in St. Marys, before the 1958 fire; the blades were blue and yellow in alternating sequence. Larger 1-inch Cat Eye shooters with single-colored blades were packaged under the Peltier and Marble King labels.

After the 1958 fire and the relocation to Paden City, Marble King produced a four-colored, four-vaned Cat Eye. The four-colored type has blades of red, dark blue, dark green, and yellow. Made only in 1959–1960, this design was short-lived, as it was expensive to make and did not sell well. It occurred in both 5/8-inch and 1-inch sizes. Recently Marble King revived this design, but in 1-inch and 1¼-inch sizes.

At present, the Cat Eye with a single-color blade is made in red, green, white, and blue in 1 inch, and the yellow Cat Eye is made in 1 inch, 7/8 inch, 3/4 inch, 5/8 inch, and 9/16 inch.

Marble King, Inc., is the only United States company to produce Cat Eyes with two or four different colors of blades in each marble.

Opaques: Sizes as above, plus a 3/8-inch black industrial variety produced in the early 1980s. Eleven colors are available—opal pink, ivory, blue, blue-gray, gray, black, yellow, jade, seafoam, white, and red; and three types of body finish—iridescent, frosted, and standard. Opaques were produced from the earliest days of Marble King's operations (1949-present).

Opaque Patched and Ribboned: The Rainbow is made in green-white, red-white, blue-white, black-white, and red-yellow and white. The famous black-yellow Bumble Bee, black-red Black Widow, and yellow (gold)-blue Cub Scout were discontinued several years ago; these are now quite collectible, particularly in larger sizes.

Opaque Patched and Ribboned types made by Marble

Des Moines, Iowa, took over sponsorship in 1988. Howdyshell was a member of the executive committee of the National Marbles Tournament, and the tournament in 1991 was sponsored by Marble King in his memory. The Howdyshells' daughter, Beri Howdyshell Fox (named for Berry Pink) was appointed to fill her father's position on the executive committee and assumed responsibility for news and publicity at the 1991 meet. (Beri is very active in promoting marbles tournaments and fields her own team called "Marble Kings." Her team won second-place honors at the World's Marbles Championship at the Greyhound Pub, Tinsley Green, England, on April 17, 1992, and was awarded a sterling silver cup called the "Roger Howdyshell Memorial Cup.")

Howdyshell was a leading figure in the marble industry, and he remains a treasured legend of West Virginia. Honoring his progression from office manager to president and owner of Marble King, the June 1993 issue of *Entrepreneur* magazine designated Roger

Contemporary Rainbows and Cat Eyes produced by Marble King, Inc., in sizes ranging from ⅞ inch to 1¼ inch. These marbles have the same classic designs as previous versions, but some slight change in color is evident. These designs are unusual and quite collectible in these sizes. Marble King is one of the five U.S. companies still manufacturing marbles. Courtesy Roger W. Howdyshell.

King appear in both veneered and non-veneered varieties. The non-veneered types include color combinations of red and black, yellow and black, and blue and white.

This type was also distributed in a promotional package for Coca-Cola and Pepsi-Cola in colors of red, blue, yellow, green, and black, all with white body glass; also black and yellow; and blue and burgundy.

Mr. Peanuts promotional packages also contained Opaque Patched and Ribbons, in the same colors as the soda pop packages.

Opaque Swirls: colors of green, blue, red, purple, and orange in white body glass from pre-1958 St. Marys fire; red, green, blue, and yellow in white body glass, as seen in the bottle hanger packages.

Patched Opaques: Sold at first in cotton mesh, later in poly bags, and finally in rigid plastic blister packs, in sizes from ⁵⁄₁₆ inch to 1 inch. Color combinations of red on white; blue on white; blue and red on white; red and yellow on white; green and red and yellow and blue on white; red-orange and light green and yellow and blue and purple on bluish-white.

Promotional Marbles: A wide variety of promotional marbles and packages have been produced by Marble King, including the Big Blue Marble made in 1974 as part of International Telephone and Telegraph's promotion of the National Marbles Tournament (see Chapter V), as well as marbles promoting the state of West Virginia and Marble King itself. "Wild and Wonderful West Virginia" and "Almost Heaven West Virginia" adorn that state's promotional marble, and the words "Marble King" accompanied by a round-faced boy with a crown hat are on the company's marble.

Special production promotional marbles are usually opaque, so that logos and slogans show up on the surface. There is usually some other design as well, such as patches or ribbons, with the logos and words placed between the design colors—on the West Virginia marbles in particular.

While Marble King was still located in St. Marys, the Esso Oil Company placed loose Marble King marbles (Cat Eyes and Rainbows) as a promotion in large blue-striped barrels with an Esso decal at their stations, and customers were offered a handful of marbles with fill-ups.

Promotions with regular marbles were also produced, including bottle-hanger packages for Coca-Cola and Pepsi-Cola, Mr. Peanuts packages, and the General Foods Post Toasties premium of the mid-1950s, all mentioned above.

Translucent Ribboned: Still being made; yellow, green,

red, orange, and red and green on milky white body.

Patched Translucents: This variety is still being made.

Transparents: Produced in various sizes and colors.

Transparent Patched: Sold under the brand name of Rainbows. Produced in $9/16$-inch size normally, but also in $1\frac{1}{4}$ inches in 1984; a $1\frac{1}{2}$-inch diameter is anticipated in the near future.

In addition to regular marbles, Howdyshell also produced glass spheres as small as 5 millimeters for the deco market; this is believed to be the smallest sphere to be produced on a marble-making machine.

Currently, Marble King, Inc., is producing Sparklet Gems with three body finishes—iridescent, frosted, and standard—in thirty-two color combinations. These objects are also produced by other marble makers and are called flats, nuggets, or pebbles. They are used in the hobbies, crafts, and decorating industries.

THE MASTER GLASS COMPANY
Bridgeport, West Virginia (mailing address Clarksburg)

In August 1941, Clinton F. Israel bought all the equipment and supplies of the Master Marble Company and began business as the Master Glass Company in the Old Chimney Glass plant in Bridgeport. Production of marbles began in the same year using the old Master Marble machines designed by John F. Early. The letterhead on a September 1, 1952, price list to jobbers and wholesalers shows Master Glass Company as a manufacturer of signal and automotive lenses, pressed ware, Master Marbles, and glass balls.

When the Akro Agate Company closed in 1951, Israel purchased a considerable stock of Akro boxes, some Akro marbles, the Akro glass formulas, and the right to use the Akro trademark. For some time, Master Glass sold both this old Akro stock and some of its own marbles in boxes marked Akro Agates. Master Glass also had boxes made that used the Akro Agate trade name, in which they placed Master Marbles and sold them after 1951.[57]

In Master Glass advertising dated September 1952, both Master Made Marbles and Akro Agates are shown (Chinese Checkers in this case). Marble packages and advertising produced by the Master Glass Company are sometimes confused with those of the Master Marble Company, as the term "Master Marbles" is often used on the products of Master Glass.

The company closed on September 1, 1973; the plant was in ruins by the next year and was bulldozed for a public parking lot. Clinton F. Israel, who had been active in the marble industry since its heyday in the 1920s, died in 1975.

Marbles produced by the Master Glass Company include many types. The list below is probably not a complete list of this company's production. Colors listed under each type are known examples; however, there is no reason why any color produced under one particular type could not be used in any other types.

The same is true of the sizes of marbles—a particular machine is built or set to produce a 1-inch marble; it could just as easily be one design as another. It is safe to assume that the size range known for Transparents could be seen in Opaques or other types as well. The sizes known range from approximately $5/8$ inch up to $1\frac{1}{8}$ inches, but the

marbles vary slightly off the $1/16$-inch standard increments. That is, what the maker would have sold as a $5/8$-inch marble might be $1/32$ inch more or less than the ideal $5/8$-inch measurement. This characteristic was true of many marbles, not just those made by Master Glass. It was not necessarily a fault; perfect diameters were not that critical to children.

Marbles Produced by Master Glass

Cat Eyes: Blades rather indefinite (thin, slightly transparent), some examples cage-like. Colors include white, green, red, and purple.

Opaques: Colors of white, light blue, blue, light green, green, dark green, and yellow; sometimes "gathered" like the Transparents.

Opaque Brushed: Purple brushed on black body.

Opaque Patched: Colors of red on white, blue on white, blue-black on white, green on blue, and red-orange on yellow.

Opaque Patched and Ribboned: Orange patch and ribbon on yellow body.

Transparents: Colors including clear, red, dark red, blue, green, dark green, yellow, gold, orange-yellow, and more unusual colors such as dark burgundy and dark gray. In some of the Transparents the coloring itself seems to have a faint pattern, as if it were gathered together at the two poles of the marble. This may be due to incomplete mixing of the coloring material and the body glass; the gathering at two points would be caused by the mechanics of the glass feed and cutoff operations.

Transparent Brushed: Orange-yellow on clear; partially gathered at poles.

THE MASTER MARBLE COMPANY
Anmoore, West Virginia

After resigning over disagreements with their employer, key personnel of the Akro Agate Company at Clarksburg, West Virginia, organized and formed their own company, the Master Marble Company, on May 20, 1930. The factory was located at Anmoore, West Virginia, and the mailing address was at Clarksburg.

The initial founders of the new company were John F. Early, Claude C. Grimmett, and John E. Moulton; they later invited Clinton F. Israel, who had also just resigned from Akro, to join them. Their positions in the new company were: Claude C. Grimmett, president; John E. Moulton, vice president and sales manager; Clinton F. Israel, secretary and chemist; and John F. Early, treasurer and factory superintendent. The new company was not long in producing its first marbles, which were shipped on or about October 25, 1930.

The marble machine used by Master Marble was

designed in 1930 by John F. Early. The new company spent some $9,000 in experimenting and producing its own machine. An earlier machine scrapped by Akro Agate was used only for experimental purposes. While it was not patented, it still had several significant differences from Early's earlier patented machines then in use by the Akro Agate Company. Initially Master Marble experimented with the use of offset grooves but found that offset grooves were not suited to the type of rolls Master Marble contemplated using; any misalignment resulted in imperfect and unmarketable marbles. The machine developed and used by Master Marble had opposed rolls with helical grooves, the centers of which were directly opposite to one another and were not offset; the grooves of the lower roll were shallower and narrower than the grooves on the upper roll, which were deeper and

The Master Marble Company at Anmoore, West Virginia. This photo comes from "Master Marble Makers," an article in the October 1931 West Virginia Review. Author and photographer are unknown.

partially overlapped the lower roll on both sides; there was a slight taper of about $1/32$ inch on one roll. Nevertheless, the machine produced marbles of equal quality to the Akro machines. The new Early machines were made by Fisher Brothers, Washington Mold and Foundry, Pennsylvania.

During Master Marble's first year of business, Akro Agate tried to buy them out, but the new partners refused to sell. This refusal resulted in a price war, in which Akro Agate cut its prices 30 percent, endeavoring to lower the price to the point that the new company could not remain in business. Akro Agate, still believing it had been wronged by the owners of Master Marble, induced one of its employees to spy upon the new company to obtain evidence of patent infringements. He was caught on the premises, arrested, tried, convicted, sentenced and fined. Akro Agate paid the fine to get him released from jail.

Since its attempt to gather evidence of wrongful conduct or unfair trade practices by Master Marble had failed, Akro Agate filed suit in District Court of the United States for the Northern District of West Virginia, charging the Master Marble Company and its officers with patent infringement and conspiracy to create and enter into business of manufacturing and selling marbles in competition with Akro Agate The court proceedings lasted from 1933 to 1937, but in the end the case was decided in favor of Master Marble. (See Chapter XIII on Patent Suits.)

Master Marble was the sole concessionaire for marbles at the 1933 Chicago World's Fair. Their exhibit was called the House of Marbles, with walls of plate glass filled with five million marbles. The building had a sign reading "Master Marble Shop," and inside were displays of marbles produced by the company, most notably the famous College Edition. (An illustration of the Master Marbles Shop appeared in *Ripley's Believe It or Not* on December 1, 1991.) This building is displayed on the cardboard covers of the College Edition and another special edition for the Fair. The covers also displayed a color panorama of the Fair itself.

Former Akro Agate officials at their newly formed Master Marble Company factory. From left to right, they are: Clinton F. Israel, in charge of shipping and assistant to Early; John E. Moulton, sales manager; John F. Early, plant superintendent; and Claude C. Grimmett, general manager. Courtesy of J. Fred Early.

The College Edition boxes were produced exclusively for the Fair but contained current marbles (i.e., the marbles were not specially produced for the Fair). The College Edition included an assortment of varieties packaged in a red box with a velour-like surface; besides the marbles, it included a knuckle pad and chamois marble bag. Another edition contained only the marbles and the bag.

A 1936 magazine article says Master Marble sold one-half million "premium" boxes of marbles to Popsicle,[58] but the main point of the article was that the heyday of marbles had passed.

In 1935-1936 Claude Grimmett lost his Master Marble Company stock in a bank foreclosure, and John Moulton also dropped out of company ownership, leaving only

1933 Century of Progress special edition of one hundred assorted marbles and a highly decorated leather pouch with a panorama of the House of Marbles. These editions were only sold at the fair at the Master Marble Shop. This particular boxed edition had the fair panorama on the outside cover; another edition had the panorama on the inside cover. A highly collectible boxed item and rather rare. Photo by Dennis E. Webb.

"Master Made Marbles" by the Master Marble Company. The package on the right was a promotional item for Posicle-Fudgsicle, a popular frozen treat. The message on the bottom of the box reads, "This is your reward for being a booster of delicious frozen confections on a stick." J. Fred Early Collection.

Clinton Israel and John F. Early of the original owners. In 1939 or 1940 Early was voted out of management by Israel and outside owners. Early still owned stock, which he sold to George Moore; Early later retired and moved back to Ohio.

The Master Marble Company closed in early 1941 and sold its land and buildings to the National Carbon Company on April 18, 1941. In August of the same year, the only remaining original founder, Clinton Israel, bought all of the equipment and remaining supplies of the Master Marble Company and went into business as the Master Glass Company at the location of the Old Chimney Glass plant at Bridgeport.

Marbles Made by The Master Marble Company

Opaques: Known to have made black Opaques, probably many other colors as well.
Patched Opaques: Red-brown on light green, black on yellow, red on yellow, red on white, black on white, blue on white.
Tiger Eyes: Made from 1930 to 1935, this distinctive type had a transparent body glass with many different colors of striping running between two poles of the marble. Striping colors included black, green, blue, red, yellow, and white. The Tiger Eye is a scarce, beautiful, and collectible marble.
Translucents: Opal glass in single colors of ivory, yellow, green, blue, red, white, and purple; brand name Comet. Also known as Milkies or Alabaster Solids; included in the 1933 World's Fair packages.
Brushed Translucents: This type had a red design in milky white body glass.
Patched Translucents: Known as Meteors, or Alabasters; milky white body glass with patch of dark green, red, blue, black, or yellow; also in yellow body glass with white, green, or red patches. They were sold in 1933 World's Fair packages.
Transparents: Brand names Clearie and Litho; made in crystal (no color), yellow, green, red, amethyst, and azure.
Brushed Transparents: Mixtures of colors brushed on surface and interior of clear body; colors include red, white, and black.

MID-ATLANTIC OF WEST VIRGINIA, INCORPORATED
Ellenboro, West Virginia

The Mid-Atlantic Glass Corporation was founded in 1937 by a group of enterprising and experienced glassworkers. Over the years, Mid-Atlantic Glass became well known in the glass industry for its good quality and competitive prices. The company ceased operations in March 1987.

In May 1987 Mid-Atlantic Glass reorganized under new ownership to become Mid-Atlantic of West

Virginia, Inc.; the company remained at the same location in Ellenboro on Route 18. The officers are Ronald Spencer, president; Michael Hall, vice president; and Charlotte Hall (Michael's spouse), secretary.

With the purchase of molds from West Virginia Glass Specialty Company, Inc., the reformed product line

Mid-Atlantic of West Virginia, Ellenboro, West Virginia. This rear view of its marble-making building shows three machines, with the one at right in use. Note the cullet in the foreground. Photo by Dennis Webb.

greatly expanded, still stressing high grade soda-lime crystal products.

The new company increased its sales line with "gems" (flats) purchased locally from a marble factory. However, the customer demand could not be filled. Since a marble machine is necessary to produce gems, which in reality are gobs of glass that do not go through the marble-forming rollers, the company decided to further extend its line of glassware with marbles.

A nearby company-owned building became the site for this venture, and around November 2, 1990, production began with gems and crystal marbles of 9/16 inch in colors of dark blue, azure, clear crystal, pink, teal green, black, white opaque, and amethyst. Toy marbles are also made in 5/8 inch. Gems and marbles are sometimes given a frosted or iridescent finish.

The company makes high-quality marbles and gems using three new duplex marble machines. The recruitment of experienced glassmen from the nearby Champion Agate Company and Lewis L. Moore, former plant manager of Vitro Agate, as consultant makes Mid-Atlantic a leading contender. Moore has many years' experience in making marbles, and Mid-Atlantic will probably extend its marble line with multicolored marbles in new designs.

A display and salesroom in the main building contains a wide range of company-made crystal products, novelty items, paperweights, eggs, canes, ash trays, marbles, and gems. Of interest to marble collectors is the availability of marbles and gems at reasonable prices, as well as eggs and paperweights that contain antique marble colors and

designs such as Cloud, Swirl, and End of Day. Contemporary handmade marbles by the resident craftsman James C. "Jim" Davis in sizes up to three inches are also available. Some new designs are evident and are sold at a reasonable price.

Mid-Atlantic acquired the machine for making large marbles (up to 1¼ inch) owned by the House of Marbles in London in September 1992. Unfortunately, only Lewis L. Moore of Vitro Agate, Parkersburg, was ever able to produce acceptable marbles on this machine, and in 1994 it was shipped to the House of Marbles museum in England.

The Mid-Atlantic factory was the scene of the Mid-Atlantic Festival of Marbles held July 11, 1992. Members of the West Virginia Marbles Association earned top honors. Some of the youths entering the competition participated in the National Marbles Tournament in Wildwood, New Jersey, in 1992. The theme of the West Virginia Marbles Association is "Shoot Marbles, Not Drugs."

THE NAVARRE GLASS MARBLE AND SPECIALTY COMPANY
Navarre and Steubenville, Ohio

One of the earliest American attempts in the glass marble-making industry was the Navarre Glass Marble and Specialty Glass Company, which was founded in Navarre, Ohio, in 1897. The company produced handmade glass marbles but soon failed in business. It reopened in Steubenville in 1902 under the direction of Emile P. Converse.[59]

Jeremiah J. Leiter, of Canton, Ohio, had invented and patented a "Tool for Making Marbles" in 1903, which was assigned to Converse. Leiter's device was a technological step behind an 1898 patent by Christian C. Hill, which was called a "Machine for Rolling Balls." Even though Hill's 1898 device was superior to Leiter's, Hill's was apparently never used to make marbles. Even so, Leiter's machine was not enough to make Navarre successful, and the company again failed.[60]

The company's factory was purchased by Martin F. Christensen and reopened by the company bearing his name sometime before 1905.[61]

THE NIVISON-WEISKOPF COMPANY
Cincinnati, Ohio

The Nivison-Weiskopf Company is referred to in the court records of the Akro Agate Company vs. Master Marble Company lawsuit as being in the marble-making business during the years 1921–1924.

Specifically, the records refer to the "Miller-Nivison-Weiskopf machine," which was built in 1919–1920, and sold and delivered to Nivison-Weiskopf in March 1920 by W. J. Miller of Swissvale, Pennsylvania. (See Chapter XII on Patents.)

The machine was put into use in February 1921 and used until January 1924. It produced the following quantities of marbles for Nivison-Weiskopf:

1921	854,940
1922	474,842
1923	1,374,075

Specific designs produced by the Nivison-Weiskopf Company are unknown.

THE PELTIER GLASS COMPANY
Ottawa, Illinois

The Peltier Glass Company is the oldest surviving marble maker in the United States and continues to produce high-quality pressware and colorful marbles. The company was founded in 1886 as the Novelty Glass Company by Victor J. Peltier. The name was changed to the Peltier Glass Company after the original factory burned down in 1919. The *Ottawa (Ill.) Daily Republican-Times*, October 21, 1919, headlined the Novelty Glass fire with a total loss of the factory at an estimated loss of $150,000. The fire was believed to have been caused by oil pipes that ignited in the furnace room. Two main buildings were destroyed: the main building of the plant and the abutting warehouse, both of tile and wood construction. Firemen saved the residence of Marie Peltier, not over 150 feet away from the flames.

Victor Peltier's sons Sellers and Joseph succeeded him in the business. His grandson Duncan (Don) Peltier also joined the business.[62] Joseph L. Jankowski, a widely known and respected glassman and long-term member of the Peltier organization, is the current president.

Documented sources show that Peltier began making marbles in 1927. Marbles were sold under several brand names and distributed by M. Gropper & Sons, Inc. An early inventory shows that in 1928 thirty-three million marbles were made.

Before the fire, art opalescent plate glass was the main product. This beautiful pane glass was sold for use in cathedral and Pullman car windows. After the fire, however, the immediate plan in addition to rebuilding was to produce marbles using the same recipe as for the company's opalescent glass.

The *American Flint* magazine of 1927 in an article "William J. Miller's Semi-Automatic Marble Machine" describes the machine used by Peltier in its marble-making effort.[63] Peltier's genius produced a marble that would retail at thirty marbles for a nickel. In addition to marbles, Peltier made glass gear shift knobs for automobiles in the late 1920s and early 1930s. A colorful flyer depicting an Indian chief shooting an arrow notes that twenty-seven different sizes of replacement headlamp lenses were available for automobiles made from 1928 to 1939. Peltier used a high-grade white quartz sand from the nearby Ottawa Silica Company.

Uranium oxide was used to make a bright chartreuse fluorescent color. No other types of oxides were used to produce this effect or color. The use of uranium oxide ceased with the advent of World War II, when no uranium was available. Peltier used cold cream jars (white opal glass) as a base for the variegated style of marbles and, of course, for Opaque marbles. However, Peltier's own glass formulas were used for striping. Hence, the Marine Crystals (Transparent colored) marbles that Peltier manufactured were all made using a Peltier formula or were formulas that Sellers Peltier had derived to suit particular needs.

An early historical and biographical sketch of Peltier is contained in *Ottawa in Nineteen Hundred*, compiled and privately published by E. Nattinger, Ottawa, Illinois.

The most famous of all marbles produced by Peltier were the "Picture Marbles" that featured the faces of famous comic strip characters. The process of applying an indicia to the surface of marbles was quite a coup for Peltier at the time. The process was apparently invented and patented by George W. Angerstein of Chicago, and Peltier used Angerstein's process under a contractual agreement. The agreement was dated October 1933, the same date that Angerstein applied for patent on his process. The patent was granted a year later, in September 1934 (Patent 1,972,854).

Knowledgeable informants in the Ottawa area described the patented process as follows: The marble blanks were stamped with a sticky oil substance in the shape of the desired picture, then powdered graphite was applied to the area. The marble was then placed on a tray of asbestos and heated until the graphite was fused into the marble glass. Flour sand was then sprinkled onto the marble and reheated; the sand melted and covered the picture with a thin layer of glass.

An old photo of the Novelty Glass Company in Ottawa, Illinois. The company was renamed the Peltier Glass Company in 1919 after this building was destroyed by fire. Courtesy of Joseph L. Jankowski.

All figures are black. Body glass of the blanks consisted of the following color combinations: black-white, red-white, green-white, blue-white, or green with yellow, blue and yellow (very rare), and blue and red (rare).[64]

The patent shows boiled linseed oil or sandalwood oil as the sticky oil substance. The heavier the oil and the finer the powder or dust, the more clean-cut the picture that resulted.

At that time the retail price of the Picture Marbles was two cents each, twice the price of other popular machine-made glass marbles. In spite of the technological triumph of this marble type, the design was not popular enough with buyers to sustain a very long life, and the Picture Marbles (Comic Strip) faded from popularity in the mid-1930s.

The faces on the comic marbles produced by Peltier were Orphan Annie, Skeezix, Betty Boop, Bimbo, Andy Gump, Koko, Kayo, Emma, Sandy, Smitty, Herbie, and Moon Mullins. The rare Cotes Bakery and Tom Mix marbles were also produced.

In order to determine how long ago the Picture Marbles were produced, James H. "Jim" Davis of New Orleans, Louisiana, a highly respected marbles researcher, targeted one marble, the Betty Boop marble, as the key figure in his research. He concluded that Picture Marbles were not made until the early 1930s.[65] This time period is confirmed. Examination of Peltier's payroll records show that $16.75 was expended on an "experimental lehr" and $8.40 on "experimental marble printing" on April 21, 1933. Then $2.13 was expended for "printing marbles" on April 28, 1933.[66] Apparently the experimental lehr was related to the annealing of Picture Marbles, which was different from the annealing process for other types of marbles.

On October 3, 1933, W. E. Weatherly, president of the Picture Marbles Glass Company of Chicago, advised the Peltier Glass Company that two salesmen took "ninety imperfect marbles to a school at dismissal time and that they were mobbed." The salesmen "gave a few to some kiddies and all wanted to know where they could be bought. They are placing some in the nearby store. The reaction was marvelous."

The letter concluded with a request to ship 8,800 to San Francisco on October 25; 16,320 to Jersey City on November 5; 12,600 to Baltimore on November 5; and 15,600 to Dallas on November 15. All of these were in boxes of five or twelve. Weatherly also asked that the

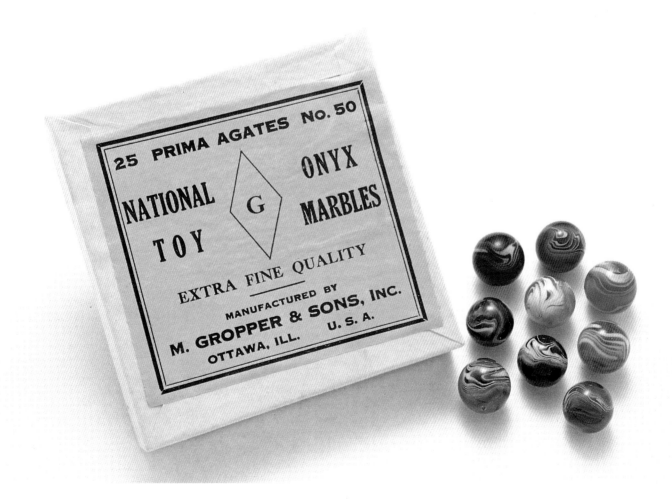

These early machine-made glass onyx marbles were made by Peltier Glass Company and marketed by M. Gropper and Sons, Inc., of Ottawa, Illinois. Complete sets of marbles and boxes in mint condition are rare and command high prices. (See Chapter XVI, Price Guide.) Peltier made onyx marbles in a variety of colors, all with white opaque swirls. Gino Biffany Collection.

marbles "all be rubbed in some way so as to make them shine as that is a great improvement." The Peltier Glass Company responded on October 4, 1933, and stated that the shipment was not up to the quality that was expected to be maintained and that "it is only by continuous every day operation with the glass itself and in this particular case it was mostly with the burning kiln which when heated up from a cold start does not maintain an even temperature that is so much desired and is better accomplished by continuous operation. A lot of 2,000 which we are sending today appears to us to be a much better grade." Apparently the Picture Marble Company did not manufacture Picture Marbles but rather retailed them for Peltier.

The patent and copyright then came into play. A December 7, 1933, letter from the law offices of Angerstein, Piggott & Angerstein of Chicago advised S. H. Peltier, president of the Peltier Glass Company, that they had written to Washington relative to Peltier's securing copyright of trademark of the words "Picture Marble." This letter also agrees with the contractual agreement dated October 1933 between George W. Angerstein and Peltier. Prior to the above exchange of letters, George Angerstein had filed an application to the U.S. Patent Office for a patent titled "Methods of Applying Indicia to Rounded Small Radius." The patent office gave it an application file date of October 13, 1933, Serial Number 693,441. Protection under the patent commenced on the filing date.

Picture Marbles became an instant success. The *Ceramic Industry* magazine of January 1934, in a story titled "Cartoon Glass Marbles Build Up New Business," stated that Peltier had already received orders for more than 500,000 and said, "the idea is 'cartoon' marbles have the picture of comic characters on it such as Andy Gump, Moon Mullins, Mutt & Jeff and others. Soon all well-known comic characters will appear on these marbles, and later it is expected to reproduce pictures of motion picture stars, big league ball players, and special marbles for Boy Scouts with the Boy Scout insignia on them." So far, there are no known examples of baseball players or Boy Scout insignia marbles.

Another promotional gimmick arose. James H. Forbes Tea & Coffee Company of St. Louis, Missouri, told grocers by a letter dated January 1934 that they would "redeem six Forbes Santa Fe Trail Coffee price tags for one box containing five picture marbles featuring characters from daily comic strips and movie screen cartoons. A suitable display card would be furnished by their salesmen."

Going back to the name of this fantastic collectible, several well-known authors label the type as "Comic" or "Comic Strip." However, the official factory name is "Picture Marbles."

The Peltier Glass Company was defendant in a 1929 lawsuit by the Akro Agate Company which charged that Peltier's marble-making machine (William J. Miller's 1926 Patent 1,601,699) was an infringement on Akro's Horace C.

Hill machine, patented 1915 (Patent 1,164,718). The suit was decided in favor of Akro but was reversed on appeal by Peltier. (See Patents and Patent Suits chapters.) Historically, this decision is referred to as the "breaking of the patent," which opened up the marble industry by allowing many other companies to start up in the marble business, using technologies already developed without fear of patent infringement.

Peltier experienced the same decline in sales as did other domestic makers due to the incursion of the Japanese Cat Eye in the mid-1950s. Peltier's total output for 1954 was 141 million marbles; sales fell 25 percent the next year, to 106 million.

Peltier entered the Cat Eye market a few years later than other United States makers due to the company's wish to design a marble that looked more like an actual cat's eye than the other Cat Eye designs on the market. Peltier's unique style had a single thick blade in the center rather than the "X" pattern of other makers.

Some Peltier marbles were sold by Berry Pink Industries Marble King, and some marbles made by Marble King were sold by Peltier Glass at Marble King's St. Marys factory.

Duncan Peltier died in 1973 and was succeeded as president by Joe Jankowski,[67] who served until about 1983, when he was succeeded by Karen Armstrong. Jankowski resumed the presidency in 1986. The company changed hands in early 1984; no Peltiers remain in the business, but the company name remains the same.

The Peltier Glass Company has made only industrial marbles for the past few years but resumed making colorful toy marbles to satisfy demand generated by a renewed interest in marbles. Peltier used stock in hand to satisfy the demand in the interim period. Peltier's big volume comes from gems, or nuggets, which sell by the ton.[68]

Gino Biffany possesses the most complete examples of Peltier marbles and has mounted them on a display board. The board has appeared at many marble shows and enjoyed publicity in several newspapers. Biffany's sharing of valuable information concerning the Peltier factory and its marbles is highly appreciated by collectors.

Marbles Produced By The Peltier Glass Company

Cat Eye: Champion brand; green label on poly bag; marbles have red, white, blue, and light green striping; center design is a single large blade. Early Peltier packages contained five large Cat Eye shooters with the "X" blade, but the marbles were made by Marble King.

Opaques: Bloodies, a white Translucent with random broad red stripes; Chinese Checkers in twelve colors, including two shades of red and three shades of green; National Opaques (half colors) in red-white, blue-yellow, red-yellow, black-yellow, and green-yellow; Peerless, also used to make the Picture Marble (half and half colors) in red-blue, green-yellow, green-white, red-white, blue-yellow, blue-opaque white, black-opaque white, and green-yellow.

Ribboned Opaques: Ribbons of blue, light green, and red-orange on white body, in poly bags with yellow label that is printed on the bag: "Peltier Glass Marbles / DECORATIONS SPARKLETS SHOOTERS ALL COLORS HOBBIES MARINE CRYSTALS GIRLS BOYS."

Translucent: Milkies, an opalescent white; White Milkie, an opalescent Pee Wee in ¼ inch (rare).
Transparents: Crystals; these marbles came in a wide assortment of colors, including blue, red, gold, light green, and purple in sizes of 1 inch, ⅞ inch, ⅝ inch, ⅜ inch; and Pee Wees in 5/16 inch and ¼ inch.
Transparent Swirls: Cerise Agates, red with white striping; an early type, produced in the 1920s but probably not surviving far into the 1930s.
Other types: Beside the famous Comic Strips, according to a 1975 newspaper article,[69] Peltier had at some time made all of the following types of marbles: Aggies, Rainbos, Plains, Bomboliers, and Pints. Exactly which types the article meant by Aggies, Bomboliers, and Pints is not certain.

In addition to the above, the following brand-named designs include:
Canaries: A yellow-green tint, translucent body glass.
Champion: A contemporary type with blue or black opaque body glass with multicolored stripes; the earlier type was of blue opaque glass.
Imitation Carnelian: White opaque body and reddish swirls. An attempt by Peltier to imitate the color and design of the carnelian stone (agate) marble. This is quite a collectible design, particularly in the larger sizes.
Moons: Beige or orange tint, translucent body glass.
National Rainbo: Agates (1920s) in ⅝-inch size in green-red, blue-red, blue-yellow, black-white, green-yellow, and red-white.
Onyx: In yellow, light blue, green, amber, red, clear, and purple, all with swirls of white opaque glass.
Rainbo: In white opaque body glass with stripes of orange, blue, yellow, red, and green and combinations thereof; also a white transparent body glass with the same coloring scheme. The ⅞-inch Rainbo was called Big Boy. The header shows "big Boy" without any other data.

PLAYRITE MARBLE AND NOVELTY COMPANY
Ellenboro, West Virginia

The Playrite Marble and Novelty Company was situated in the present I. Tucker building between the abandoned B & O Railroad right of way and Highway 18 in midtown Ellenboro, and near Mid-Atlantic of West Virginia. Operations began on November 8, 1945. The list of officers consisted of O. Krupp, president; Andy Long, secretary-treasurer; and Lawrence Jones, production. Stock was sold in the company with C. A. and Joseph Jones purchasing stock in the spring of 1946. Operations ceased December 31, 1947.[70] The abandoned building is constructed of concrete block with a metal roof. There are no known examples made by this short-lived marble and novelty company.

THE RAVENSWOOD NOVELTY WORKS
Ravenswood, West Virginia

Charles Turnbull founded the Ravenswood Novelty Works at 20 Wood Street in 1931 or 1932 and ran it for several years. After his death, his wife ran the company until her own death, and at that time the ownership and management of the company passed to their son-in-law, Paul Cox.

The firm was diversified, producing utility pottery greenware and marbles in two separate locations. The marble factory and the office were located at Wood and Washington Streets in Ravenswood, in a building constructed of concrete block with a metal roof. It is currently still standing and in use by its present owner, Bobby J. King, for storage. The ceramic factory was in two wooden buildings a short distance away.

The company apparently quit producing its own marbles at some point in the early 1950s but sold marbles made by other companies under the brand name Paul Bunyans. The marbles actually produced by Ravenswood's five machines were called Buddy Brand. Marbles sold by Ravenswood were packaged in either polyethylene or mesh bags with paper labels, and in cardboard boxes with cut-out designs on the face of the box.

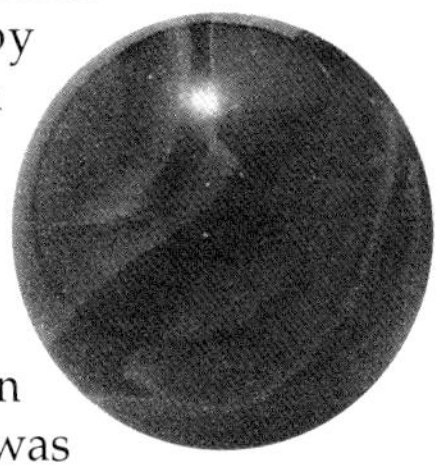

In the early 1950s, the incursion of the Japanese Cat Eye marbles was causing serious problems for American marble makers. To be sure, beginning in 1955 or 1956 a couple of American companies had succeeded in developing their own Cat Eye designs. But Ravenswood's Paul Cox still decided that that was the time to "quit, when the quitting was good."

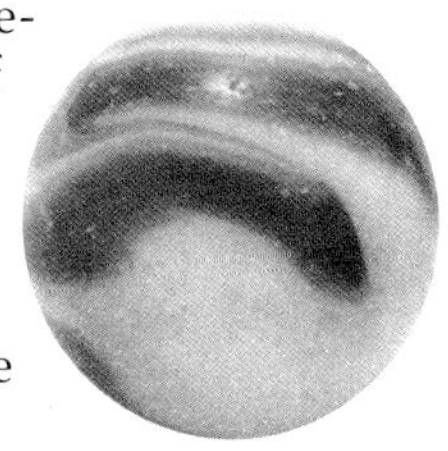

The company went out of business in 1954 or 1955, and the plant, equipment, and stock of marbles in ⅝-inch and 9/16-inch sizes were bought by O. K. Griffith. The stock of marbles on hand included a large number of 1-inch marbles made by Master Glass. The marble-making machines were sold to the Bogard Company and the Champion Agate Company.

A subsequent general clean-up of the marble factory resulted in the dumping of a large amount of marbles on the banks of and into a nearby river.

Marbles Marketed and Produced By the Ravenswood Novelty Works

Opaque Swirled: Sizes vary from approximately ½ inch to ⅝ inch, in colors of red and white, green and white, blue and white, purple and white, orange and white, brown and brown, blue and brown and gray, burgundy and light blue, black and white, and blue and light brown.
Patched Opaques: Paul Bunyans, made by Master Glass Company, large size, in cloth mesh bag with paper label. Colors: blue on white, red on yellow, blue on green, green on blue, light purple on white.
Transparents: Examples only in 9/16 inch, green or blue.
Transparent Swirls: Ravenswood brand; sizes vary from marble to marble rather than being in standard 1/16-inch increments; they range from approximately ½ inch to ⅝ inch. Color combinations include white in clear, white in blue, blue in clear, greenish-white in clear, brown and white in clear, white in dark blue-green, and white in light blue-green.

The Transparent and Opaque Swirls were duplicated at a later date by Champion Agate and called Whirlwinds and Old Fashioneds.

121

THE VITRO AGATE COMPANY /
GLADDING-VITRO AGATE COMPANY
Parkersburg, West Virginia

In early 1992, Vitro Agate Corporation, the latest incarnation of Vitro Agate Company, closed its doors and sold its marble machines to other manufacturers. Thus ended what may be the last chapter in the colorful history of a well-known and respected U.S. marble maker.

That history began on April 19, 1932, when Henri Arthur (Art) Fisher, Lawrence E. Alley, and Press Lindsey founded the Vitro Agate Company in Parkersburg, West Virginia. Over its six decades of operation, Vitro Agate's management changed a number of times. The first switch came in the late 1930s, when Fisher and Lindsey bought out Alley's interest in Vitro Agate. Later, Fisher bought out Lindsey. But these and later developments seemed to have little effect on manufacturing procedures or on the marbles produced.

In many ways, the story of Vitro Agate is the story of Art Fisher's life.[71] He brought to this new venture a variety of experiences that contributed to his success. Most notably, Fisher had served as an official with the nearby Vitrolite Glass company, which helped him considerably. He designed and built the original marble-making machines at Vitro Agate.

Fisher grew up near Hereford, Texas, which also influenced his time at Vitro. While living on the 7-Bar Ranch, he participated in a roundup with the reformed outlaw Cole Younger. Fisher also rode with Cash Whitsett and Tom Bassett, former members of Quantrill's Raiders. Fisher would occasionally wear his six-shooters around the Vitro Agate plant to recall the memories of his youth.

Among the more significant events in Vitro Agate's history was the return of Art Fisher's son from the Orient, where he had been stationed after World War II. While there, the younger Fisher learned how the Japanese-style Cat Eye design was produced. He brought this information back to Vitro, and in late 1955 Vitro began production of its own Cat Eye design.

Even though inspired by the Japanese style, the Cat Eye made by Vitro Agate is easily distinguished from the Japanese. Indeed, Vitro's design may have prompted the Japanese to introduce a revised version of their original design in the early 1960s, which was made for only a few years. Also a cage design, the modified Japanese style is distinguishable from the Vitro marble in that it has very regular and evenly spaced blades running from a central point at one end of the body to another point at the other end. In Vitro's style the spacing between the blades is irregular, and even though the design stripes run more or less from one end to the other, the gathering point is not nearly as definite as in this short-lived Japanese style.

Vitro, along with other American marble makers,

enjoyed a boost in business in the early to mid-1950s with the advent of premiums, which were marbles included with other products. Vitro sold the total output of two of its machines over several months in 1956 to General Foods to use as prizes in cereal packages. An advertisement for General Foods shows a child "All set for the best breakfast in the world before the marble-shooting tournament. . . . Get Eagle Eye marbles—regulation Tournament size—FREE in every marble-pack box of Post Toasties."[72]

In 1956 and early in the production of the Cat Eye design, Art Fisher went to Guadalajara, Mexico, to negotiate a partnership with a Mexican firm to make marbles for Vitro Agate. This arrangement would have given Vitro a cost advantage over other United States marble producers due to lower labor costs and subsidized natural gas. Reportedly, the deal fell through because Fisher wanted his name first on the letterhead, before that of his Mexican counterpart. Further contention centered on whether the Mexican partner would own the building and furnish the gas, with Fisher providing the machinery and expertise to make Cat Eye marbles.

In 1969, however, the son of the original Mexican partner and a contingent of his employees visited the Parkersburg plant to renew negotiations. The Mexican marble maker entertained Fisher. D. I. Gandee, the Vitro Agate manager, was also entertained by his counterparts, and Fisher, knowing the possibility of losing trade secrets, ignored the risk. He allowed the Mexicans to inspect Vitro Agate machinery and to take measurements inside the plant. Key components of a marble machine were subsequently removed and shipped to Mexico. Again, the joint venture did not go through, but a Cat Eye design was soon in production in Mexico in competition with United States companies, including Vitro Agate. Cheap labor, subsidized natural gas, and newly gained technical knowledge gave the Mexican factory a definite edge in marble manufacture worldwide.[73]

Vitro Agate remained a strong company in the early 1960s, producing 2,164,000 marbles daily during peak operation in 1964. Fisher discovered a way of making a marble of white opaque body glass and coating it with a color veneer in 1966.

In 1969, the first of several major changes at the corporate level occurred when Vitro was purchased by the Gladding Corporation, and the name was changed to Gladding-Vitro Agate. The Paris Manufacturing Company bought Gladding-Vitro in 1982 and changed the name back to Vitro Agate. The company's decline continued until it went bankrupt in 1987. The factory closed on June 30, 1987.

A selection of Slag (opaque body and transparent body) and Transparent types manufactured by the Ravenswood Novelty works. Note the strong resemblance to the later Champion Agate Old Fashioneds and Whirlwinds. Champion attempted to duplicate the Ravenswood designs (see photo on page 49 for comparison). Bobby J. King and Dennis Webb Collections.

Two years later, the Viking Rope Company purchased the defunct Vitro Agate. The new owners, Richard J. "Dick" Ryan and Timothy C. Sullivan, a former Vitro plant manager, revived the company and christened it the Vitro Agate Corporation.

Vitro Agate had suffered during two decades under the Gladding Corporation Vitro and the Paris Corporation, and lacked capital. The new owners tried to make a go of it but were forced to close the Parkersburg plant. In an effort to salvage the business, they moved the operation to Anacortes, Washington, in mid-1989. Machinery and marbles were shipped west, but Vitro dumped all scrap glass, cullet, and other glass ingredients instead of selling them to a local glass buyer who might have resold the materials to a competitor. Personnel and glass formulas long employed at the Parkersburg plant also remained in Parkersburg.[74]

A personal visit to the site of the abandoned factory in April 1987 showed an appearance of disarray, and the entrance to the plant area was blocked and posted "No trespassing."

ANACORTES, WASHINGTON

Despite all that was left behind, twenty tractor trailers were needed to haul machinery and tools to Anacortes. The shipment included six regular marble machines; two machines capable of making $3/8$-inch marbles; one capable of making marbles $7/8$ inch to 1 inch; one capable of making a marble 1 inch to $1\frac{1}{4}$ inches, owned by the House of Marbles, England; two nugget machines; and a new duplex machine.

The newly constructed plant in Anacortes was about the same size as the old one. The officers of the Anacortes plant included Timothy C. Sullivan, president, and Richard J. Ryan (former plant manager at Parkersburg), vice president. The foreman was Richard "Dick" J. Kilburn, and Shirley Chapman was office manager and assistant to Ryan. The new Vitro Agate Corporation's line included game marbles, decorative marbles, industrial marbles, and VitroGrow Kits.

Game marbles included the Cat Eye, All Reds, Chinas (Rainbows), and Chinese Checkers. The Cat Eye marbles were made with a crystal clear body glass containing six

The former Vitro Agate Co. factory in Parkersburg, West Virginia. In 1992 the building was sold to a firm that planned to manufacture Styrofoam. Photo by Dennis Webb.

colored, swirled strips through the marble. The All Reds and Chinas were made with a multicolored veneer surface. Chinese Checkers are opaque marbles designed for use in the original Chinese Checker board game but are now used in a variety of marble games.

A new multicolored mix of transparent and opaque marbles called Classic was introduced in 1991. The variety of color designs are beyond description; at least sixteen varieties have been identified by collectors.

Decorative marbles are used in a variety of applications, including floral arrangements, fish tank decoration, potted plant cover, craft projects, and others, and are made with standard and iridized colors and custom colors. Vitro packaged decorative marbles in samplers or assortments.

Vitro Agate used a variety of packaging—mesh bags, plastic jars (clear plastic with white lid, ideal for storage and display), poly bags, and bulk cartons.

Vitro Agate introduced a new use for marbles in its VitroGrow Kit, a hydroponic kit for growing houseplants in glass marbles instead of potting soil. Each plastic tub contained 350 ⁹⁄₁₆-inch diameter glass marbles, along with instructions and VitroGrow hydroponic plant food. These kits were often seen in garden and flower shops; it is unknown if they are still available.

Vitro also produced a variety of industrial marbles in several different diameters: 1 inch, ⅞ inch, ¾ inch, ⅝ inch, ⁹⁄₁₆ inch, and ½ inch.

Marbles Produced by Vitro Agate/Gladding-Vitro Parkersburg, West Virginia

All Reds: Streaked by various colors with a red stripe or spot; as the marble rolls across the play area it appears to be all red. This factory design and brand contained

various swirling colors of yellow, red, green, orange, and blue in a white opaque body glass and made in 1¼-inch and ⅞-inch sizes. The larger size was made on a British-owned machine for export only; therefore, it is highly collectible in the United States. Vitro ceased production of the original All Reds design in mid-1986 and changed to a new color design with stronger, darker colors.

Brushed Transparents: Conqueror; small size in same cloth mesh bag as Patched Transparents below, but patch not well-defined. Very faint brushed-on looking whitish area on clear body.

Cat Eyes: As discussed above, Vitro produced the Cat Eye type in late 1955. The early Vitro Cat Eyes were much different from those produced later, however. The type produced in the late 1950s and early 1960s was very similar to the type made by Marble King—four wavy blades joined in the center. But Vitro modified its design during the late 1960s, making it quite distinct from that of any other maker.

The later design has been called a "cage-style" Cat Eye, referring to the fact that the blades or vanes do not stay close to the center of the marble, but spread out to about halfway between the center and the outside. The blades are not as thick and predictably shaped as the Japanese style. A carry-over from the early Vitro type is the waviness of the blades; however, in the new design the bending and waving is more extreme, like filaments in a liquid. They are not evenly spaced; while they run more or less from one "end" of the marble to the other, they do not meet at such a definite gathering place as do the early Vitro or other makers' styles. It is a unique and most attractive style of marble.

Vitro's Cat Eyes were also sold packaged under the "5 Star Brand" name in ⅝-inch diameter, colors including blue, red, orange, and green. Another characteristic of

Vitro Agate's Cat Eye is that some of the blades will be slightly tinted with another color toward the edges; light blue with orange edges, green with yellow edges, and red with gray edges, among other combinations.

Cat Eyes also sold under the Gladding-Vitro label, in poly bags with labels printed on the bag, or with paper labels: large size marbles in red, green, blue, white, yellow, and red-yellow; small-size marbles in red, white, and blue. Standard sizes are $\frac{5}{8}$ inch and $\frac{7}{8}$ inch.

In 1984 a special run for the House of Marbles produced Cat Eyes in $1\frac{1}{4}$-inch diameter with crystal clear body glass and erratic swirls of one color—green, blue, yellow, orange, azure, or white opaque. Some did contain a combination of the above colors. Hardly any two are alike. These were made for export and sale by the House of Marbles (a world-wide company) only and are scarce.

Dotted/Spotted: Confetti, white Transparent and black Opaque with colored dots sprinkled on the surface; $\frac{5}{8}$ inch and $\frac{7}{8}$ inch made experimentally in 1984. Dot colors are white, red, orange, yellow, blue, turquoise, and green.

Frosteds: Produced experimentally at one time, never for sale. They were produced in 1988 in $1\frac{1}{2}$-inch size. See Transparents below.

Half and Half: This type comprises two different colors, splitting an opaque body fairly evenly in half. It was made during the 1940s and 1950s, and packaged in gift boxes. The unusual $\frac{3}{4}$-inch size of this type faded from popularity in the 1950s. Pressman Toy Corporation bought many of this type from Vitro.

Nugget Gems and Industrials: The Nugget Gems, which are flat on one side, great for craft and flower arrangements, were available in the same colors as the Exotic Gems and Aqua Jewels (see Transparents, below). Industrial marbles were made in sizes of $\frac{9}{16}$ and $\frac{5}{8}$ inch.

Opaques: Chinese Checkers have been produced since 1932. Marbles in $\frac{9}{16}$-inch size in colors of blue, white, red, green, light green, yellow, black, and tan have been made, as well as the large $1\frac{1}{4}$-inch black Opaque that was made for the House of Marbles.

At one time Vitro produced veneered Chinese Checkers marbles, the only company known to have done so.

Tomato, a special order of a particular color of red Opaque, is favored among British marble players, first produced in 1983, solely for export to the House of Marbles, London. The House sells in the United States, so this type may be seen here as well as internationally. Available in $\frac{9}{16}$-inch and $\frac{7}{8}$-inch sizes.

In 1985 Vitro began producing opalescent pink marbles, similar to the Carnival Glass of the Depression period. Another beautiful color produced in limited quantities in the late 1980s was chocolate brown. it is not well known to collectors, but is quite collectible.

Opaque Swirls: (Veneered) 1964 to the present.

Patched Opaques: Designated "Type A" and described by the company as having a spot with white base, and produced from 1932 to 1954.

Patched and Brushed: Well-defined patch covering one-fourth to one-third surface area, the remainder of the body glass filled with thread-like strands of white or greenish-bluish-white; the body glass is colorless, but depending on the amount of white added the body may be slightly transparent or almost entirely opaque. $\frac{5}{8}$-inch size, patches of yellow, blue, red, orange, green, and greenish-

blue. A major customer requested that a certain color in the All Reds line be "darkened"; the company recipe was altered and thereafter this particular color design was called "Blackie" by company personnel.

Patched and Ribboned: All Reds, Opaques only; made about 1963 to the present.

Patched Translucents: "Type B," having a spot with little milk white, made during 1932–1954.

Patched Transparents: "Type C," a spot with clear base, same period, 1932–1954.

Patched Transparents: Conqueror, small size ($\frac{5}{16}$ inch) in cloth mesh bag with paper label. Usually well-defined patches, but in some cases a Brushed Transparent. Patches of white, light blue, or green on a clear body.

Another variation in the same cloth mesh as above, light brown and white on honey body; coloring almost covers the outside, much like a veneer, but not thick enough to be true veneering.

It is apparent that the term Conqueror was as much a brand name as a marble type, unless this particular batch just had wide variation in the amounts of color striping applied to various marbles. That is, perhaps the ideal Conqueror is a well-defined Patched Transparent, but for whatever reason, several of the marbles in this particular bag did not get as much coloring as they should have.

This might be the case if they were all the same color; the color glass might have run out and this bag might have been one of the last from that run. But as these are of different colors, this means they came from different runs. Therefore, it seems that the name Conqueror was used for at least a group of similar marbles—Patched or Brushed Transparents, but not Chinese Checkers or Clears.

Transparents: Made since the beginning of the company in 1932. Exotic Gems and Aqua Jewels (same marbles, different names according to whether they are packaged by a single color or mixed). Clear, azure blue, dark blue, light green, dark green, light amber, dark amber, orange, ruby, purple. According to a 1975 ad, white and black Opaques were sold as a part of the Gems and Jewels poly bag packages as well as the Transparents.

The 1983 and 1985 offerings of Exotic Gems and Aqua Jewels included the same colors as above with the addition of "golden topaz."

Vitro's Transparents come in very small ($\frac{3}{8}$ inch), medium ($\frac{9}{16}$ inch), and large ($\frac{7}{8}$ inch) sizes, in the usual colors, including crystal (clear), azure (blue), and red.

A 1962 memo from H. A. Fisher to the factory employees stresses the importance and care necessary to produce pink glass marbles, noting, "Colorwise there is no color so difficult in production as **PINK**. . . . The cullet for PINK must be DRY, it must be hand picked, the greens, heavily muddied and terribly dirty material rejected." Truly pink marbles (not faint red), whether made by Vitro or anyone else, are quite rare. A light pink with considerable seedy glass was produced in 1986. This was a short production run, not listed as a standard marble.

A special order of large clear Transparents were produced solely for the House of Marbles and made on a British-owned machine capable of producing diameters from $1\frac{1}{4}$ inches to 2 inches. The colors include crystal, red, azure, green, gray, gold, and a black Opaque sold as part of this package. Made beginning in 1984, this scarce type was also frosted.

Occasionally marble factories are requested to produce a special industrial marble. In 1988 Vitro Agate was asked to make a "borasilica" marble. Purpose or use of the marble was not disclosed by the customer. The marble was produced, but additional shipments were declined since the marble tended to "eat" the inside of the melting tank. The exact formula is not known. The marble is a dark, straw-colored Transparent, ⅝ inch in diameter. A recent commercial advertisement for fire-resistant glass made of borasilicate glass indicated that it can stand a temperature of 1,832 degrees Fahrenheit for four hours.

Transparent and Brushed Deco: In 1988 a new design called Deco Mate, which has a tinted surface (iridescent-like) in clear crystal, white Opaque, dark blue crystal, and chocolate-brown Opaque, was produced in 1¼-inch size.

Marble production ceased in early 1992; however, stock on hand was sold as late as September 1992. The large marble machine owned by the House of Marbles, London, was shipped to Mid-Atlantic of West Virginia in September 1992. The Anacortes factory is for sale. The management said it wants to devote more time and energy to its Puget Sound Rope Company.[75] Earlier that year, the vacated Parkersburg factory was sold to a firm that planned to manufacture Styrofoam.

RENO, OHIO

The above remaining machines and marbles were purchased by JABO, Inc., and Jack Bogard, JABO's general manager, made arrangements to ship the newly acquired materials to Reno, Ohio, home of the company. Operations resumed in a separate building near the JABO building, and assumed the name of Vitro Agate, A Division of JABO, Incorporated. It is noteworthy to collectors that any marbles produced by the Anacortes factory—the packaged items in particular—are instant collectibles because of the factory's short life.

At this time there are six factories making marbles in the United States: Marble King, Champion Agate, and Mid-Atlantic in West Virginia; Peltier in Illinois; and JABO and Vitro Agate, a Division of JABO, in Ohio.

[1]Sophia C. Pappanou, *Akro Agate's Children's Line and Price Guide* (Syracuse, N.Y.: Estabrook Printing Company, 1973), p. 8.

[2]Darlene M. Bourque and Joseph A. A. Bourque, Sr, "A Treatise on the Akro Agate," *The Akro Agate Gem*, newsletter of the Akro Agate Art Association, Box 758, Salem, NH 03079, Vol. 1, No. 1 (June 1983), p. 5.

[3]Roger Howdyshell, personal comment.

[4]*The Akro Agate Gem*, Vol. 3, No. 3, p. 4.

[5]J. Fred Early, personal correspondence.

[6]Early, personal comment.

[7]Heather Wright, "Little Charmers," *Traditional Home* magazine, April 1991, pp. 38 and 116.

[8]Gene Florence, *The Collectors Encyclopedia of Akro Agate Glassware* (Collector Books, 1975), p. 6.

[9]Roger W. Howdyshell, personal comment.

[10]Edwin Sweeney, "Marbles and Pressed Glass— Remembering Akro Agate of Clarksburg," *Goldenseal*, Vol. 10, No. 2 (Summer 1984), p. 23.

[11]*The Akro Agate Gem*, Vol. 3, No. 3, p. 1; and J. Fred Early, personal comment.

[12]Sweeney, ibid., p. 6.

[13]Early, personal comments.

[14]Early, personal comment.

[15]Dr. Budd Appleton, *Akro Agate*, private publication, 1972, p. 18.

[16]Florence, ibid., p. 62.

[17]Florence, ibid., p. 9.

[18]Early, personal correspondence.

[19]Papapanu, ibid, p. 38.

[20]Early, personal correspondence.

[21]Early, personal correspondence, and *Clarksburg Telegram*, October 14 and 18, 1991.

[22]Early, personal correspondence.

[23]John Doll, general manager since 1947, Pennsboro Glass Company, personal conversation.

[24]Enrique Canova, "West Virginia: Treasure Chest of Industry," *National Geographic Magazine*, Vol. 78, No. 2 (August 1960), p. 183.

[25]Jack Frier, personal comment.

[26]Frier, personal comment.

[27]Howdyshell, personal comment.

[28]Ron Mawson in *Marble-Mania*, Vol. 36.

[29]Frier, personal comment.

[30]Louise Ada Boger and H. Batterson Boger, *The Dictionary of Antiques and the Decorative Arts* (New York: Scribner, 1957).

[31]Mel Morrison and Carl Terrison, *Marbles— Identification and Price Guide*, private publication, Falmouth, Maine, 1968.

[32]Merrill.

[33]Dave McCullough, personal conversation.

[34]Jeff Carskadden and Mark Randall, "The Christensen Agate Company, Cambridge, Ohio (1927–1933)," *Muskingum Annals*, Vol. 4 (1987), pp. 48–52.

[35]*Crockery and Glass Journal*, November 17, 1927.

[36]Kim Novak, "The Christensen Agate Co.," unpublished report by the Degenhart Paperweight and Glass Museum, Cambridge, Ohio, 1984.

[37]Ralph and Lana Watkins, personal conversation.

[38]Watkins, ibid.

[39]*Fortune*, "Immies," Vol. 13 (June 1936), p. 36.

[40]Jeff Carskadden, personal comment.

[41]Carskadden, personal comment.

[42]Watkins, ibid.

[43]Ralph Watkins, personal conversation, August 7–8, 1992.

[44]Watkins, ibid.

[45]J. Fred Early, personal conversation.

[46]Michael C. Cohill, *M. F. Christensen* (Akron, Ohio: Group Ideate Publishing), p. 45.

[47]Michael C. Cohill, personal conversation.

[48]Dean Six, West Virginia historian, personal correspondence.

[49]Mariam Righter, *Iowa City Glass*, private publication, copyright by Dr. J. W. Carberry, 1982, p. 32.

[50]Ibid., Plate 6.

[51]Ibid., Plate 34.

[52]Righter, p. 14.

[53]Bud Sweiger, personal correspondence, September 21, 1992.

[54]Wallace S. Huffman, Kokomo, Ind., personal conversation and correspondence; and *Glassology*, News Magazine of the Kokomo Opalescent Glass Company (second quarter, 1989).

[55]Oliver Butterfield, "Marble Collecting for Keeps," *Yankee*, September 1977, pp. 174-184.

[56]Roger W. Howdyshell, personal conversation.

[57]Bourque personal comment.

[58]"Immies," ibid.

[59]Paul Baumann, *Collecting Antique Marbles* (Leon, Iowa: Prairie Winds Press, 1970), p. 38.

[60]Fred Feretti, *The Great American Marble Book* (New York: Workman, 1973), pp. 32-33.

[61]Baumann, ibid, p. 38.

[62]Joan Hustis, "Ottawa's Marble Company One of Only Three in U.S.," *Ottawa (Ill.) Daily Times*, April 18, 1969.

[63]Harry H. Cook, Editor, *The American Flint* magazine, "William J. Miller's Semi-Automatic Marble Machine," 1927, p. 14.

[64]Gino Biffany, Bob Hutchinson, and Carmelo Tripodi, of Ottawa, Ill.

[65]Jim Davis, "Betty Boop Reveals Age . . . of Peltier Picture Marbles!," *Marble-Mania*, Vol. 59 (July 1990), pp. 2-3.

[66]Joseph L. Jankowski, long-term employee and president, the Peltier Glass Company.

[67]Ed Callahan, "Peltier Glass Company is Oldest Ottawa Industry," *Ottawa (Ill.) Daily Times*, July 2, 1978, p. 13.

[68]Joseph L. Jankowski and Gino Biffany, personal correspondence.

[69]Callahan, ibid.

[70]Dean Six, personal correspondence.

[71]Lewis L. Moore, personal conversation.

[72]"Who Ate My Post Toasties?," *Life* magazine, March 28, 1955, p. 61.

[73]Lewis L. Moore, personal conversation.

[74]Lewis L. Moore, personal conversation.

[75]Shirley Chapman, personal conversation, September 28, 1992.

Chapter XV

● ● ●

Foreign Marble Companies and Glass Houses

The business of marbles has always been international. From the earliest days of marbles in the United States, German imports were more common in America than American-made marbles. By the end of the first World War, the German marble business was much less important than it had been internationally, and the new American machine-made glass marbles were the new leaders.

By the late 1940s American marbles were being exported all over the world; even as early as the 1930s other countries were trying to build their own glass marble businesses. Belgium, for instance, succeeded in obtaining a marble-making machine designed by Lawrence Alley. Other foreign companies produced marbles as well, particularly Vacor de Mexico, with the largest factory in the world.

JAPAN

The most famous imports of the twentieth century are the Cat Eyes, made by the Japanese and imported into the United States beginning in the early to mid-1950s and continuing to the present day. This single design caused a great upheaval in the marble industry, very quickly dominating the American market and almost putting American makers out of business. In the early 1950s, just following the importation of the Japanese Cat Eyes, employment in the United States marble industry fell by two-thirds.

Recently a one-inch Cat Eye made in Japan appeared on the United States market. It is a striking and well-made design of six blades in three colors: yellow, orange, and opaque white; yellow, orange, and light green; and orange, yellow, and black. The blades are broad and reach from pole cutoff to cutoff point. This is the first known example of the use of black in a Cat Eye. Efforts to obtain additional information about the Japanese factory or factories were futile.

ENGLAND

The House of Marbles, Teignmouth, South Devon, England, is internationally known for quality glass products. The company claims to "make some marbles ourselves, cause others to be made for us and also buy other manufacturers' marbles unchanged." This causes problems for United States marble collectors who, without

research, arbitrarily assign names to marbles. The foreign manufacturer's and the glass house's names for a marble may be quite different, and then a third name is given by an enthusiastic collector. The House is also supplied by its own glass house, Teign Valley Glass, which makes a large variety of glass objects, such as art deco spheres, eggs, paperweights, novelty items, and marbles. The marbles are of museum quality, attractively packaged and supplied with a novel plastic display case. A wide variety of handmade glass marbles is made to duplicate earlier types. In fact, the display box shows a "Handmade Victorian Reproduction Marble." All early handmade marble types and designs are made except Sulphides.

Marbles sold by the House are made by foreign marble factories, including those in the United States, and are available in four sizes—Giants, 34 millimeters (1½ inch); Large, 30 millimeters (1¼ inch); Medium, 22–25 millimeters (⅞ inch–1 inch); and Small, 14–17 millimeters (⁹⁄₁₆ inch–¹¹⁄₁₆ inch). The machine-made marbles are complemented with a large array of board and table games. Highly likely to become a collectible is their "Pocket Pack," an introductory offer consisting of ten out of a selection of twelve brightly packed games on a metal display board, an inexpensive collection of marble-shooting games and other traditional games on one striking display stand. The accompanying cloth bag with company logo in red is outstanding.

A broad range of nuggets, which are supplied in bulk or clear plastic jars, are available for interior design, flower arrangements, and other uses. A wide array of semiprecious stone marbles in an attractive plastic jar and with a company booklet attached rounds out the company's line of products. They are "made in traditional water-driven grinding mills, in the same way as some of the earliest marbles."

The head office of the House of Marbles is Devon, England, with a United States office in Belle Mead, New Jersey. The house is not geared to handle inquiries from individuals and does not run a mail-order service.[1]

MEXICO

Closer to home is Vacor de Mexico, in Guadalajara, Mexico, which first entered the marble-manufacturing business in 1930. Its first products were clay marbles with a production rate of one million per month. Four years later, Vacor commenced making glass crystal marbles in

In business for over 60 years, Vacor de Mexico in Guadelajara has become the largest marble-making company in the world.

blue, green, amber and clear, with two marble machines at the rate of eighty thousand marbles per day.

Vacor's first Cat Eye marbles were made in 1944, and the company enjoyed growth and production to satisfy the Mexican market. Vacor entered the export market twenty-five years later due to improvement in the quality of its marbles. The rapid growth and improvements in Vacor's marble machines resulted in the capability to produce twelve million marbles per day in ten sizes from 10 millimeters to 35 millimeters, and twenty-five designs for each size. Vacor employs about five hundred people and exports marbles to thirty-five countries. Vacor de Mexico

produced the sampler set of marbles contained in the Travel Game, which was marketed under the trade name of Qualatex and sold by the Pioneer Balloon Company, Wichita, Kansas. Production of this game ceased due to non-interest of marble players. It is now a highly collectible packaged set of marbles.

Vacor USA is the sole distributor of marbles made by Vacor de Mexico.[2] The new trade name that replaced Qualatex is MEGA marbles. It reflects Vacor's colors, styles, and MEGA sizes, which set them apart from other U.S. manufacturers. National Sales Manager Margaret K. Phillips heads Vacor USA.

Contemporary machine-made clay marbles by H. E. Hopf of Coburn, Germany. The splotchy colors, left, and the solids, right, are sold in plastic net bags with uncommon plastic carrying devices.

A selection of paired marbles made by Vacor de Mexico. Back row: Pandas, Pirates, Flames, Turtles, Black and Blue.
Center row: Glitters. Front row: Galaxies.

A large selection of Vacor marbles is contained in various decorative types of blister packs called "Qualatex Collector Marbles." The net bags with limited edition sampler sets, imprinted marbles, and decorated leather pouches are products for United States sale. The limited edition sampler sets make an especially good addition to a marble collection.

Vacor is noted for new designs and offers a new design of marble each year. Two major categories of marble produced are the decorator marbles and glass toy marbles. Decorator marbles are made in black, champagne gold, "diamond" crystal, green, ice clear, light blue, quartz pink, winter lilac, and white. Glass toy marbles are made in the following color designs: Candy, Cat Eye, Corsair, Crystal, Diamond, Galaxy, Glitter, Iris, Meteor, Opal, Sparkle, Pearl, Pirate, Polar Ice, Sky Blue, and White Pearl. Opals are made in opaque white and opaque black; Crystals are made in blue, green, ice clear, lilac, and pink; Frosties are made in blue, green, ice clear, lilac, pink, and transparent; and Diamonds are made in blue, green, ice clear, lilac, and pink. All of these colors and designs are factory names.[3]

Vacor de Mexico continues to introduce colorful designs and names for their glass marbles. The most recent 1992 designs have stripes similar to but wider than Marble King's Rainbow line. The following are examples of Vacor's 1993 line:[4]

Name	Color
Devil	Orange/yellow
Pirate & Black Panthers	Yellow, Yellow/black, white/black, blue/black
Turtle	Green/yellow, red/green
Panda	Iridescent white/ tints of purplish black

Based on all available data and production rates, Vacor is the largest marble maker in the world.

GERMANY

The H. E. Hopf Marble Factory (Spielwarenfabrik) is located in Coburg, Germany. H. E. Hopf is not well known to marble collectors of America. Although its products appear in the United States, they are unrecognized except by seasoned collectors. Clay, glass, and plastic marbles with a variety of marble games are advertised in its catalog.

Hopf clays were sold in import specialty houses as early as 1983 and 1984, produced in three sizes in a variety of colors and packaged in plastic mesh bags with an attractive carrying handle. Plastic bags and plastic bags with a cardboard fastener at the top round out their package styles.

H. E. Hopf produces clay marbles in three sizes: $^{21}/_{32}$ inch, white surface with single blue, green, red, or yellow splotches (spongeware); $^{25}/_{32}$ inch, solid color surface with single red, green, white, yellow, or blue dots; $1^{3}/_{16}$ inch, white surface with a combination of green, red, and yellow splotches (spongeware).

The distinguishing features of the Hopf clays are their colors and roundness, which are superior to clay marbles made in earlier years. This is an attractive line of clay marbles not often seen in today's markets or shows.

Hopf produces a single design of glass marble in which a single color of blue, yellow, red, or green random striping appears in a clear body glass. There are no known combinations of colors. Of interest is the inner design with a very random wavy appearance. It is highly likely that this is the Wirepull described by Castle and Peterson in their identification guides.

Plastic marbles round out the Hopf line of spheres and are advertised as several games as "stick game with plastic sticks [pick-up sticks], billiard game, bead game with nylon thread, calculator with plastic marbles and wood frame, and mosaic game."[5]

[1]W. R. Bavin, president, House of Marbles, personal correspondence.

[2]Margaret K. Phillips, Vacor USA, personal conversation.

[3]Claudia M. Del Toro, export manager, Vacor de Mexico, personal communication.

[4]Claudia M. Del Toro.

[5]Translation by Jim Davis.

Chapter XVI

● ● ●

Price Guide

As with any collectible, the value of any marble or piece of marble paraphernalia is determined by the question of how badly someone wants what someone else has. Supply and demand may come into play, and prices may suddenly fluctuate, particularly when there is a cache found "in an old warehouse." As the saying goes, a willing buyer, a willing seller, and an agreed-upon price consummates a sale.

The very best investments are those marbles that were rare to begin with. Factors in determining value are rarity, size, condition, type of marble, and—in some rare instances—a pedigree.

The price of collectible marbles and marble paraphernalia skyrocketed in the early 1970s, when more people became aware of marbles as collectible items. Additional marble clubs and societies were formed; shows, sales, and exhibitions followed. Since that time, however, price levels of most marbles have risen much more modestly, and only the rarer types and unique specimens have continued to increase significantly in price. However, modern machine-made marbles have also shown increases in price and have attracted collectors. When does a marble become a collectible? In the 1990s the startling answer is, the minute it is produced.

Obviously, it is impossible to cover every collectible item, but this is an attempt to cover most of the types of marbles and representative marble-related items a collector will encounter. The main thrust is with packaged marbles, which afford identifying features and marbles produced or marketed by or for a particular factory.

In some cases, very rare or unique items are listed which have not been sold recently, and so no actual prices are available. In these cases, estimated values were used based on regional prices, advertisements, dealer prices at various shows, and "For Sale" items and ads in the newsletters of various marble societies.

In the case of packaged marbles, price may vary according to rarity, condition, logos, and designs. Package materials, in descending order of rarity, are wood (early), metal, cardboard, cloth, cotton mesh, cutout cardboard, blister packs, and plastic (solid or net). The prices for early cotton net bags are high due to their deteriorating nature. Boxed items may or may not have their spacers.

A penlight with two AA batteries and adjustable focus is often useful to a buyer

to "look through and inside" a marble to determine its design and condition.

Archaeological artifacts are not listed, since the sale, trade, or purchase of them is contrary to the objectives and principles of archaeologists.

A standard guide to determine condition or grade of a marble became necessary for a growing number of marble collectors. The standard generally accepted is:

Mint (M): Unmarred and in original condition. The best possible condition with a clear surface.

Near Mint (NM): The next highest classification refers to a clear surface with a couple of minor digs. Other terms used to describe this condition are "very good" and "excellent."

Good (G): May have a few small digs, surface scratches, and minor surface cloudiness. However, the core must be easily seen and it must be without large chips or fractures.

Collectible (C): May have minor surface chips, dings, and cloudy surface. May also have minor fractures under the surface, but the marble must be whole.[1]

STONE MARBLES

Limestone Marbles: In the boom since the 1970s, prices for limestone marbles have increased only slightly, largely due to the fact that there is so little variation in "plain" stone marbles, except in size. Each collector needs only a few different sizes to have a fairly complete collection of this type. Limestones become more scarce as their size increases above $5/8$ inch, and the prices rise accordingly.

Less than $1/2$ inch	**$1**
$3/4$ inch	**$5**
1 inch	**$10**
Larger than 1 inch	**$30**

Artificially colored limestone marbles command a higher price.

Agates and Other Semiprecious
Stone Marbles (Antique): The Aggie has kept up its fascination for collectors, and antique hand-turned examples of agates and other semiprecious stone marbles have kept up in value with most other collectible marbles except rare handmade glass types.

With all semiprecious stone marbles, but agates especially, size alone does not determine value. Agates vary from bland gray or brown one-colored specimens to

CERAMICS, CLAYS	½″	¾″	1″	Large
Clay (Earthenware)				
Undecorated or one color	$.25	$.45	$1.45	$4.00
Decorated	.35	2.50	4.00	6.00
Yellowware	.50	1.00	3.50	5.00
Crockery (Stoneware)				
Benningtons				
Brown	.50	1.50	3.75	20.00
Blue	.60	.90	4.00	12.00
Agateware				
Fancy (Several colors)	5.00	2.00	7.00	12.00
Salt-Glazed Stoneware	2.00	4.00	7.00	15.00
China (Porcelain)				
Unglazed				
No Design	.15	.50	2.00	3.00
Simple Design (Lines, Leaves Bull's-Eyes)	3.00	7.00	12.00	15.00
Glazed				
No Design	1.00	10.00	15.00	25.00
Simple Design (As Geometrics Above)	8.00	15.00	35.00	60.00
Fancy Design (Flowers, Much As in Simple Designs Above)	25.00	50.00	75.00	100.00
Scenes		2500.00	3000.00	4000.00

the beautiful classic Bull's-Eye of four colors. The latter, Bull's-Eyes, are the most sought-after type and command a higher premium than other agates of the same size.

½ inch	$15
¾ inch	$30
1 inch	$45
Larger than 1 inch	$50

Agates of natural black color double the above prices.

Agates and other Semiprecious

Stone Marbles (Modern): In the past five years or so, large numbers of agate marbles have been imported from India. These are primarily gray in color, not always very round, and generally run about ½ inch to ¾ inch in diameter. Prices asked run anywhere from 50 cents to $7 per marble, but they are commonly available for $1.50.

"Mineral spheres" of diameters larger than typical marbles have been made for many years for rock and mineral buffs. They are still being produced by a few individual makers and by one major manufacturer in Germany (Otto & Dieter Jerusalem). They are available in sizes up to about 6 inches in diameter and in a multitude of different mineral types. While the larger spheres are definitely not marbles, the smaller sizes are usually considered marbles, and their price is determined by the mineral, rather than their rarity as a standard marble type.

CERAMIC MARBLES

Modern Machine-Made Clay

"Metallic Clay" packets of marbles contained in "Chen Check Chinese Checkers" or "Marble Mosaics" cardboard box, American Toy Works. **$85–125**

Modern Handmade Clay (Ceramics)
Robert A. Brown (United States): Signed and dated.

(A) Bennington-style, Spongeware, and Spatterware (minimum of 1 ½ inch). **$15–20**

(B) Big Blue, small version, 1991. **$40**

(C) Big Blue III, hand-signed, numbered, and dated. Limited edition of one hundred in 3 inch (plus or minus) diameter with matching stand. **$100–125**

(D) Corkscrew **$30**

(E) First dated (1986) clay (six made). Contains a hallmark of "RB 86." Rare. This is the first known dated handmade marble made for sale to the public. Subsequent ones are signed (by hand or decal) and dated by full year. **Not priced**

(F) Geometrics. **$15–30**

(G) Handpainted; American flag band of white specks on blue band, fifteen stripes to each end; red, white, and blue. Scarce. **Not priced**

(H) Handpainted; fish bait (worm crawling across razor blade). Scarce. **$45**

(I) Handpainted; fruit (apples, pears, strawberries, grapes, etc.). **$35–60**

(J) Handpainted; Pennsylvania Dutch motif (flowers, petals, leaves, chicken scratches, etc.). **$25–45**

(K) Handpainted; (Rosalita—small rose) band of roses with sixteen spokes going out to each end. Scarce. **$65–75**

(L) Limited editions of Spirit of St. Louis, Osprey, Clipper Ship, and Funny Faces; handpainted, numbered, signed, and dated. Additional scenes are anticipated. **$55**

(M) Line Crockery. **$25**

(N) "Mexican Agate," unglazed. **$20**

(O) Milidot, more than 2,000 handpainted dots. **$50**

(P) Polka Dot. **$15**

(Q) Special or commemorative (by commission). **$150–1,000**

(R) Sugar Daddies (only three made; in private collections). Rare. **No reported sales**

(S) Whirligigs (priced according to size). Rare. **$25–45**

H. E. Hopf (Germany): Plastic bag or plastic mesh containing single color or speckled (spongeware) clays. **$20**

Gene Weber (United States): Circa 1989.

(A) Innovative and colorful decal designs, single marble with stand. **$25**

(B) Varied colors (two) appearing as a Slag, single marble with stand. **$25**

(C) Handpainted Peppermint (red, white, and blue), numbered. **$35**

HANDMADE GLASS MARBLES

Antique Handmade Glass Marbles
Sulphides

Sulphides have always been a favorite collectible, and even common types that could be purchased for $25 in the 1970s are demanding three to five times that price now. Rare examples of Sulphides have sold for over $8,000.

HANDMADE GLASS MARBLES (ANTIQUE)	3/4″	1″	1 3/4″	2″	2 1/2″
Transparent					
No core					
Interior Swirls	$30.	$75.	$200.	$300.	$450.
Exterior Swirls	30.	75.	250.	325.	450.
(Banded)					
Solid Core	35.	90.	300.	425.	500.
Lobed or Ribbon Core	90.	100.	200.	300.	400.
Divided Core	15.	35.	95.	150.	200.
Latticino Core	20.	45.	150.	125.	225.
Translucent					
Single Color	20.	90.	150.		
Opaque					
Single Color	20.	100.	200.		
Slag	35.	60.			
Peppermint	75.	200.	900.	1000.	
Clambroth	90.	200.	950.		
Indian or Joseph	110.	300.	900.		
Banded (Swirl)	100.	400.	1000.		
Mica					
All Colors Except Red	30.	60.	400.		
Red	350.	700.			
Lutz	80.	150.	400.		
Onionskins, Clouds,					
End of Days	75.	130.	325.	400.	500.
Goldstones	25.	40.	75.		

Sulphides fall into five price groupings, depending on the figure and the body glass. Prices below are for sizes up to about 1 1/4 inch; 2-inch sizes run almost twice the price of the smaller examples.

Bear, bird, boar, buffalo, camel, cat, cow, deer, dog, donkey, duck, eagle, elephant, fish, fox, frog, goat, hedgehog, hen, horse, lamb, lion, monkey, owl, parrot, pigeon, pig, rabbit, raccoon, rooster, sheep, squirrel.
$100–150
Crane, flying bird, lizard. **$150–175**
Child, man, numbers, owl with wings spread, woman.
$200–300
Angel, baby, bust, child with dog, crucifix, Madonna, Santa Claus. **$325–375**
Rare types such as combinations: Pair of doves, pair of fish. **$900–8,000**
Any tinted glass will roughly double the value of a Sulphide.

U.S. Modern Handmade Glass Marbles

Rarity does not enter into the pricing of these marbles yet. Since all or most of the artists who produce them are still active, there is no reason that a particular design could not be produced for many years. Rather, the prices are dictated by the artists themselves, who decide what the craftsmanship in that piece is worth, tempered by the price that collectors are willing to pay. Generally, the larger the piece, the higher the price.

At present there is not a large premium for any one artist's work over another's, in spite of the fact that some differences in quality do exist. Some artists have begun

signing, numbering, and dating their larger pieces.

The inspiration for these pieces was the traditional handmade marble of the nineteenth century, and for this reason they are sought after by some marble collectors.

One may distinguish modern United States handmade marbles from the antique types. Modern ones are a near-perfect sphere, do not have pontil marks, and show considerable design imagination. But beware—some antique types have been refinished on a sphere machine or heat-treated to obliterate a scar or ding. The best advice is to compare a known example with an unknown example for identification.

Styles Inspired by Traditional (Nineteenth Century) Designs.

3/4 inch	**$15**
1 1/4 inch	**$30**
Larger than 2 inches	**$50–75**

Modern Sulphides: Special edition (six made and numbered) Sulphide by Brown and Gibson for ARMCO (promotional/advertising). **$1,000**

Larger than 2 inches **$50–75**

St. Clair: Quite colorful figures; some examples have the St. Clair hallmark, some do not. Now becoming scarce.
$40–50

Gibson Glass: With or without St. Clair figure. **$25–35**

Gibson Glass: With "G" on bottom of figure. **$100**

MACHINE-MADE GLASS MARBLES	5/8″	3/4″	1″	1 1/4″
Translucent				
Alabaster, Vaseline,				
Milk Glass	$10.00			
Opalescent	20.00			
Tiger Eye (Not Cat Eye:				
Master Marble)	500.00			
Guinea (Christensen)	300.00			
Swirls, Slags				
(Transparent,				
Translucent, or				
Opaque:				
Akro Agate)	1.00	5.00	8.00	20.00
Spirals or Corkscrews				
(Transparent,				
Translucent or Opaque)				
Two Colors (Opaque)	10.00	25.00		
Two Colors (Transparent)	7.00	20.00		
Three Colors				
(Transparent)	5.00	7.00		
Four Colors				
(Transparent)	10.00	15.00		
Patched and Ribboned				
Opaques (Marble King:				
Cub Scouts, Bumble				
Bees, Black Widows;				
Rainbows)	1.00	5.00		

Modern Imprinted (Decal) Picture Marbles or Comics: Made by Harold D. Bennett, $7/8$-inch diameter imprints on Marble King Rainbow. Figures are larger than those contained on the Peltier Picture Marbles and have single or double color designs.

    (A) Single, $7/8$ inch. **$10**

    (B) Boxed set of twelve with autograph, $7/8$ inch. **$75**

    (C) Single, $5/8$ inch or $3/4$ inch. **$2**

    (D) Boxed set of twelve, $5/8$ inch or $3/4$ inch. **$35**

    (E) Chambered Nautilus glass marble made from the Snakeskin by Robert A. Brown **$20–50**

    (F) Contemporary Tom Mix, Hopalong Cassidy, Topsy, and Sambo, sold as single marbles. **$5**

Foreign Modern Handmade Glass Marbles

The House of Marbles, England, is the only known foreign glass house making handmade glass marbles. They are of high quality and design. Each marble is packaged individually in an attractive display box with appropriate silver on black printing showing the company logo and address and declaring that the marble is a "Handmade Victorian reproduced marble." Prices may vary for individual marbles according to type and design. Marbles with a colored transparent body command a higher price.

MACHINE-MADE GLASS MARBLES

Several leading catalogs carry a variety of marbles for sale in wooden boxes and leather pouches. A very colorful set is the Norman Rockwell Museum at Stockbridge bag of marbles in a leather pouch with booklet on how to play marbles, which features Rockwell's famous painting, "Marbles Champion," on its cover. Catalog price is $10.

Of the hundreds of different types of machine-made glass marbles, only a small percentage are considered collectible at this time. Only those types are listed in the following text and chart.

Promotional or Special Edition Marbles

Limited quantities of single marbles were produced for special purposes; these were not advertised or sold on the normal market at the time of production.

Marble King Logo: $7/8$ inch. **$100**
West Virginia Promotional Slogans: Marble King, $7/8$ inch. **$100**
Big Blue Marble: Marble King, $7/8$ inch. **$100**
Tom Mix and Cotes Bakery: See Peltier **$300**
Orange Crush. **$400**
Hoover 1932 President: One known example; extremely rare. **No price**

Big Game Bagatelle is a colorful toy pinball machine made by Marx Toys. It contains nine white marbles and one black marble.

Chicago Worlds Fair—Century of Progress: One known example, extremely rare. **No price**

The Collector Series: Plastic mesh bag containing Qualatex marbles—Meteors, Silvers, Glitters, Galaxies, Corsairs, and Cat Eyes. Thirty-five playing marbles and one shooter. This is a wonderful selection of marbles produced by Vacor de Mexico is reflected in the Collector Series. **$5**

ING-RICH BEAVER FALLS PA: Red lettering on a variety of glass body colors and designs. Examination of a collection of over nineteen types indicates that Akro Agate made the marbles for the imprinting. Two types are outstanding—Lemonade and Oxblood, and a Spiral (Corkscrew) light green in white Transparent body glass. This promotional marble was made for the Ingram-Richardson Manufacturing Company, Beaver Falls,

Pennsylvania, in operation from 1901 to 1965. Price for individual marble, depending on type/design/color of marble used. **$250–300**

Greenberg's Guide to Marbles: Promotional marble, blue lettering on white Opaque body glass, and a promotional item for first edition hardback book. This is the first dated glass promotional marble—1988. **No reported sales**

MARBLES OF OTHER MATERIALS

Metal Marbles

The most common metal "marbles" are solid steel ball bearings, which have no value as collectibles, even though some of these solid balls were actually sold as marbles (1914). Those steel marbles are, however, indistinguishable from their industrial counterparts, the ball bearings.

The other type of steel marble is fairly scarce. This is the hollow steel marble, sold during the early teens (1910–1914). It measures ½ inch to ¹¹⁄₁₆ inch in diameter and is recognizable by an X mark where the metal was crimped together.

"Cannonball Steel Marbles," Steelee Company, Hopkins, Minnesota, price per package. **$35**

"Genuine Steelies" steel marbles, price per package. **$25**

Hollow steel marble. **$30**

"Ottumwa" Steelie Marbles (colored), price per package. Rare. **$600**

Other Materials

Plastic, wood: Valued only as a curiosity in a collection. **No dollar value**

Ivory: Ivory "marbles" also exist, but are scarce. **$5**

Fiber-optic glass: Prices vary according to color, size, and availability. **$35–$100**

GAME BOARDS AND MISCELLANEOUS ITEMS

Chinese Checkers Boards

Chen Check Chinese Checkers: American Toy Works, New York, USA Assembler of Toys. Contains "metallic clay" marbles in a waxed paper envelope. **$150**

"CHING-KA-CHEK": Made by Gotham Pressed Steel Corporation, New York; Oriental motif, highly ornamental. **$35**

"HOP CHING": Made for J. Pressman Toy Company, New York; Oriental motif, highly ornamental. **$40**

"MAH TONG": Sold by the Alox Manufacturing Company, all red lettering and design, depicting Chinese junk and couple. **$30**

"MAN-DAR-IN": Plywood board made by Baldwin Manufacturing Co., Inc., Brooklyn, New York. **$75**

San Lo: Made by Northwestern Products Company, St. Louis. Unique board with hollow copper tubing around the edge and two butterfly closures for storing marbles. **$50**

"Ting Tong Tan" Marble Board: A variation of Chinese Checkers sold by Alox Manufacturing Company. The board is pressed wood with red paint and pictures six Chinese men running around it. **$35**

Chinese Checkers Board with no caption; all red lettering and design, depicting junk and dragon; sold by the Alox Manufacturing Company. **$25**

Four-Sided Chinese Checkers Board with no caption or ornamental design; two sides are green, two sides blue; sold by the Alox Manufacturing Company (scarce). **$80**

Other Game Boards

"BET-CHU-CAN'T": Solitaire game by Marietta Games, Incorporated, Marietta, Georgia. **$75**

"The Big Game—Bagatelle": Pinball game made by Marx Toys, with nine white marbles and one black marble. **$50**

Crystal Solitaire No. 37: Manufactured and Distributed by S. A. Derwik, Yonkers, New York. Wood board with 37 playing marbles; boxed. A variety of General Grant's game. **$600**

'Melican Checkee King Fuu Checkee': Cardboard with wood frame; checkerboard on reverse. Manufactured by Straits Manufacturing Company, Detroit, Michigan. **$25**

Three Great 13 Puzzle (Solitaire) patented July 25, 1899: Boxed set advertising the N. Y. Tea Company, Lancaster, Pennsylvania. **$125**

Miscellaneous Items

Fisher Jewel Trays: Made by Vitro Agate.

(A) No brand markings; tray has brass or old-like finish. **$65**

(B) "The Vitro Agate Co., Parkersburg, WV Patent Pending." **$35**

(C) Design Patent No. 99,857. **$30**

(D) Both Patent and Design Numbers. **$30**

(E) New York World's Fair Special Edition—1939. **$75**

(F) "Fisher-Master-Jewel Tray Pat 2,094,529 Des 99,857," fourteen marbles, silver finish, and 5¼ inch in diameter. **$50**

Fortune-Telling Marble: from Czechoslovakia. **$35**

Plastic Presentation Box with Genuine Agate Marble: Inscribed "Berry Pink"; very rare. Berry Pink of Marble King would sometimes compliment a tournament player with a present of a genuine agate marble made in Germany—a highly prized shooter. Another of Berry's marble gifts that opened many doors was a present to the secretary guarding the office; this was a special plastic jewelry box with an agate marble inside and "Berry Pink" inscribed on top. Many sales were made by using this unique and rare calling card. **$3,000**

Razor Blade Sharpener: This device was designed for sharpening safety razor blades and was sold in dime stores during the Great Depression years. The razor blade was pulled between the two marbles, thus sharpening the edge. **$20**

AMERICAN MARBLE COMPANIES

Akro Agate Products

Cardboard Box: Mixed types including shooters, plus drawstring pouch. Cover illustration shows three boys playing marbles. **$200–900**

Cardboard Box:

(A) Red; "Cardinal Reds," twenty-five red transparent Swirls. **$200–250**

(B) Partitioned; one hundred marbles plus shooter and one hundred sticks of gum. **$1,000**

(C) "Chinese Akro-Agate Checkers," sixty count. **$50**

(D) With cutout cardboard playing board inside plus twenty-five marbles. **$80**

(E) Solitary Chinese Checker set (board and marbles). **$75**

(F) Large boxed set labeled "Akro Agates" with colorful marble player scene on cover, includes knee pad. **$200**

(G) Boxed game, "Click." **$450**

(H) Boxed game, "Kings." Rare. **$925**

(I) Boxed set of fifteen marbles and pouch with "Popeye" on pouch and cover. **$800–900**

(J) Boxed set No. 230 containing marbles with pouch; central figure in a marble playing scene on the cover is a girl rather than a boy. Rare. **No reported sales**

Cutout Cardboard Box:

(A) Blue; "Superior Quality Assorted Colors No. 16," with five Transparent Swirls. **$40**

(B) Red; "Akro Agates Superior Quality," ten assorted, mainly Transparent Swirls. **$35–40**

Metal Box: Blue, five children pictured playing marbles, Akro logo. **$300–$500**

Net Bag:

(A) Paper label: "HY-Grade," thirty marbles. **$175**

(B) "Hot Shot Akro Agates 5-1." **$175**

Alley (St. Marys) Products

"Bull's Eye Marbles, Pressman Toy Corporation, New York, Made in USA": Appears to be made by L. E. Alley at St. Marys. Plastic Bag. **$35**

Alox Products

Cutout Cardboard Box: "Tit-Tat-Toe Three in a Row." Contains ten solid colors for playing the game plus twenty assorted colors. **$30**

Mesh and Poly Bags: Two different selections of marbles, Cat Eyes or assorted. Bags were packaged in quantities of twenty-five, thirty, fifty, sixty, or six hundred. Labels are a colorful red and white or red, white, and blue with two boys shown playing the ringer game. **$25–30**

Promotion Poly Bag: With printed header made for "Weatherbird Shoes." **$35**

Bogard Products

"Mountaineer Shooters, Made by Mountain Craftsmen in W. Va."; Cat Eyes. C. E. Bogard & Sons. Colorful yellow cardboard with blister pack. Scarce. **$35**

Poly Bag: Double headers. Bogard label stapled on top of Heaton Agate label; "Cat Eyes—The Cat's eye in Glass 19 Count." Rare. **$300**

Cairo Products

Cardboard Box: With marbles game "Trap The Fox." No known examples of a complete box or set of marbles. Rare. **No reported sales**

Champion Agate Products

Backlash: Unique, only one run made. **$10**

Bicentennial Pack: 1976, poly bag. **$50**

"Flame": In smaller size made by Champion Agate for a major toy company. **$3**

Single "Flame": $7/16$ inch red-white Opaque Swirl with a hint of yellow (company-named marble). A unique marble made in only one run. **$10**

60 Chinese Checkers Marbles: Made for Steven Manufacturing Company. **$20**

White Label, Red Lettering:

(A) "4 Champion Agates." **$10**

(B) "5 Champion Agates." Most packages contain the transparent Clearies, but an occasional package may contain an Opaque Slag-type marble. **$15**

(C) "20 Champion Agates." Contains a wonderful assortment of early machine-made marbles. **$25**

Christensen Agate Company Products

Boxed Set of 25: American Agates (glass). **$2,000**

Boxed Set of 25: World's Best Guineas. **$7,500**

Single Marble: Guinea. **$300**

The above prices are not realistic but are current prices paid. Prices may drop when other equally beautiful but unknown color and design types appear, such as the glass Tiger Eye by Master Marble. Price may fluctuate in the event a cache or hoard is discovered.

Heaton Products

Big Shot 60 Count Chinese Checkers: Plastic bag. **$60**

Big Shot 60 Count: Mesh bag, red label. **$75**

Big Shot 60 Count: Mesh bag, brown label. **$75**

Big Shot 10 Count Cat Eye Marbles: Plastic. **$50**

Kokomo Opalescent Glass Company Products

Chief Kokomo: Cotton mesh bag. Rare. **No reported sales**

Chief Kokomo: Cardboard box. Rare. **No reported sales**

Single Marble: **$5**

Marble King Products

Marble King's earlier packages had plain white labels; the later ones had black and white labels with the Marble King logo. The earliest types indicate Berry Pink Industries, while the later packages are labeled Marble King Incorporated. Marble King produced a very wide range and number of items, many of them very collectible. Early Marble King packets containing Peltier's Rainbo are very collectible, and the price is doubled.

Blister Pack of Cat Eyes: Five count including shooters. Reverse side lettered "Words that Players Use and What they Mean" and "'Tips' to Remember." **$15**

Blister Pack of Rainbows: Five count including shooters. Reverse side lettered "Words that Players Use and What they Mean" and "'Tips' to Remember." **$20**

Boxed Set: Labeled "60 Solid Color Marbles—Red, yellow, blue, green, black, white for Chinko-Checko-Marblo." Berry Pink, Inc. **$45**

Bumble Bee, Cub Scout, or Black Widow: Single marble, in large size. **$20–35**

Cat Eyes: Single marble, $1\frac{1}{4}$ inches. **$15**

Cat Eyes: Single marble, four vanes—red, dark blue, dark green, and yellow. Short-lived design. **$5**

"Cat's Eye": Fourteen count; all red label with no logo. **$20**

Cellophane Tube containing six early Cat Eyes promoting General Foods Post Toasties. **$45**

Coca-Cola Bottle Hanger: With Rainbow marble types.

This box contains one hundred Number 8 assorted mint Master Marble Company marbles. The marble types include Sunbursts, Alabasters, Meteors, Ivories, and Clearies. This collection is not *common in mint box or assorted designs. Note the company logo, "Master Made/M M M/Marbles." The box includes dividers. J. Fred Early Collection.*

    (A) All-red label (earlier type). **$30**
    (B) Red and white label. **$20**
    (C) Red and white label containing six ⅞-inch Rainbo (Peltier) marbles. **$35**
Display Board: With "J"-shaped tube blister pack on cardboard with an empty plastic mesh bag and closure carrier. Contains forty marbles (four red Opaques and thirty-six cobalt blue Transparents). Featuring Spider Man. **$200**
Display Board: With caption "Marble King says 'Knuckle Down' with American marbles." Reverse says, "The Game of Marbles How Ringer is Played." Contains forty marbles of various types with reusable leather bag. **$80**
Leather Pouch of Marble King marbles sold as a promotional item with Fred Ferretti's *The Great American Marble Book*, 1973. Recent but now quite rare. Price for book with marbles. **$250**
"Marble King Says 'Knuckle Down' with American

Marbles": Marble King's latest package, a "J"-shaped blister pack on display board, plastic mesh bag, and forty Rainbow and Cat Eye marbles. The back of the board, like "Secrets of a Marble Champ," explains the basic rules of the Ringer game and gives advice to shooters. The package does not contain the Bumble Bee, Cub Scout, or Black Widow. **$300**
Marble King Tournament Assortment: Cat Eyes, Rainbows, Moonies, Marine Crystals, and large shooters. The colorful cloth bag alone is quite collectible ($25).
    (A) Cloth bag (228 marbles) **$90**
    (B) Poly bag (140 marbles) **$40**
Maryland 350th Celebration Commemorative Marble 1635–1984: Commissioned exclusively for the event. Leather bag and commemorative label. Colors are black and yellow (Maryland's state colors), similar in design to the Rainbow (Bumble Bee). **$200**
Plastic Mesh Bag: With plastic closure and carrying

handle with fifty assorted Rainbow marbles featuring "The Incredible Hulk" on the label. **$60**

Poly Bag: Containing "14 Rainbow Marble King Marbles 14." Red label. Includes their Bumble Bee. **$25**

Poly Bag: Containing an assortment of marbles labeled, "Compliments of Marble King, Inc. 1st Avenue Paden City, W. VA 26159," distributed at the 1989 National Marble Tournament. **$20**

Poly Pack 60 Chinese Checkers: With Marble King header. **$12**

Poly Pack 60 Chinese Checkers: Without Marble King header. **$8**

Poly Pack: Early red and white header "Glass Shooters," twelve count Transparent marbles. Contains a pink-colored type. **$15**

Poly Pack: Header of red and white "American Made Glass Marbles," twenty-five count Transparent marbles with shooter. **$20**

Poly Pack: Header of black and white "Glass Marbles," 45 count Transparent marbles with shooter. **$30**

Red and White Label: With logo and caption "American Made Glass Marbles" Cat Eyes, twelve count. **$10**

"Secrets of a Marble Champ": Unusual display board containing the Marble King booklet "The Game of Marbles," a leather marble bag, and fifty marbles plus shooter in blister pack. **$100**

Special Packages for marbles were also produced. The best known are the bottle-hanger packages for Coca-Cola and Pepsi-Cola, and regular packets for Dolly Madison Dairy products, Mr. Peanuts, and "Elsie," of the Borden Company. These contained the ever-popular Rainbow marbles, and the header gave marble player guidance and caution in playing. Double the price for packets containing the Rainbo made by Peltier. **$10–25**

Master Glass Products

Chinese Checker Set: Sixty marbles in six colors. **$50**

Marble Set: Containing thirty or sixty size 0 marbles in assorted colors. **$45**

Master Shooter Bag: Poly bag containing five 1-inch marbles. **$12**

Mesh Bag: Size 0 marbles, quantities of twelve, seventeen, twenty-six, and thirty-six in assorted colors. **$12–35**

Plastic Packet: Five Translucent assorted shooters mislabeled as "Cat's eye." **$12**

Plastic Packet: "Master Marbles" containing five shooters. **$10**

Poly Bag: Size 0 marbles, containing fourteen, nineteen, thirty, and forty marbles in assorted colors. **$40–100**

Shooter Assortment: Thirteen marbles, assorted sizes and colors. **$200**

Master Marble Products

Box of 100: Assorted (ten each of ten types) with caption "Master Made Marbles" and "MMM" logo in center; lid designed for folding display. Scarce. **$300**

College Edition: For 1933 Chicago World's Fair (A and B).

(A) Red velour-like carton containing decorated leather marble bag and knuckle pad. Inside of cover is a color panorama of the Fair. Rare. **$600**

(B) Cardboard box with top of cover containing a color panorama of the Fair. Forty and sixty various type Master Made marbles and decorated chamois bag. Cardboard dust cover shows the World's Fair "Master Marbles Shop"

and group of children at play. Rare. **$700–800**

(C) No. 130 boxed set with double plastic cutouts on top with eighteen marbles of assorted design, and the caption "Master Made Marbles." **$25**

(D) No. 13 boxed set with five cutouts on top and thirteen marbles of assorted design, and the caption "Master Made Marbles." Bottom of box had advertisement for Popsicle-Fudgsicle. **$35**

(E) Glass Tiger Eye (single marble), quite rare. **$500**

Peltier Products

Big Value: Boxed assortment containing approximately one hundred Rainbo marbles. **$75–100**

Boxed Set of twenty-five Cerise Agates, M. Gropper & Sons, Inc. **$250–300**

"Champion Jr. Glass Marbles": Plastic bag containing a colorful assortment of eighteen early marbles. **$15–20**

Morton's Salt: Promotional mesh bag containing an assortment of Rainbo marbles. **$30**

Picture Marbles: Andy Gump, Betty Boop, Bimbo, Emma, Herbie, Kayo, Koko, Moon Mullins, Orphan Annie, Sandy, Skeezix, and Smitty. Often called Comics. Tom Mix and Coates Bakery marbles also are found. Prices may vary according to character, color scheme, condition of character, grade of marble, and rarity (rare, scarce, standard).

(A) Boxed set of five Picture Marbles. **$600 & Up**

(B) Boxed set of twelve Picture Marbles. Standard colors (first color is the patch color): Andy—green/yellow; Betty—red/yellow; Bimbo—green/white and red/yellow; Kayo—black/white; Emma—blue;white; Herbie—black/white; Moon Mullins—green/yellow; Orphan Annie—red/white; Koko—green/white; Sandy—blue;white; Smitty—green/yellow; and Skeezix—blue/white. **$1,300 & Up**

(C) Set of twelve in black/white, blue/white, red/white, dark yellow/dark green—priced much higher than the standard color sets above. Sets are very scarce and it is hard to determine prices. **No reported sales**

(D) Tom Mix, individual marble. **$700 & Up**

(E) Cotes Bakery, individual marble. **$500 & Up**

(F) Individual Picture Marble (Comics). Rare color combination is blue with a yellow patch. Scarce color combinations are dark green/dark yellow patch; blue/red patch; light green/light yellow patch (lighter than standard yellow/green). Standard color combinations (first color listed is the patch color:

Andy, green/yellow.	**$110**
Annie, red/white.	**$85**
Betty, red/yellow.	**$110**
Bimbo, green/white.	**$65**
Emma, blue/white.	**$70**
Herbie, black/white.	**$80**
Kayo, black/white.	**$225 & Up**
This particular marble is in great demand and the price is going up.	
Koko, green/white.	**$85**
Moon Mullins, green/yellow	**$135 & Up**
Sandy, blue/white.	**$100**
Skeezix, blue/white.	**$85**
Smitty, green/yellow.	**$65**

The price for the above marbles varies depending on what color and what character on that color.

Old and new Vitro Agate packages. From left, Vitro "Aqua Jewels," which were made in a variety of colors; Vitro "45 + 1," the last of the design series made in 1989, before the plant was moved to Anacortes, Washington; mesh bag, the earliest known marbles made by Vitro Agate at the Parkersburg factory and very collectible in mint condition; Vitro Cat Eyes, of the early 1950s type with pronounced vanes. This package is unique because it contains a Clearie shooter. Courtesy Lewis L. Moore, former Vitro Agate plant manager.

Prima Agates boxes: Four small boxes fit in one large box. Empty boxes sell for about $35 and up.
"Sparklets": In plastic bag. **$20**
"Sparklets": Containing the Peltier single-vane Cat Eye. **$30**
"30 Marine Crystals": In plastic bag with blue label. **$10**

The classic Peltier Rainbo may appear in early promotional packages made up by Marble King at the St. Marys factory. (See Chapter XIV.)

Ravenswood Products
Buddy Brand:
    (A) Poly bags, forty or one hundred marbles. **$40–200**
    (B) Cut-out cardboard box, nineteen or thirty marbles. **$40–90**
Cardboard Box: With "Buddy" or plain green box with caption "Made in USA" and eighteen white stars around the top and sides. **$30**
Paul Bunyans: Five 1-inch shooters in assorted colors. **$15**

Vitro Agate (Parkersburg Products)
Bag of thirty count Cat Eyes in blue, yellow, green, red, and white vanes. "The Pride of Young Americans Made in U.S.A. Vitro-Agate Co., Parkersburg, W.Va." **$25**
"Blackbeard's Treasure Chest of Marbles": Cardboard boxed selection of Gladding Vitro agate marbles (243 pieces plus eight shooters) with colorful label. Considered quite rare since only two hundred samples were sent to sales representatives and toy stores; they were not acceptable and production ceased. Twelve boxes were packed to a carton. **$200**
Bottle Hanger: "Double Cola—Free—This bag of Vitro Agates with the purchase of this 6 bottle carton of Double Cola." Eighteen count plastic bag. **$25**
Boxed Set: Sixty game marbles No. 00 made for Chinese Checkers games. Six colors, ten each. Early type company logo in center of box cover—"The Vitro Agate Company, Parkersburg, W.Va." **$60**
Cotton Mesh Bag: "25 Vitro Agates 25," light brown label. Early marble design. **$25**
Cotton Mesh Bag: "Vitro's Victory Agates—30," light brown label. Early marble design. **$35**
Earliest Vitro Agate Company Price List: No. 5 Shooter bag (mesh) with five marbles, label reads "5 Shooters 5." **$10**
No. 0 Tri-Lite Marbles: Boxed, one hundred marbles. **$60**
No. 1 Tri-Lite Marbles: Boxed, one hundred marbles. **$65**
No. 1 Clear-Lite Marbles: Boxed, one hundred marbles. **$75**
No. 2 Tri-Lite Marbles: Boxed, fifty marbles. **$65**
No. 2 Tri-Lite Marbles: Boxed, one hundred marbles. **$75**
No. 2 Clear-Lite Marbles: Boxed, fifty marbles. **$60**
No. 10 Gift Box: Twenty-eight marbles and leather marble bag. **$75**
No. 30 Mesh Bag: Thirty marbles, with label "30 Spinners 30." **$20**
No. 40 Pee-Wee Bag: Forty marbles, with label "40 Pee Wees 40." **$25**

No. 60 Mesh Bag: Sixty marbles, with label "60 Sunny Boy 60" **$30**
Plastic Bag: With label "Vitro Agate Corporation—Subsidiary of Paris Manufacturing Co. Parkersburg, West Virginia." Containing forty-five marbles and one shooter (Cat Eyes, cage type). The vanes are single-color red, azure, and opaque white. **$50**
Poly Bag: With drawstring; "Gladding Vitro Marbles—100 Marbles—The Pride of Young Americans." Bag illustration shows marble game scene. **$75**
Special Design-Experimental "Confetti": Made in Parkersburg. Body glass may be transparent white, transparent light green, or opaque black.
    (A) White or green. **$5–25**
    (B) Black. **$25**
Vitro Agate Jewels: Thirty count Five Star Brand Transparent $9/16$-inch diameter marbles, wide assortment of colors. The blue is deep, with no seeds. Green printing on white label. **$40**
"Vitro Cat Eyes 6 Count—Five Star Brand Shooters 10¢": Reverse side "The Pride of Young Americans Vitro-Agate-Co." Plastic bag. **$12**

Various header designs appear on their packaged marbles throughout their history. The earliest is "The Vitro Agate Company," followed by two subsidiary owners, "Gladding-Vitro-Agate" and "Vitro-Agate Corporation." All packages have a Parkersburg, West Virginia, address.

Vitro Agate (Anacortes, Washington) Products
Vitro Agate made toy marbles in designs and colors similar to but not exactly like those previously made at the Parkersburg factory. Two different header designs for their packaged marbles exist. The first one is similar to the header used at Parkersburg but with an Anacortes address. The header contains an altogether new design with the Anacortes address. Collectors are cautioned to read the headers on the Vitro Agate packages in view of various changes in design, ownership, and location.

The Anacortes factory stopped production in early 1993. Stock on hand continued to be sold; remaining stock, consisting of packaged and lose marbles, was purchased by JABO, Incorporated. The short period of production of the Anacortes design marbles should make this an instant collectible—a so-called "sleeper."

FOREIGN MAKER MACHINE-MADE GLASS MARBLES

"Fifty of the World's Best Marbles": Contains a canvas marble bag and instruction booklet attached to the top of a clear plastic canister. Made in Devon, England. **$15**

H. E. Hopf (Germany): Plastic bag or plastic mesh single colors with clear transparent body glass; colors in a random design resembling the so-called Wirepull. **$15**

Vacor de Mexico: Vacor USA is the sole distributor of marbles made by Vacor de Mexico, in a large variety of designs and colors.
    (A) "Collector Marbles," an assortment of eighty 16mm marbles and two 25mm shooters in genuine leather pouch, marble game rules, and two marble display rings. **$30**

(B) Limited Edition, Collector Sampler, comes in plastic mesh bag. **$25**

(C) Travelog Collector Marbles, nineteen marbles and one shooter with imprinted United States city; entire set consists of fourteen cities. Price is for single set, one city. **$5**

[1]"Marble Sizing and Conditions," *Marble-Mania*, Vol. 55 (July 1989), p. 4.

Dictionary of Marble Terms

AGATE: Also Aggie; a taw or shooter made of agate stone; the perennial favorite shooter of generations of players. Agates were famous for their tendency to develop "moons," which were concoidal fractures just under the surface, due to the concussions suffered in hard play. A folk remedy for such scars is to soak the marble in lard or grease for a few days; the lard is supposedly absorbed into the fractures, which become less noticeable. The hardness of agate varies and on Mohs' hardness scale is listed as being from 6.5 to 7.

ALABASTER GLASS: Translucent milky-white glass popular from the late 1920s through the 1930s; the main coloring agent was common table salt. Fred Carder, founder of the Steuben Glass Works at Corning, New York, called milky translucent glass "alabaster"; it diffuses light without a fiery color.

ANNEALING: The process of heating and cooling glass to produce a durable end product. Properly annealed marbles bounce on hard surfaces rather than breaking; poorly annealed marbles will shatter. It is accomplished by placing marbles in a lehr.

AVENTURINE: Either the mineral, which is a quartz with mica flecks in it, or its glass imitation. According to Professor E. Peligot of France, "Aventurine is a yellowish glass in which there are an infinite number of small crystals of copper, protoxide of copper, or silicate of that oxide." Hautefeuill, a skilled chemist in the Societé d'Encouragement, in October 1860 described the above process—"when the glass is very liquid, iron or fine brass turnings enclosed in paper are added, these are incorporated into it by stirring the glass with a red-hot iron rod. The glass becomes blood red, opaque, and at the same time milky and full of bubbles; the draught of the furnace is then stopped, the ash-pan closed, the pot with its lid on is covered with ashes, and it is allowed to cool very slowly. The next day on breaking the pot the Aventurine is seen formed."[1] Shortly before, Fremy and Clemandot succeeded with a recipe consisting of "three hundred parts pounded glass, forty parts copper scales, and eighty parts iron scales, cooked for twenty hours and then slowly cooled."[2] As noted above, the operative words "crystals of copper" and "scales of copper" do not necessarily mean that the ingredient was the metal copper alone, but could mean that it was a salt or oxide thereof.

BAG: Personalized containers for a player's marbles; often included as part of a manufacturer's package of marbles. Akro Agate and Master Marble at one time included a highly decorated chamois marble bag in some of their premiere edition packages. Marble King also offered a leather bag with certain of their packages. During the Great Depression, children often kept their marbles in empty cloth tobacco bags.

BALL AND LIGHT TEST: A method currently in general use for testing the alignment of grooves in rollers. A steel ball is placed between the rolls and an electric light placed underneath the rolls to observe the position of the ball in the grooves. When the rolls are in proper alignment, a black spot will show at the contact point between each side of the ball and the bottom of each groove. When the rolls are set with the lead on one roll, a black spot will occur if the upper groove is leading, since the ball would naturally contact the groove beyond the center.

BATCH: The component parts of a single melting, comparable to a cake recipe.

BATCH BOOK: An in-house notebook containing glass formulas.

BATCH ROOM: Area in glass marble manufacturing plant where glass colors and recipes are weighed and mixed.

BLADE: See VANES.

BLISTER PACK: A modern package for marbles with a large plastic container holding the marbles in place.

BLOCKING: The forming of a gather of glass into a sphere by twisting in a semi-circular concave block of wood, metal, or carbon (graphite).

BODY: The basic part of a glass marble, upon which or into which the design glass ("striping") is put. The basic framework or non-design portion of the marble.

BODY GLASS: Glass used to form the body of glass marbles; may be transparent to opaque. In the case of veneered marbles, the body glass is often made of scrap glass to reduce production cost.

BOTTLE HANGER: A particular kind of package of promotional marbles with header, designed to hang around the necks of bottles. The Marble King Coca-Cola packages are an example.

BOTTLE MARBLES: Handmade or mold-made marbles used as a stoppering device in soda bottles beginning about 1870 and continuing well into the twentieth century.

BURN SPOTS: Black circular spots on a Bennington marble; players call them "black eyes." Most contemporary handmade or machine-made marbles do not have them.

CAGE MARBLE: A particular style of Cat Eye, wherein the vanes are well-separated at the middle and tend toward the outside of the marble, forming a cage-like network. Not a factory brand name.

CANDY STRIPES: Handmade Spirals or Swirls.

CANE: Long slender thin rod of glass made for the glass industry; it may be a single cane or a bundle of canes fused together.

CAT EYE: Type of glass machine-made marble introduced into the United States market by the Japanese in 1950–1951; characterized by the presence of colored vanes or blades in a clear body.

CHAIR: Wooden bench with two arms that supports the punty (or iron) of the gatherer. One hand rolls the shaft of the iron while the other hand shapes the glass by blocking.

CHARGE: Loading the melting pot, furnace, or tank with a batch.

CHINESE CHECKERS MARBLES: Opaque marbles made to play the game and normally packaged at the factory in "60 count" bags. Nor normally collected as a single marble, but highly collectible if contained in a factory package marked as "Chinese Checkers Marbles."

CHRYSOPRASE: A very fine-grained translucent to transparent green quartz.

CLAMBROTH: A handmade glass marble, distinguished by a series of fine regularly spaced threads of glass on the outer surface of the body, running from one pole of the marble to the other in a gently spiraling curve

CLEARIE: A single-colored transparent marble.

COLD SHEAR: A method of cutting a gob of molten glass without any preforming of the gob before it hits the rolls.

COMICS or COMIC STRIP MARBLES: Machine-made glass marbles made by the Peltier Glass Company commencing in 1933 and containing a picture; erroneously named, since the official records of the company and their labeled boxes show them to be called Picture Marbles.

COMMERCIAL MARBLES: Glass spheres manufactured for commercial or industrial use; may be used as ball bearings, aerosol can mixing balls, or in the perforation of oil-bearing geological strata. Also called Industrials.

COMMIES: Common or inexpensive marbles; used over a long period of time to describe a variety of marble types, particularly clay types in the early twentieth century. Also a glass marble made by Peltier.

CONFETTI: Machine-made glass marble with numerous colored dots on the surface. Number and color may vary according to the factory; body glass may be opaque or transparent. Confetti marbles with colored body glass are scarce.

CORNELIAN: A variety of red agate, a prime stone for agate marbles in the late nineteenth and early twentieth centuries; also spelled "carnelian" and sometimes called "blood cornelian" in the pre-World War I catalogs. Color

of this stone may be altered (light to dark) by exposure to a direct flame or to the direct rays of the sun, as practiced in India.

CROCKERY: See Chapter III.

CRYPTOCRYSTALLINE QUARTZ: Category of quartz that includes the microscopically grained quartzes, chalcedony, agate, jasper, chert, and flint.

CULLET: Broken glass used as an ingredient of a batch of glass. The glass may consist of formula glass made from scratch at the marble factory or purchased from another glass factory. A mix of scrap glass, which may include glass soda bottles or milk glass from cold cream jars, that is added to the melting furnace or day tank and mixed with cullet. Scrap glass is cheaper than formula (recipe) cullet and can be used as body glass when a veneer of better quality glass is to be applied.

CULLET WAGON: Used to transport cullet glass in manufacturing areas.

DAY TANK: The main melting tank erected on grade (at ground level) for full stock, capable of melting from one to five tons of recipe or recycled glass. In modern production methods, the molten glass is poured from the day tank to the kettle for transport to an area where it may be dumped and broken into cullet. The name derives from the fact that the usual method is to fill in and work out the glass daily, loading it in at the end of the day and melting overnight.

DUPLEX MACHINE: A marble machine with two sets of rolls. May be fed at the center or from the end.

END OF DAY: One-of-a-kind marbles, generally of a large diameter; according to popular belief, made by glassworkers at the end of the day for presents for their children. The usual method of glassworkers was to fill in and work out the glass daily, loading it at the end of the day and melting overnight.

FIRE POLISHING: Reheating a finished contemporary handmade marble by melting scars or the punty mark. Contemporary handmade marble makers use a torch.

FLATWARE: Also "pressware"; basically, any glassware other than marbles. Many marble makers did and do produce flatware as well as marbles.

FLATS: See NUGGETS.

FLINTIE: Early hand-ground marble made of chalcedony-flint; color is a translucent light to dark gray. A type of agate. Grinding facets are visible. Flintie is also a Master Marble factory name. See Chapter XI on marble recipes and formulas.

FLUX: An alkaline substance, such as potash or soda, which aids the fusion of the silica; it produces a rapid chemical activity, causing the batch to melt together. Potassium oxide also acts as a flux.

FRIED MARBLES: Popular for a short time in the 1960s; individuals produced "fried marbles" by heating marbles in a frying pan and then plunging the marbles into cold water. They fractured internally, producing beautiful designs that reflected light like small mirrors. Often used in jewelry and do-it-yourself knickknacks. Modern mass production of fried marbles has been accomplished. The hot marbles from the marble rollers are directed into a large flat metal pan instead of the lehr and then jet-sprayed with a fine mist of cold water. Shipping of fried marbles is a problem, since they have a tendency to break apart due to internal fractures.

GAME MARBLES: More correctly called "toy marbles" in earlier days. A term used by marble makers to distinguish marbles that will be used as toys from marbles that are designed for industrial usage. Often marbles originally intended for industrial use are later employed by children as game marbles.

GATHER: A gob of molten glass on the tip of the punty.

GATHERER: The primary team member in the hand-assisted production of machine-made marbles prior to about 1926. See Chapter X for details of the gatherer's role. The gatherer was paid according to the number of marbles of a proper size he made. The unit of pay was based on one thousand marbles. The marbles produced were screened and sorted according to size; acceptable ones were placed in buckets of one thousand. The job of the gatherer, as well as those of the other team members, was eventually eliminated by the full automation of the process. Some of the most beautiful glass marbles were made by the gatherer. Sometimes called "gathering boy" at the Akro Agate factory. Not really a boy, but an adult male.

GEMS: See NUGGETS.

GLASS HOUSE: Earlier name for a glass factory.

GLASS MARBLE SCISSORS: A hand-held tool used to cut and form a marble from a cane. Invented by Johann Christoph Simon Karl Greiner of the famous Greiner family of glassmakers. A similar type of scissors had already been used for the creation of animal's eyes and glass blobs.[3]

GLASSMAN: An employee of a glass house or glass factory.

GLAZE: In ceramics, the liquid mixture applied to the outside of a clay object which, when fired, produces a very hard, high-glass finish. In marbles, seen on Chinas and Benningtons. Various metal oxides when painted on (dipped) or mixed into a glaze give different colors. Copper oxide produces green, iron oxide produces brown or green, and cobalt oxide produces blue. Glazing can also be accomplished by a method called "salt glazing," wherein salt is added to the kiln during the firing. The salt vaporizes, then condenses on the surface of the clay and fuses with the silica in it.

GLORY HOLE: An opening in a monkey pot or open pot (tank), from which molten glass is withdrawn or into which a punty or blow pipe may be inserted for the purpose of preliminary heating and withdrawing of a gob of molten glass.

GOB: A mass of molten glass. It may be glass cut from the tip of the punty or glass sheared from the molten stream of glass coming out of the orifice in a modern marble machine.

GOLDSTONE: Not a mineral, but glass with a gold sparkling effect. Goldstone stripes are the mark of "Lutz" marbles.

GROUND BURNER: A marble shot from ten feet or more that "scorches the ground" on its way to your marble, then scorches your psyche.

HANDSHOP: Term used by Akro Agate officers to describe a working unit (three-man or two-man team) on a Hill marble machine.

HEADER: Top part of a package or bag containing advertising or factory information; usually stapled onto the package and made of heavy paper or cardboard.

HOT END: That part of a marble factory containing the melting tanks and furnaces.

HOT SHEAR: A mechanical device located between the orifice of the melting furnace and the rolls. The hot shear cut the teardrop-shaped flow of molten glass into a gob for one marble.

IMITATION AGATE: Term used in catalogs of the late nineteenth and early twentieth centuries to designate a variety of marbles, from brown crockeries to machine-made glass. The term was meant to appeal to the players' attraction to genuine agate marbles.

IMITATION ONYX: Use in the same manner and time as Imitation Agate, above.

INCRUSTATION: The art of incrusting a Sulphide figure in glass to form a cameo, paperweight, or toy marble.

INDIAN OR JOSEPH SWIRL: Handmade glass marble characterized by vividly colored strips of several colors on the surface of a dark body.

INDUSTRIALS See COMMERCIAL MARBLES.

KETTLE: A three-wheeled cast-iron container used to prepare cullet or to transport molten glass.

KNUCKLE PAD: A part of many a seasoned marble player's game kit, along with a marble bag and perhaps a knee pad. Used to protect the player's knuckles against the ground. The favorite material for a pad was a piece of sheepskin. Some players scorned the use of such pads, preferring to display their well-worn knuckles.

LAMP OR LAMPWORK: Melting a glass cane or canes over a burner.

LATTICINO: A fine pattern or network of fine threads of colored glass in the body of handmade glass marbles.

LEAD: See OFFSET.

LEHR: As used in the marble industry, the heated metal bucket or annealing can at the end of the production process. Also, a small oven with controlled heat to anneal handmade marbles.

LUTZ: Any marble with goldstone-like stripes. See Chapter XIV, section on the Boston and Sandwich Glass Company.

MAPLE SUGAR SYRUP: An ingredient in clay marbles recipes as long ago as 130 years. It was thought that the sugar was converted to carbon in the firing process and made a harder marble.[4] Raw sugar was used by Robert A. Brown to make his Sugar Daddy.[5]

MARBLE YARD: A specially prepared arena with three equally spaced holes, 10 feet apart on a 25 by 40 foot of packed red clay for playing the Rolley Hole game. Most yards have wood side bumpers.

MARVER: Polished metal or lithic stone on which a gather is rolled or shaped for further processing.

MELTING TANK: An elevated tank positioned above the modern marble machine. Cullet or scrap glass are shoveled into it through the rear opening.

METAL: The glassmakers' name for molten glass.

MIB: The marble used by the mibster.

MIBSTER: What marble players call each other.

MICAS: Also "micaceous marbles"; handmade glass marbles with flecks of ground mica included in transparent body glass. Some contemporary marbles made by Gibson Glass Company contain iron pyrite flakes instead of mica, which achieves the same glitter.

MILKIES: Translucent marbles, usually without decoration other than a single coloring of the body glass. Also known as Cloudies, Vaselines, milk glass, etc.

MOLD MARK: Fine ring or ridge around the circumference of a marble caused by excess glass in a hand-held mold. Not to be confused with a "roll mark."

MONKEY POT: A closed cylindrical vessel about 5½ feet high with a hole in one side about a foot down from the top. Six or more of these pots are arranged in a circle with openings facing out on the floor of a cone-shaped furnace that is fired from a pit below the floor. The fire surrounds the pots, and the glass is charged and drawn out through the side openings in the pots. This melting procedure was used before the advent of the modern day tank.

NUGGETS: Also known as gems or flats, according to various makers; not marbles, but produced on marble-making machines, in many cases using recipes identical to marbles. Used in board games, flat on one side, and generally square or ovoid in shape.

OFFSET: The intentional non-alignment of the grooves in the rollers of marble-making machines. The offset more thoroughly knead the gob of glass, producing a smoother surfaced marble. The rollers can be shifted slightly forward or backward to change the diameter of the marbles produced. Synonymous with "lead."

ONIONSKIN: Handmade glass marbles characterized by a solid layer of colors just under the surface; produced by rolling in tiny flecks of colored glass, then adding another layer of clear body glass.

ONYX: Very soft mineral used in commercial marble-making in the late nineteenth century. May have been used in imitation of true agate, but due to the minereal's soft nature, few onyx marbles have survived. Some early machine-made glass marbles were called "onyx" marbles in catalogs.

OPEN POT: A vessel that looks like a thick-walled washtub. It rests on the floor of a furnace with the fire surrounding it, as a monkey pot does when it is heated. However, the intense heat passes over the top of the melting glass. This is the same principle as the modern day tank except that the day tank is much larger. The open pot is normally lifted and moved by a pot chariot.

ORIFICE: A hole in the bottom of the flow tank through which molten glass flows by gravity into the shearing/feeding device.

PEE WEE: A small marble, about ⅜ inch in diameter; the term was used for a long period of time and varied from region to region in the exact types of marble denoted. Also Pee Dad.

PEPPERMINT SWIRL: A handmade glass marble, usually opaque or translucent white body glass with red and blue stripes on the surface, alternating to form a red, white, and blue pattern like peppermint candy.

POLES: Two points on opposite ends of the marble where design elements begin and end, or come together.

POLKA DOT: A contemporary ceramic design by Robert A. Brown, Ironton, Ohio. A time-consuming marble to decorate because of hand application of many colors of dots and the number of firings required—a separate firing for each color. Quite scarce and highly prized.

PONTIL: See PUNTY.

PONTIL MARK: In most cases, the term "pontil mark" is a misuse of a glass-making term, meant as the scar on the finished product where the glass was cut from the hot metal rod or blowpipe. Since the pontil was used only in one-of-a-kind marbles like End of Day marbles and some

Sulphides, only these two types have a true pontil mark. Other handmade glass marbles have a similar scar that should properly be called a cutoff mark.

POT CHARIOT: A prefabricated two-wheeled cart used to transport the pot from one area to another. It has long handles to protect the operator from heat and a lifting capability like a fork on one end.

PROMOTIONAL MARBLES: Specially packaged or specially designed marbles promoting a particular commercial venture or product. Marble King's Mr. Peanuts, Coca-Cola, and Pepsi-Cola packages are prime examples of a regular production marble that was packaged for a particular commercial application. The Coca-Cola marbles package label had a hole in it so that it hung around the neck of the bottles (bottle hanger). Included was advice for the players, such as "stay out of the streets" and "play a fair game." During the late 1920s and 1930s, marbles were used in the sale of divinity candy. A marble was stuck on top of each piece of candy, slightly covered with frosting so that it was not clearly visible. The purchaser might get a cheap clay or a fine machine-made glass marble. In the early 1950s, Cat Eye marbles were placed in gum ball machines. The purchaser might get a ball of gum or a new, popular Cat Eye marble.

PUNTY: Also called a punty iron or pontil. The primary glass-handling tool used by the gatherer in the making of glass marbles in the first three decades of the twentieth century. A typical punty was a handmade $3/8$-inch steel rod 30 inches long with a rivet welded to the end. The size of the head determined the size of the gather and marble.

PURIE: Single-colored Translucent marble.

RAINBO OR RAINBOW: Brand names for types of machine-made glass marbles. See Chapter XIV, Peltier and Marble King sections. The Rainbow is also the name of a contemporary Swirl made by Mark Matthews of Matthews Art Glass.

RECIPE: The formula for making marble glass; also the ingredients themselves. A marble recipe is like a cake recipe; it can be made from scratch or can be bought ready-mixed from another maker in the form of cullet.

REFINING STATE: The time in the glassmaking process after the batch is melted and the day tank is opened, allowing the molten glass to give off gas.

RIBBON CORE: A handmade marble with a single ribbon-like strip of colored glass at its core.

ROLL MARK: Incused, circular surface defects in a machine-made marble considered a reject. Similar defects are found in early machine-made "transitionals" and were not considered as rejects by the early factories.

ROULETTE BALL: Glass ball with thirty-two facets, each numbered; also called "fortune-telling marble." See Chapter VIII, Game Boards and Miscellaneous Items.

SAND: Principal ingredient of glass. West Virginia glassmakers use Oriskany sand, from Berkeley Springs, West Virginia, which has very small angular grains and is pure white. Similar high-grade sand used by Peltier is obtained from the famous sand pits in Ottawa, Illinois.

SEED: An extremely small gaseous inclusion in body glass.

SEEDY GLASS: Glass containing minute bubbles of gas. In the early days of marble production, this trait was thought to be undesirable, but more recently has been seen as an acceptable design characteristic in certain machine-made marble types. Transparent marbles that are completely free of bubbles generally predate the "seedy" examples.

SHEAR MARK: A noticeable scar remaining when a marble is sheared from the glass mass or a cane.

SHOOTER: The main marble in play, and usually the most prized marble of a player; usually at least $7/8$ inch in diameter. The marble with which the player shoots at his opponents' marbles.

SLAG GLASS: Glass having the appearance of slag. Historically, the term is the derivation of the material silicate slag skimmed off molten steel and then mixed with clear glass.

SOLID CORE: A handmade glass marble with a central core of one piece, either one color or several colors in one solid strip from pole to pole.

SPIRAL: Catch-all term used by marble collectors to designate any handmade glass marble with a spiraling design. In machine-made glass marbles, a distinctive style made by the Akro Agate Company after about 1926, which consisted of two to four colors of glass interlocking in a definite spiral or corkscrew pattern. Not to be confused with Swirls, which have a much more random pattern of colors mixed together.

SPONGEWARE: A marble similar to yellowware, except that its clay body has been decorated. Large crockery items were decorated with a sponge, and the same applied to marbles. Often called "mottled" in catalogs.

STEELIE: A steel ball bearing employed as a marble; generally not allowed in games with glass marbles, and definitely not allowed in tournament play. Even so, Steelies were quite common and were in every child's collection of marbles. A hollow Steelie was also made but was not popular. Also called Ironies in Ottumwa, Iowa, place of manufacture.

STRIPING POT: A fire clay pot usually containing about 25 pounds of molten glass, hand-carried from main melting furnace in a cast-iron ladle to the pot.

SULPHIDES: Large transparent handmade glass marbles with enclosed ceramic figures or numbers. See INCRUSTATION.

SWEET GLASS: Easily workable glass, which in the terms

of marble workers, one "can do anything with." A disadvantage is that it shatters easily if dropped.

SWIRLS: In describing handmade glass marbles, the term Swirls is often used interchangeably with Spirals. (See SPIRAL.) The term also designates the earliest type of glass marble made by machine, characterized by a swirling of two or more colors of glass intermingled in a much more random pattern than the Spiral type.

TANK: A melting unit in which the container for molten glass is constructed of refractory (fire clay) blocks or bricks.

TAWS: Designates a marble used as a shooter; a functional name rather than any particular design of marble.

TIGER EYE: A machine-made glass marble produced by the Master Marble Company from 1930 to 1935. Quite rare and very beautiful.

TIGER'S-EYE: Semi-precious stone marble made from silicified crocidolite; generally glossy brown, but can be green or blue. The tiger's-eye stone may be altered through the use of heat. A quick and not-recommended do-it-yourself method is to wave the sphere back and forth over a flame. A safer and more practical method is to place the sphere in a small metal container and embed the sphere in clean white sand, then put it in the hot coals of a charcoal grill and allow to remain until completely cooled. Several attempts may be necessary to achieve the color desired, from a light yellow to reddish-chocolate color.[6]

TOY MARBLES: See GAME MARBLES.

URANIUM GLASS: Glass containing an oxide of uranium; color may vary according to other coloring additives and will display a vivid green under ultraviolet light. It is not used in modern marble production.

VANES: The inner design elements of Cat Eye marbles, also called blades or petals. Consists of colored strips of glass in clear body glass.

VARIEGATED CLAY: Various-colored clay that is commingled with the body glass such as in the modern handmade Big Blue and Corkscrew by Robert A. Brown.

VARIEGATED GLASS: Various-colored glass that is commingled with the body glass before flowing through the orifice to the shearing mechanism.

VASELINE: Custard or milk glass; translucent with small bubbles, usually greenish color.

VENEER: A layer of colored glass added to surface of glass marbles; may be from $\frac{1}{64}$ inch to $\frac{1}{4}$ inch in thickness. Veneering was introduced and first used by Roger Howdyshell of Marble King.

WHITEWARE: White, out-of-round, porous, partially glazed ceramic marble, often decorated with a few concentric lines or spirals.

WORKING END: The front end of the tank from which glass flows through the orifice and into the rollers. It is opposite to the rear of the tank into which cullet is fed for melting.

WORKING POINT: The place in the grooves of the marble machine rollers where the marble is rolled or preformed.

YELLOWWARE: A yellowish ceramic marble fired at around 2,200 degrees Fahrenheit with a clear glaze. Color may vary from dark yellow to extremely pale yellow, depending upon the type of clay and temperature at which it is fired. Some may be fired twice—the first or bisque firing is at maximum temperature to vitrify the body, and the second or gloss firing is at a lower temperature to fix the decoration and glaze that might have been applied.

[1] Albert Christian Revi, *Nineteenth Century Glass* (1967), p. 103.

[2] *The Cyclopedia of Useful Arts and Manufacturers* Vol. 1 (New York, 1854).

[3] Herbert Kuhnert, *Recordbook of the Thurning Glass Factory Stories* (Wiesbaden: Franz Steiner Verlag, 1973), p. 247. The records address a factory in Sonnenberg, May 16, 1950.

[4] Hinton, personal comment.

[5] Robert A. Brown, personal conversation.

[6] June Culp Zeitner, special assistant editor, *Lapidary Journal*, personal correspondence.

Bibliography and Selected Literature

"The Aesthetic of the Mib." *Esquire,* Vol. 70, August 1968, pp. 86–87.

The Akro Agate Gem. *Newsletter of the Akro Agate Art Association,* Box 758, Salem, NH 03079.

All About Marbles. Booklet by the Akro Agate Company, 1926.

"All About Marbles: A Little Book for Boys." The Akro Agate Company, Clarksburg, W.Va., 1926.

"All About Marbles and 20 Games to Play," House of Marbles, London, England.

Allen, Shirley "Windy." *The Game of Marbles.* Private publication of Marble King, Inc., Paden City, W.Va., c. 1975.

"America's Interesting People." (Includes Berry Pink.) *The American Magazine.* Vol. 123, No. 3, March 1937, p. 97.

"Anybody remember how to play marbles?" *Changing Times,* Vol. 12, March 1958, pp. 45–46.

Appleton, Budd. *Akro Agate.* Privately published, 1972.

Arnold, Arnold. *The World Book of Children's Games.* The World Publishing Company, 1972, pp. 75-76.

Bank, Professor Dr. Herman. *Das Schaubergwerk Steinkaulenberg In Idar Oberstein.*

Baumann, Paul. *Collecting Antique Marbles.* Radnor, Pa: Wallace-Homestead Book Company, 1991.

Bavin, William R. *Marbles—The Pocket Book of Marble Collecting History and Games.* London: Outline Press, 1991.

Bell, R. C. *The Board Game Book.* New York: Exeter Books, 1983.

Bernard, Betty. "Chocolate Covered Marbles." Buckeye Marble Collectors Club Newsletter, June 1991, p. 2.

Bernard, Jame. *La Bille.* France: Herault Editions, c. l991.

Blizzard, William C. "West Virginia's Marble King." *Sunday Gazette-Mail* [Charleston, W.Va.], October 4, 1959, p. 4.

Block, Stanley A. "The Akro Agate Company." *Antiques & Collecting,* April 1988, pp. 38–40.

Block, Stanley A. "Marbles-Playing for Fun and for Keeps." *The Encyclopedia of Collectibles—Lalique to Marbles,* 1983, pp. 151–160.

Boger, Louise Ada and H. Batterson Boger. *The Dictionary of Antiques and the Decorative Arts.* New York: Scribner, 1957.

Bourque, Darlene M. and Joseph A. A. Bourque, Sr. "A Treatise on the Akro Agate," *The Akro Agate Gem,* Newsletter of the Akro Agate Art Association, Box 758, Salem, NH 03079, June 1983, Vol. 1, No. 1, p. 5.

Brinckloe, Julie. *Playing Marbles.* New York: Morrow Junior Books, 1988.

Buckeye Marble Collectors Club Newsletter, 473 Meadowbrook Drive, Newark, OH 43055.

Burrows, Fredrika A. "Marbles—Another Fun Hobby." *Hobbies,* April 1977, Vol. 82, No. 2, p. 117.

Butterfield, Oliver. "Marble Collecting for Keeps." *Yankee,* September 1977, pp. 174–184.

Callahan, Ed. "Peltier Glass Company is Oldest Ottawa Industry." *Ottawa (Ill.) Daily Times,* July 2, 1978, p. 13.

Canfield, Dorothy, et al. *What Shall We Do Now?* Toronto: F. D. Goodchild Company, 1907.

Canova, Enrique C. "West Virginia: Treasure Chest of Industry." *The National Geographic Magazine,* Vol. 78, No. 2, August 1940.

Carberry, Dr. J. W. *Iowa City Flint Glass Manufacturing Company 1880–1882 Price Guide.* Private publication, 1982; obtainable from the author along with Mariam Righter's Iowa City Glass.

Carskadden, Jeff, and Richard Gartley. *Chinas— Handpainted marbles of the late 19th Century.* The Muskingum Valley Archaeological Survey, Zanesville, Ohio, 1990.

Carskadden, Jeff, and Richard Gartley. "A Preliminary Seriation of l9th Century Decorated Porcelain Marbles," *Historical Archaeology,* Vol. 24, No. 2, 1990, pp. 55–69.

Carskadden, Jeff, Richard Gartley, and Elizabeth Reeb. "Marble Making and Marble Playing in Eastern Ohio: The Significance of Ceramic, Stone, and Glass Marbles in Historic Archaeology." Paper presented at the Third Annual Symposium on Ohio Valley Urban and Historic Archaeology, March 23, 1985.

Carskadden, Jeff, and Mark Randall. "The Christensen Agate Company, Cambridge, Ohio (1927–1933)." *Muskingum Annals,* Vol. 4, 1987, pp. 48–52.

Cassidy, John. *The Klutz Book of Marbles.* Palo Alto, Calif.: Klutz Press, 1989.

Castle, Larry, and Marlow Peterson. *Marbles: The Guide to Machine Made Marbles.* Private publication of Utah Marble Connection, Inc., Ogden, Utah, 1992.

Castle, Larry, and Marlow Peterson. *Collectable Machine-Made Marbles—Identification and Price Guide.* Private publication of Utah Marble Connection, Inc., Ogden, Utah, 1989.

Charles, Russell J. "It's Magic Time in Idar-Oberstein." *Lapidary Journal,* Vol. 17, No. 2, May 1963, p. 282 ff.

Childress, William. "How I Lost My Marbles." *Ford Times,* Vol. 72, No. 4, April 1979, pp. 12–17.

"Chinese Checkers." *Popular Science,* Vol. 133, September 1938, p. 56.

Clark, Agnes. "Collectors Shoot for Swirls, Sulphides." *The Boston Globe Calendar,* Changing Times, Vol. 2, No. 23, April 8, 1976.

The Coevolution Quarterly. No. 20, Winter 1978 (cover photos of Richard Marquis' work).

Cohill, Michael C. *M. F. Christensen and The Perfect Glass Ball Machine.* Akron, Ohio: Group Ideate Publishing, 1990.

Combs, Josiah H. *More Marble Words.* Publication of the American Dialectic Society, No. 23, Center for Applied Linguistics, Arlington, Va., 1955, pp. 33–34.

Cook, Harry H., Editor. "William J. Miller's Semi-

Automatic Marble Machine." *The American Flint* magazine, 1927, p. 14.

Cope, Cathleen. "The Rolley Holers." *The Tennessee Magazine,* September 1972, pp. 7–10.

Cowgill, Mary R. "Searching for Pieces of the Past." *Maryland,* Winter 1984, pp. 34–38.

Daiken, Leslie. *Children's Toys Throughout the Ages.* New York: Frederick A. Praeger, 1953.

David, Derek, and Keith Middlemas. *Colored Glass.* 1968, p. 118.

Davis, Jim. "Betty Boop Reveals Age . . . of Peltier Picture Marbles!" *Marble-Mania,* Vol. 59, July 1990, pp. 2–3.

Davis, Kenneth C. *Don't Know Much About History.* New York: Crown Pubishers Inc., 1990, pp. 274–275.

Davis, Rod. "Shoot Not To Kill." *American Way,* September 15, 1987, Vol. 20, No. 18, American Airlines Magazine Publications, Dallas-Fort Worth Airport, Tex., pp. 58–63.

Dickson, Paul. "Marbles." *Smithsonian* magazine, April 1988, pp. 94–103.

Dickson, Paul. *The Mature Person's Guide to Kites, Yo-Yos, Frisbees, and Other Child Like Diversions.* A Plume Book, New American Library, 1977.

Douthat, Strat. "The Magic Marble of West Virginia." *Washington Star,* August 13, 1980, pp. C1–C2.

Drew, Lisa. "Crazy for Quartz." *National Wildlife,* June–July 1993, pp. 46–51.

Dusing, Allen F. "Rolley Hole Championships." *Trailer Life,* September 1989, pp. 120, 122–123.

Edwards, Janet. "Shortage Sets Machine-Made Marbles in Motion." *Antique Week* Eastern Edition, October 1, 1990, Vol. 23, No. 27, pp. 1, 40.

Ely, Bill. *The Sulphide Marble—A Handbook.* Private printing, Vancouver, Washington.

Eogan, George. *Knowth.* London: Thames and Hudson, 1986, pp. 140, 144, 210.

Every Little Boy's Book, A New Edition. London: George Routledge and Sons, 1880.

Ferretti, Fred. *The Great American Book of Sidewalk, Stoop, Dirt, Curb and Alley Games.* New York: Workman Publishing Company, 1975.

Ferretti, Fred. *The Great American Marble Book.* New York: Workman Publishing Company, 1973.

Florence, Gene. *The Collectors Encyclopedia of Akro Agate Glassware.* Collector Books, 1975.

Frazier, Si and Ann. "Quartz Building Blocks," *Lapidary Journal,* February 1990, p. 91.

Freeman, Ruth, and Larry. *Cavalcade of Toys.* New York: Century House, 1942, p. 113.

Garland, Bob. "That's Marbles, Son." *The Saturday Evening Post,* Vol. 219, July 13, 1946, p. 69.

Garrett, Wilbur E. "George Washington's Patowmack Canal." *National Geographic,* Vol. 171, No. 6, June 1987, pp. 744–745.

Gartley, Richard, and Jeff Carskadden. "Marbles From an Irish Channel Cistern, New Orleans, Louisiana." *Proceedings of the Symposium on Ohio Valley Urban and Historic Archaeology,* Vol. 5, 1978, pp. 112–125.

Gibbs-Smith, T. H. *The Great Exhibition of 1851, A Commemorative Album.* London: Victoria and Albert Museum, 1950, p. 17.

Gilbert, Anne. *Collecting the New Antiques.* New York: Grosset and Dunlap, 1977, pp. 25–27.

Gomme, Alice Bertha. *The Traditional Games of England, Scotland, and Ireland 1894.* New York: Vol. 1, Dover Pub., 1964, p. 364.

Grist, Everett. *Machine-Made & Contemporary Marbles.* Paducah, Ky.: Collector Books, 1984 and 1992.

Grist, Everett. *Antique and Collectible Marbles.* Paducah, Ky.: Collector Books, 1992, Third Edition.

Grossman, John. "A Man with All His Marbles." *U.S. Air Magazine,* June 1993, pp. 54–58.

Grunfeld, Frederic V., ed. *Games of the World.* Holt, Rinehart and Winston, 1975.

Guralnick, Margot. "The High Roller of Marbles." *HG House and Garden,* June 1992, p. 62.

Hamblin, Dora Jane. *The First Cities.* Time-Life Books, p. 126.

Hannum, Jill. "Marbles." *Glass,* Vol. 6, No. 1, January 1978, pp. 20–25.

Harder, Kelsie B. "The Vocabulary of Marble Playing." *Publication of the American Dialectic Society,* No. 23, Center for Applied Linguistics, Arlington, Va., 1955, pp. 3–33.

Hardy, Roger, and Claudia Hardy. *The Complete Line of the Akro Agate Company.* Private publication, Clarksburg, W.Va., 1992.

Hobbies, November 1941, p. 56 (article on sulphides).

Hollister, Paul Jr. *The Encyclopedia of Glass Paperweights,* 1969, p. 255.

Hoxter, Curtis J. "The Marble Business Rolls Ahead." *Coronet,* Vol. 26, September 1949, pp. 119–120.

Howe, Bea. *Antiques from the Victorian Home.* New York: Scribner, 1973, pp. 114 and 116.

Huffer, Lloyd, and Chris. "Marbles—Today's Game is Collecting." *Antiques, and The Arts Weekly,* May 11, 1990. Newtown, Ct.: The Bee Publishing Company, 1990, pp. 107–110.

Hume, Ivor Noel. *A Guide to Artifacts of Colonial America.* New York: Alfred A. Knopf, 1969.

Hustis, Joan. "Ottawa's Marble Company One of Only Three in U.S.," *Ottawa (Ill.) Daily Times,* April 18, 1969.

Hyde, Christopher. "Knuckling Down to Marble Collecting." *The Franklin Mint Almanac,* September 1979, Vol. 10, No. 8, pp. 9–13.

"Immies." *Fortune,* Vol. 13, June 1936, p. 36.

Ingram, Clara. *The Collector's Encyclopedia of Antique Marbles.* Paducah, Ky.: Collector Books, 1972.

"Interesting Antiques—Marbles." *The Antique Trader,* May 16, 1972, p. 43.

"It's Not Kids Who Are Playing with Marbles." *Press Herald* [Portland, Maine], March 20, 1980.

"It's Spring—Get Out Your Aggies and Immies." *Changing Times,* Vol. 12, March 1958, pp. 46–47.

Jhaveri, Ravindra. "Flying Fingers." (Agate marble and bead making in India.) *Lapidary Journal,* Vol. 39, No. 12, March 1986.

Jokelson, Paul. *Sulphides: The Art of Cameo Incrustation.* New York: Thomas Nelson and Sons, 1968.

Johnson, George Ellsworth. *Education by Plays and Games.*

Boston: Ginn & Company, 1907.

Johnson, Owen. "In Marble Time." *Collier's Outdoor America*, Vol. 47, April 1911, p. 23, 42 (marble terms).

Katskee, Roy. "Playing for Keeps." *Collector's Showcase*, November 1992, pp. 32–35.

Kelly, Roger E., and Albert E. Ward. "Lessons from the Zeyouma Trading Post near Flagstaff, Arizona." *Historical Archaeology*, Vol. VI, 1972, pp. 65–76.

Kern, G. I. "Marbles—An Old Game." *Recreation*, Vol. 34, May 1940, pp. 109–110.

Ketchum, Richard. *Will Rogers—The Man and His Times*. American Heritage Publishing Company, Inc., 1973.

Klamkin, Marian. *The Collector's Book of Bottles*. New York: Dodd, Mead & Company, 1971 (marble-stoppered bottles).

"Knuckling Down to Job," *The New York Times*. March 30, 1955, p. 23 (tariff legislation to protect United States marble industry).

Kuhnert, Herbert. *Recordbook of the Thurning Glass Factory Stories*. Wiesbaden: Franz Steiner Verlag, 1973, p. 247.

Life magazine, "Who Ate My Post Toasties?," March 28, 1955, p. 61.

"Linguistics of Marbles." *Playground*, Vol. 21, No. 4, July 1927, p. 205.

Little Charley's Games and Sports. Philadelphia: C. G. Henderson & Co., 1853.

Lissner, Ivar. *Man, God and Magic*. Translated from the German by J. Maxwell Brourejohn, M.A. New York: C. P. Putnam and Sons; and London: Jonathan Cape, 1961, pp. 183, 188–189 and Figure 55.

Long, C. E. "Notes on Antique Marbles." *Hobbies*, Vol. 55, May 1950, pp. 98–99.

Lorraine, Dessamae. "An Archaeologist's Guide to 19th Century American Glass." *Historical Archaeology*, Vol. 2, 1968, pp. 35–44 (marble-stoppered bottles).

"The Marble Business Rolls Ahead." *Coronet*, Vol. 26, September 1949, pp. 119–120.

The Marble Circle News, newsletter of the Blue Ridge Marble Collectors Club, 3410 Plymouth Place, Lynchburg, VA 24503.

The Marble Connection, newsletter, P. O. Box 132, Norton, MA 02766.

"Marble Golf." *Playground and Recreation*, Vol. 24, October 1930, p. 407.

Marble-Mania, newsletter of the Marble Collectors Society of America, Trumbull, Ct., published periodically since 1976.

Marble Mart, Newsletter. Marble Collectors Unlimited, P. O. Box 206, Northboro, MA 01532.

Marble Mate, newsletter of the Japan Marbles Association. Moritex Corporation, 210 Nomura Building, 2-10-9, Shibuya, Shibuya-ku, Tokyo 150, Japan.

The Marble Network, publication of the Midwest Marble Club, Center City, Minnesota, 55012.

"Marbles." *Cub Scouts Sports*; Boy Scouts of America, Irving, Texas 1985.

"Marbles." *The New York Times Magazine*, July 20, 1941, p. 2.

"Marbles." *Pic Magazine*, July 25, 1939, pp. 31–33.

"Marbles Grow Up." *Literary Digest*, Vol. 122, Oct. 31, 1936, p. 122.

"Marbles—Mad Beloit Crowns a New Mibs King." *Life*, Vol. 12, June 22, 1942, pp. 56–57.

"Marbles Shoot-out Brings Home Second Place." *Tyler Star News*, Sistersville, W.Va., April 22, 1992, pp. 1, 4.

Martin, Mary. "The Crystal Cameos of France," *House and Garden*, December, 1926.

"Master Marble Makers." *The West Virginia Review*, Charleston, W.Va., October 1931, p. 40.

McCarthy, Sam. *Sussex Marble—A Short History*. Private publication, Horsham, Sussex, England: 1989.

McCarthy, Sam. *All About Marbles and Rules of the Game*. Printed by Tolly's Marble Promotions for the British Marbles Board of Control, c. 1988, p. 2.

McCarthy, Sam. *Marbles at Tinsley Green*. Private publication, Horsham, Sussex, England: 1981.

McGilvry, Wilma. "Marbles as Collectibles." *The National Glass, Pottery and Collectables Journal*, March 1979, p. 42.

Meckley, Thad. "Timeless Appeal of a Game Known as Marbles". *Grit*, July 9–15, 1989, Vol. 31, pp. 2–3.

Metzerott, Mary. "Notes on Marble History." *Hobbies*, November 1941, pp. 56–57.

Middlemas, Keith. *Antique Glass in Color*. Garden City, N.Y.: 1971, p. 89.

Miller, Roger C. "Swirl and Sulphide Playing Marbles." *The Spinning Wheel*, November 1966, pp. 20–21.

"Millions of Marbles Rolling Out of West Virginia." *The Pittsburgh Press*, June 21, 1987, pp. D1 and D8.

Morrison, Mel, and Carl Terrison. *Marbles—Identification and Price Guide*. Private publication, Falmouth, Maine, 1968.

Mortenson, Kristine. "Marvelous Marbles." *Glass*, September 1992, pp. 28–35.

Munsey, Cecil. *The Illustrated Guide to Collecting Bottles*. New York: Hawthorn Books, 1970, pp. 104, 108–109 (marble-stoppered bottles).

Needham, Jerry. "Kids Go For All The Marbles as Game Makes Comeback." *Dallas Times Herald*, June 23, 1991, pp. 19 and A-21.

Nelson, Glenn C. *Ceramics, A Potter's Handbook*. New York: Holt, Rinehart and Winston, Inc., 1971.

Novak, Kim. "The Christensen Agate Company," unpublished report by the Degenhart Paperweight and Glass Museum, Cambridge, Ohio, 1984.

O'Brien, Richard. *The Story of American Toys*. Abbeville Press, 1990, p. 61.

The Official Rule and Game Book, Vol. 1. Old Saybrook, Ct.: The Great American Marble Company.

Olmert, Michael. "Points of Origin." *Smithsonian*, Vol. 14, No. 9, December 1983, pp. 40, 42 (mention of marbles in early European literature).

"Output of Marbles up Sharply." *The New York Times*, October 30, 1966, III, p. 16.

Papapanu, Sophia C. *Akro Agate's Children's Line and Price Guide*. Syracuse, N.Y.: Estabrook Printing Company, 1973.

The Paper, Germantown, Md., Campus of Montgomery County College, "The Big Blue Marble," October 26, 1979, pp. 6–7.

Pellat, Apsley. *Curiosities of Glassmaking*, Blackfriars

Bridge in Surrey, England, 1849.

"Peltier Glass Company is Oldest Ottawa Industry." *Ottawa (Ill.) Daily Times,* July 2, 1978, p. 13.

Plinius Secundus *The Historie of the World,* translated into English by Philemon Holland, 1634. (2nd edition).

Price Guide. Marble Collectors Society of America, Trumbull, Ct., 1985.

Proctor, John. "Marble King." *The Family Circle,* June 23, 1939, pp. 14–15.

Quick, Lelande. *The Book of Agates.* Philadelphia: Chilton Company, 1963.

Ramella, Richard. "Champions with Dirty Knuckles—Marbles in the Mountain State." *Goldenseal,* Vol. 19, No. 2, Summer 1993, pp. 35-41.

Randall, Mark E. "Early Marbles." *Historical Archaeology,* Vol. 5, pp. 102–105, 1971.

Randall, Mark E. "Identifying and Dating 19th and 20th Century Marbles." *Southwest Folklore,* Vol. 1, No. 2, pp. 1–34, Spring 1977.

Randall, Mark E. "Ceramic Marbles." *Pottery Southwest,* Vol. 5, No. 2, Albuquerque, N.M., Archaeological Society, April 1978, pp 4–6.

Randall, Mark E. *Marbles as Historical Artifacts.* Trumbull, Connecticut: Marble Collectors Society of America, 1979.

Randall, Mark E., and Dennis Webb. "Handmade Glass Marbles." *Glass Collector's Digest,* June–July 1989, Vol. 3, No. 1, pp. 40–47.

Randall, Mark E., and Dennis Webb. "Akro Agate's Spiral Marbles." Glass Collector's Digest, December–January 1990, Vol. 3, No. 4, pp. 45–46.

Randall, Mark E., and Dennis Webb. *Greenberg's Guide to Marbles.* Sykesville, Md.: Greenberg Publishing Company, Inc., 1988.

Revi, Albert Christian. *Nineteenth Century Glass.* 1967, p. 242.

Rice, Jane Ann. "The Story of St. Clair Glass." Private publication, edited and published by Richard E. Harney.

Righter, Mariam. *Iowa City Glass.* Private publication, copyright by Dr. J. W. Carberry, 1982. Obtainable along with Dr. Carberry's *Iowa City Flint Glass Manufacturing Company 1880–1882 Price Guide* from Dr. Carberry at P. O. Box 2231, Iowa City, IA 52240, for $13.50.

Roberson, Wayne R. *The Carrington-Covert House: Archaeological Investigation of a 19th-Century Residence in Austin, Texas.* Texas Historical Commission, February 1974, pp. 51–52.

Rolling Marbles, newsletter of West Virginia Marble Shooters Association, Bridgeport, W.Va., 26330.

Romaine, Anne. "In Memoriam: Robert "Bud" Garrett (1916–1987)." *Tennessee Folklore Society Bulletin,* Vol. 53, No. 1, 1988, pp. 27–28.

Roth, Jack. "Long Island Housewife Fries Marbles in Jewelry-Making Technique." *The New York Times.* August 16, 1962, p. 29.

Runyan, Cathy C. *Knuckles Down—A Fun Guide to Marble Play.* Kansas City, Mo.: Right Brain Publishing, 1985.

Sackett, S. J. "Marble Words from Hays, Kansas." *Publication of the American Dialectic Society,* No. 37, University of Alabama Press, 1963, pp. 1–3.

Shaffer, Dale E. *Marbles, A Forgotten Part of Salem History.* Privately published, 1983.

Shaub, Benjamin Martin. *The Origin of Agates, Thundereggs, Brunea Jasper, Septaria and Butterfly Agates.* Northampton, Mass.: The Agate Publishing Company, 1989.

The Shooter. Occasional publication of the Cape Fear Marble Club, Wilmington, N.C.

Short, Lisa L. "Marbles Once Made Here Enjoy Worldwide Popularity." *The Daily Jeffersonian,* Cambridge, Ohio, April 20, 1992, p. 11.

Shull, Thelma. "Old Marbles." *Victorian Antiques,* Charles E. Tuttle Company, Rutland, Vt., 1963, pp. 302–306.

Shull, Thelma. "Old Glass Marbles." *Hobbies,* November 1941, pp. 55–56.

Slusser, Esther. "Swirl and Sulphide Marbles." *The Spinning Wheel,* June 1965, pp. 10–11.

S-M-C-S, newsletter of Suncoast Marble Collectors Society, St. Petersburg, Florida, 33794-0213.

Smith, G. Hubert. "Archeological Investigations at the Site Fort Stevenson (32 ML 1), Garrison Reservoir, North Dakota." *Bureau of American Ethnology Bulletin,* Vol. 176, 1960, pp. 159–238.

Smith, G. Hubert. "Ft. Pierre II (39 ST 217): A Historic Trading Post in the Oahe Dam Area, South Dakota." *Bulletin of the Bureau of American Ethnology,* Vol. 176, pp. 83–158.

Smith, Joan. "The Marvel of Marbles." *The Bangor Daily News,* June 17, 1982, p. 8.

Smith, Linda Joan. "Lost Marbles." *Country Home,* April 1991, pp. 92–95, p. 146.

Smith, Violet Bramer. "Marble Collecting." *Hobbies,* November 1941, pp. 58–59.

Spendlove, Earl. "He Has All His Marbles." *Rock & Gem,* June 1991, pp. 56–59, 84.

Stout, Wilbur. "Coal Formation Clays of Ohio." Geological Survey of Ohio, 4th Series, Bulletin 26, Columbus, 1923.

Stanley, Mary Louise. *A Century of Glass Toys.* New York: Crown Publishing, 1972.

Strutt, Joseph. *The Sports and Pastimes of the People of England.* Methuen and Company, 1903; reprinted Detroit: Singing Tree Press, 1968, p. 222.

Sutton-Smith, Brian. *The Folklore of Children.* Austin, Tex.: University of Texas, Austin, 1972, pp. 174–176 (New Zealand games and terms).

Swanson, Emerson Regena. "Not All Grown-ups Let You Win." *Country,* December–January 1990, Vol. 2, No. 6, p. 12.

Sweeney, Edwin. "Marbles and Pressed Glass—Remembering Akro Agate of Clarksburg." *Goldenseal,* Vol. 10, No. 2, Summer 1984, pp. 20–25.

Swirls, newsletter of Canadian Marble Collectors Association, Georgetown, Ontario, Canada.

Tamulevich, Susan. "Lost Marbles." *Mid-Atlantic Country* magazine, February 1993, pp. 58–61.

Toys and Games. Alexandria, Va.: Time Life Books, A Rebus Book, c. 1991, pp. 122–124.

"A Treatise on Glass Balls and Glass Marbles." Master Glass Company, privately published, no date.

Tymorek, Stan. "The Shoot-Out by the Sea." Land's End

catalog, Vol. 26, No. 5, May 1990, pp. 87–89.

Walker, John W. *Excavations of the Arkansas Post Branch of the Bank of the State of Arkansas.* Southwest Archaeological Center, National Park Service, 1971.

Walters, J. L. "Agate Facts and Fancy." (Coloring agate.) *Lapidary Journal,* Vol. 39, No. 11, February 1986, pp. 38–39.

Watson, Henry D. "Antique Marbles of Stone, Pottery and Glass." *American Collector,* Vol. 11, No. 6, July 1942, 7, 15.

Watson, Henry W. "Marbles Among the Earliest Games." *American Collector,* Vol. 12, No. 7, July 1943, pp. 10–11.

Webb, Dennis. "A New 'Corkscrew." *Marble-Mania,* September 1991, p. 1.

Webb, Dennis. "A Marble Formula." *Swirls* (Canadian Marble Collectors Association), June 1991, p. 4.

Webb, Dennis. "Favorite Pieces—Fiber Optic Marbles." *Glass Collector's Digest,* April/May 1991, Vol. 4, No. 6, pp. 80–81.

Webb, William S. *Indian Knoll.* Knoxville, Tenn.: The University of Tennessee Press, 1974, p. 231.

White, Gwen. *Antique Toys and Their Backgrounds.* New York: ARCO, 1971, pp. 32–34.

Wills, Geoffrey. *The Collector's Pocket Book of Glass,* New York: Hawthorne Books, Inc., 1966, p. 28.

Wilson, Red, and Ann Wilson. "Marble Making and Lapidary Hints." Lubbock, Tex.: Western Printing Company, 1977.

Wolter, Scott F. *The Lake Superior Agate.* Minneapolis: Lake Superior Agate Inc., 1986.

Wright, Heather. "Little Charmers." *Traditional Home* magazine, April 1991, pp. 38 and 116.

Youth's Companion, "Making Marbles," February 15, 1912, p. 9.

Appendix: U.S. Producers of Toy Marbles

It is obvious that the Akron, Ohio, area was the scene of early marble production for clay and glass marbles. However, the birthplace of the industry may well be the Frazey Pottery Company, Zanesville, Ohio. As to the factory that was the "toy marble capitol of the world"—that claim may be made by the Akron area manufacturers, but only for a short period of time. They then "ran out of gas" and the marble capitol of the world shifted to Clarksburg, West Virginia, with the Akro Agate Company's commercial production in 1914, and continued to remain in the West Virginia Area for many years.

Historically, Akron was the birthplace of the American machine-made marble industry but soon gave way to the West Virginia marble makers due to a dwindling natural gas supply. West Virginia provided a high grade of silica for glass formulas, and river networks allowed transport to markets beyond the Ohio River valley. Added to all this was the availability of a skilled labor force made up of native craftsmen and patents granted subsequent to the M. F. Christensen patent, which made possible mass production by fully automated marble machines. The use of long rollers of the Hill and two Early patents put the marble industry in the Clarksburg area into a modern golden era of marble manufacturing. (See Chapter XII on patents.) The following companies are listed chronologically according to their entry into the toy marble industry.

COMPANY	TYPE	TIME PERIOD	YEARS IN BUSINESS
Frazey Pottery Co., Zanesville, Ohio	Ceramic (China)	1818–?	?
Indiana Pottery Co., Troy, Ohio	Ceramic	1844–?	?
Iowa City Flint Glass Mfg. Co., Iowa City, Iowa	Handmade glass	1880–1882	3
S. C. Dyke & Co., Main Street, Akron, Ohio	Ceramic	1886–1888	3
S. C. Dyke & Co., West Street, Akron, Ohio	Handmade glass	1889–1891	3
American Agate Co., Akron, Ohio	Ceramic	1889–1891	3
American Marble & Toy Mfg. Co., Akron, Ohio	Handmade and ceramic glass	1892–1905	14
Dyke Marble and Toy Works, Akron, Ohio	Ceramic and handmade glass	1892–1894	3
Akron Marble & Novelty Co., Akron, Ohio	Ceramic	1893–?	?
Akron Stone Marble, Akron, Ohio	Stone	1892–?	?
Akron Insulator & Marble Co., Akron, Ohio	Ceramic and handmade glass	1894–1904	11
Standard Toy Marble Co., Akron, Ohio	Ceramic	1894–1920s	?
J. H. Leighton and Co., Akron, Ohio	Handmade glass	1896–1899	3
M. F. Christensen & Son Co., Akron, Ohio	Machine-made glass	1901–1917	17
East End Marble Co., Akron, Ohio	Ceramic	1890–1892	3
Henry Mishler and Son Co., Mogadore, Ohio	Ceramic	Circa 1892	?
Albright and Lightcap Co., Ravenna, Ohio	Ceramic	1894–?	?
Albright and Lightcap Co., Ravenna, Ohio	Machine-made glass	1930s–?	?
Navarre Glass Marble Co., Navarre/Steubenville, Ohio	Handmade/Machine-made glass	1897–c. 1905	?
M. F. Christensen & Son Glass Co., Akron, Ohio	Machine-made glass	1905–1917	13
Akro Agate Co., Clarksburg, W.Va.	Machine-made glass	1914–1951	38
Peltier Glass Co., Ottawa, Ill.	Machine-made glass	1927–present	68
Nivison-Weiskopf, Cincinnati, Ohio	Machine-made glass	1925–1933	4
Christensen Agate Co., Cambridge, Ohio	Machine-made glass	1925–1933	9
Master Marble Glass Co., Anmoore, W.Va.	Machine-made glass	1930–1941	12
Lawrence Glass Novelty Co./L. E. Alley, W.Va.	Machine-made glass	1921–1949	29
Alox Manufacturing Co., St. Louis, Mo.	Machine-made glass	Late 1930s–1947	??
Ravenswood Novelty Works, Ravenswood, W.Va.	Machine-made glass	1931–1955	25
Vitro Agate, Parkersburg, W.Va./Anacortes, Wa./Reno, Ohio	Machine-made glass	1932–present	63
Champion Agate Co., Pennsboro, W.Va.	Machine-made glass	1938–present	57
Heaton Agate Co., Cairo., W.Va.	Machine-made glass	1939–1971	33
Kokomo Opalescent Glass Co., Kokomo, Ind.	Machine-made glass	Late 1930s–early 1940s	?
Master Glass Co., Bridgeport, W.Va.	Machine-made glass	1941–1973	21
Jackson Marble Co., Tollgate, W.Va.	Machine-made glass	Circa 1945	?
Cairo Novelty Co., Cairo, W.Va.	Machine-made glass	1948–1950	3
Playrite Marble and Novelty Co., Ellenboro, W.Va.	Machine-made glass	1945–1947	3
Davis Marble Works, Pennsboro, W.Va.	Machine-made glass	1947–48	2
Marble King, Inc., St. Marys/Paden City, W.Va.	Machine-made glass	1949–present	46
Bogard Co., Cairo, W.Va.	Machine-made glass	1971–1987	17
JABO, Inc., Reno, Ohio	Machine-made glass	1987–present	8
Mid-Atlantic of West Virginia, Ellenboro, W.Va.	Handmade and machine-made glass	1990–present	5

Index

A

Adams, Russell U., 89
Agates, 14–17, 134–135
Agateware, 19, 21, 135
Akro Agate Company, 39, 42, 46, 50–51, 52, 70, 73, 75, 79, 83, 85, 87, 88, 89, 93–94, 95–100, 106–107, 114–115, 138–139
Akro Agates, 99–100
Alabaster, 39, 83, 84, 98, 99, 116, 136; stone, 17
Alley Agate Company, *see* Alley Glass Manufacturing Company.
Alley Glass Manufacturing Company, 100–101, 139
Alley, Lawrence E., 100, 107, 122
Alox Manufacturing Company, 70, 101–102, 139
Annealing, 79
Ash tray, *see* Jewel (ash) tray.

B

Ballot marbles, 10, 30
Banded Marbles, 28–29, 136
Benningtons, 19, 21, 22, 135
Big Blue Marble, 42, 135; the water tower, 59
Bogard Company, 102–103, 108, 139
Bogard, C. E., & Sons Agate Company, *see* Bogard Company.
Bogard, Jack, 102, 109
Boston and Sandwich Glass Company, 28, 103
Bottle marbles, 10, 30
Bowen, Carole A., 10, 14, 55, 56
Brown, Robert A., 9, 23, 24–25, 36, 135
Brushed marbles, 46–47, 99, 114, 116, 124, 125
Burroughs, Edmund, 97

C

Cairo Novelty Company, 77, 89, 103–104, 139
Cambridge Glass Company, 105
Carnelian, 14, 106, 121
Carnival glass, 41
Cat Eyes, 10, 11, 47, 48–50, 102, 108, 109, 111, 112, 114, 120, 122, 124–125, 128, 129
Champion Agate Company, 41, 49, 52, 104–105, 110, 123, 139
Chinas, 19, 20, 22, 23, 135
Chinese checkers, 38, 57, 101, 107, 138. *See* also Opaque marbles.
Christensen Agate Company, 51, 105–106, 139
Christensen, Charles Frederick, 106
Christensen, M. F., and Son Glass Company, 74, 87, 106–107
Christensen, Martin F., 74, 86, 87, 106, 117
Clambroth, 29, 136
Clays, 19, 20–21, 22, 90–92, 106, 132–133, 135
Clearies, *see* Transparent marbles.

C (continued)

Clouds, 136
Codd bottle, *see* Bottle marbles.
College Edition, 115–116, 141
Comic Strip marbles, 42, 43, 118–120, 141; modern, 43, 137
Confetti, 10, 43, 125, 144
Converse, Emile P., 87
Cook, George Joseph, 87–88
Cornelian, *see* Carnelian.
Cox, Paul, 121
Crockery, 19, 22
Cullet, 11, 72–74
Custard, 10, 39, 98
Cutoff marks, 28

D

Davis Marble Works, 107–108
Davis, James C. "Jim," 117
Davis, James H. "Jim," 119
Davis, Wilson, 107–108
Day tanks, 72
Divided core, 29, 135
Double feed machines, 77–78
Duplex machines, 77–78, 89, 96
Dyke, Actaeon L., 90–91
Dyke, Samuel C., 91

E

Early, J. Fred, 85, 96
Early, John F., 38, 52, 85, 88–89, 96–97, 115
Earthenware, 19, 21, 135
End of Day marbles, 29, 31, 109, 136

F

Fiber-optic marbles, 55, 56, 138
Fiedler, Arnold, 73, 97, 105
Fisher, Henri A., 60, 122
Flint, 14, 17, 55, 84
Formula glass, 72, 81–85
Fortune-telling marble, 10, 58, 138
Freese patents, 52, 75, 88
Freese, Ira, 75, 88
Frosted marbles, 10, 40–41, 117, 125

G

Galaxy, 46
Games, 57–58, 59, 138
Gatherer, 74–75, 95–96
Gibson, Charles D., 34, 35, 59
Glazed ceramics, 9, 22, 135
Goldstone, 29, 103, 136
Grimmett, Claude C., 97, 98, 115
Guinea, 106, 136

H

Half and Half, 50, 125
Hanlon, Oris G., 89, 103
Heatherington, Ralph, 98
Heaton Agate Company, 48, 51, 104, 108–109, 139
Heaton, William, 108
Helmers, Henry, 98
Hibbs, Clyde M., 89
Hill, Christian C., 86
Hill, Horace C., 38, 75, 86, 87, 95, 96, 98, 106
Hopf, H. E., Marble Factory, 130–131, 132–133, 135, 144
House of Marbles, 40, 41, 46, 128
Howdyshell, Roger W., 110–112

I

Indian, 29, 136
Iowa City Flint Glass Manufacturing Company, 28, 109
Israel, Clinton F., 70, 97, 98, 114, 115

J

JABO, 77, 109
Jackson Marble Company, 109–110
Jackson, Carol, 109
Jenkins, Howard M., 88
Jewel (ash) tray, 60, 138
Johnston, Allen, 92

K

Kokomo Opalescent Glass Company, 110, 139

L

Lang, Matthew, 91
Latticino, 9, 29, 109, 136
Lawrence Glass Novelty Company, see Alley Glass
    Manufacturing Co.
Leiter, Jeremiah J., 86–87, 117
Limestone, 13–14, 134
Lindsey, Press, 122
Lobed core, 29, 136
Lutz, 27, 28, 29, 103, 136

M

Magnetic marbles, 55
Marble King, 41, 42–43, 48–49, 68–69, 70, 71, 76, 78, 79–80,
    101, 110–114, 139–141
Marble scissors, 27, 28
Marsh, Gilbert C., 95, 98
Master Glass Company, 49, 70, 114, 141
Master Marble Company, 50, 61, 62, 70, 79, 83, 94,
    114–116, 141
Matthews, Mark, 33–35
Micas, 30, 136
Mid-Atlantic of West Virginia, 78, 116
Milk glass, 39, 136
Miller, William J., 88
Mishler, Henry, 91

Modern marbles: ceramics, 24–26; handmade glass, 33–36
Moore, Lewis L., 73, 117
Moulton, John E., 97, 98, 115

N

Navarre Glass Marble and Specialty Company, 117
Nivison-Weiskopf Company, 88, 117–118

O

Old Fashioneds, 49, 52, 105
Onionskin, 29, 31, 136
Onyx marbles, machine-made glass type, 107, 119, 121
Opaque marbles, 7: handmade, 30, 136; machine-made,
    38–39, 46, 47, 52, 98, 101, 103, 104, 106, 109, 110,
    112–113, 114, 116, 120, 121, 125, 132, 136

P

Patched marbles, 46–47, 99, 101, 109, 110, 112, 113, 114,
    116, 121, 125, 136
Patents, 30, 31, 40, 41, 86–92, 95, 96, 100, 104, 106, 117, 118,
    120; patent suits, 93–94, 115
Peltier Glass Company, 41, 43, 49, 50, 88, 93–94, 118–121,
    141–144
Peltier, Duncan V. (Don), 111, 118, 120
Peltier, Sellers, 110, 118
Peltier, Victor J., 118
Peppermint, 29, 136
Picasso, 50
Picture marbles, see Comic strip marbles.
Pink, Berry, 79–80, 100, 101, 110–112
Playrite Marble and Novelty Company, 121
Popeyes, 51, 139
Porcelain, 19, 20, 22–24, 135
Premium marbles, 42–43, 97, 111, 116, 122
Promotional marbles, 42–43, 113–114, 137–138
Punty or pontil iron, 28, 74–75

R

Rainbos, 121
Rainbows, 46, 76, 79, 113, 136, 139
Rankin, George T., 95, 98
Ravenswood Novelty Works, 49, 79, 105, 121
Razor blade sharpener, 62, 138
Recipe glass, see Formula glass.
Ribbon core, see Lobed core.
Ribboned marbles, 47, 101, 110, 112, 113, 120, 125, 136

S

Salt glaze, 19, 135
Sandwich Glass Company, see Boston and Sandwich
    Glass Company.
Seedy glass, 73–74
Slags: handmade, 31, 136; machine-made glass type, 50,
    52, 123
Solid core, 30, 136
Spirals, machine-made glass type, 51, 52, 97, 99–100

Steelee Company, 54, 55
Steelies, 10, 54–55, 92, 138
Steimer feeders, 75, 88
Stone marbles, 10, 13–18, 134–135
Sulphides, 31, 106, 135–136
Swirls: handmade glass type, 9, 27, 28, 136; machine-made glass type, 50–52, 99, 101, 103, 104, 106, 109, 113, 121, 125, 136

T

Tiger Eyes (glass marbles), 10, 50, 84, 116, 136
Tiger's-eye (mineral), 14, 15
Translucent marbles, 7; handmade glass type, 30, 136; machine-made glass type, 39–40, 46, 47, 50–52, 98, 101, 104, 106, 109, 110, 113, 114, 116, 121, 125, 136
Transparent marbles, 7; handmade glass type, 28, 30, 136; machine-made glass type, 39, 46, 47, 50–52, 85, 98, 101, 102, 104, 106, 109, 110, 114, 116, 117, 121, 123, 124, 125, 132, 136

V

Vacor de Mexico, 41, 43, 46, 50, 128–129, 132, 144–145
Vaseline, 10, 39, 98, 136
Veneering, 47, 75–76, 111
Vitro Agate Company, 39, 46, 48, 49, 50, 60, 71, 72, 109, 122–126, 142–143, 144

W

Wetterau, Willie, 97, 98
Whirlwinds, 49, 105
Wooden marbles, 56, 138

Y

Yellowware, 19, 21, 135